MY
LIFE
IN THE
KLAN

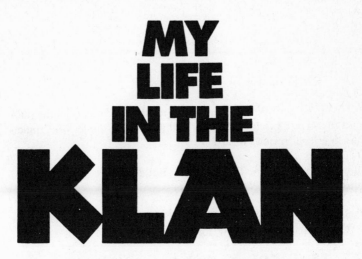

MY LIFE IN THE KLAN

JERRY THOMPSON

Introduction by
JOHN SEIGENTHALER, editorial director, *USA Today*

RUTLEDGE HILL PRESS
Nashville, Tennessee

Published in Nashville, Tennessee, by Rutledge Hill Press, Inc., 513
Third Avenue South, Nashville, Tennessee 37210.

Previous edition of MY LIFE IN THE KLAN published in hardcover
by G. P. Putnam's Sons, New York.

Library of Congress Cataloging-in-Publication Data

Thompson, Jerry.
    My life in the Klan / Jerry Thompson ; introduction by John
Seigenthaler.
        p. cm.
    ISBN 0-934395-96-9 (pbk.)
    1. Ku Klux Klan (1915-   )—Louisiana.   2. Thompson, Jerry.
3. Journalists—Tennessee—Biography.   I. Title.
[HS2330.K63T48 1988]
322.4'2'0924—dc19
[B]
                                                    88-26491
                                                    CIP

Printed in the United States of America
1 2 3 4 5 6 7 — 93 92 91 90 89 88

Acknowledgments

I lovingly thank my parents for bringing me and my brothers and sisters up in an atmosphere of sensitive respect for all people without regard to their color, religion, or nationality.

I owe a special debt of gratitude to the late Jimmy Ellis. It was his dedication, loyalty, and courage that served as an inspiration to me many times when I felt like giving up. His death, at only forty-six, stunned all of us at *The Tennessean,* but left us with the keen awareness that we had known and worked with the best.

And I offer warm acknowledgments:

To John Seigenthaler for having the confidence in me to offer me the assignment; for his guidance and support throughout the course of the story, this book, and everything since.

To Sterling Lord, my agent, who was the first to believe in the importance of this story and who urged me to expand it into a book.

To Faith Sale, my editor, whose guidance, patience, and understanding served as a constant source of encouragement through this first book.

To Mrs. Edna Gardner and Beverly Hendricks, who were always available to take the many calls, make the many excuses, and do the many things that I would never have had time to do.

To William Gralnick, southeastern director of the American Jewish Committee, for his help in providing information on the Klan before I became a member and for his continuing support and assistance.

To fellow newsmen Jon Smith, of CBS, Atlanta; Joe Holloway, the Associated Press, Atlanta; and Chris Clark and Larry Brinton, of WTVF-TV in Nashville, all of whom discovered me participating with the Klan as a member. My thanks to each of them for protecting me by refusing to expose my charade.

To David Skelton and Chris Smith, my colleagues in the woodworking shop, for not prying into my background and for not questioning my oftentimes strange excuses to explain my frequent absences, although, I know, many times they did not believe my concoctions.

To Robert Sherborne for allowing me to confide in him my fears and concerns throughout the assignment and for allowing Linda to do the same when I was away—a confidence he never once betrayed.

To Metro Nashville Sheriff Fate Thomas and deputies Jerry Burns and Mel Harders for volunteering to come to Alabama to whisk me back home after my last Klan meeting.

To Bob Mann for providing around-the-clock security at our home. His presence has been reassuring to Linda and the children on many occasions when I was away.

To Tommy Reasonover, who has provided personal security for me on numerous trips throughout the country and in Canada.

To Alfred Knight and Bill Willis, who were always available with friendly as well as legal advice.

To Jean Estes, who transcribed all the tapes and who

typed the final manuscript of this book, a woman who proved that she could keep a secret.

To Dr. Otto Billig, who helped prepare me for the people I would meet in the Klan.

To all my colleagues at *The Tennessean*—those few who knew from the early days of the assignment and others who eventually learned what I was doing—for keeping the secret.

And finally to all my friends and neighbors, far too many to name, who learned of my "drinking problem" and called Linda to share their concern and offer support.

To Linda,
whose personal sacrifice was far greater than mine.

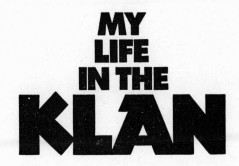

Introduction

For all of the years I have served as a staff member of *The Tennessean*—and soon I will mark my fortieth anniversary—our paper has felt a sentinel's duty to monitor and report on the periodic revivals in Ku Klux Klan activity.

The Klan, after all, is the only indigenous terrorist organization to survive for more than a century in our nation. Its birthplace was Pulaski, Tennessee, a small rural community south of Nashville well within the circulation of *The Tennessean*.

The periodic reincarnations of the Klan always have been attended by harrassment, intimidation, and violence. Klan rhetoric, always ridiculous, and Klan costumes, always clownish, have sometimes masked motives and methods that were vulgar and vicious. Klan doctrine, preached with straight-faced, fanatic fervor, appeals to the worst instincts of those who are ill-informed and those who are plainly ignorant.

In 1979, after more than a decade of relative dormancy, the seeds of racism had once more taken root in our region and had produced another crop of neo-Nazis in white sheets and hoods. In rural communities around Nashville, it was obvious that Klan members once more were raising hell and collecting money.

The leaders of the movement were calling this rebirth of the Ku Klux Klan "the new Klan." There was nothing new about it. It was still racist. It was still radical. Its existence was an outrage. An editor who is aware that such an organization is operating in his back yard can ignore it and hope that it fades away, or he can expose it and hope that the exposure rubs it out. I chose the latter course.

I assigned a team of journalists to cover, report on, and expose the Ku Klux Klan for what it was.

A crucial part of that exposure was the assignment accepted by Jerry Thompson, a reporter and editor who at the time had twenty years' experience with *The Tennessean.* I asked him to go underground, to create a new identity, to join "the new Klan" and spend a few months observing it from the inside.

Jerry accepted the assignment—a dangerous one, of course— in good faith. But the task was tougher than either of us had imagined. "A few months" became many months. Then a year. Finally six months more. The strain on Thompson and his family was enormous. To add to his stress, the newspaper was sold to the Gannett Company, even as he was going underground. Fortunately, the support of Allen Neuharth and John Quinn, the ranking executives of Gannett, was as total as had been that of Amon Carter Evans, the previous owner, who had initially agreed with me that the assignment was a vital one.

The threat to Thompson's safety would last long after he left the Klan. He and his family would have to endure the presence of security guards for many months after his assignment had ended and after the series of articles he wrote was published in *The Tennessean.* Even then his ordeal continued. Months after he left the Klan, an earlier edition of *My Life in the Klan* was published and an irate Klansman filed a libel suit in a Birmingham, Alabama, court against Thompson and G. P. Putnam's Sons, the publishers. While it was a nuisance suit, it intimidated the publishing company from continuing its sales promotion of the book and contributed to its decision not to reissue it in a paperback edition.

I testified at the libel trial for Thompson only a few hours before the case went to the jury. Before I could drive back to Nashville that afternoon, the jurors reported a verdict in favor of Thompson.

The decision by Putnam to pull back from promoting *My Life in the Klan* and printing it in a paperback was a shame. It robbed many paperback readers of the chance to know about "the new Klan."

My Life in the Klan is more than a story about the so-called "new Klan." It is a story about Jerry Thompson. To fully appreciate his account, it is important to know more about him than he tells. It is important to know him as a journalist and person.

As a reporter, he has that unique instinct that I have come to call "a sense of story." As soon as I mentioned the Klan assignment to him, he grasped the full significance and potential of what was involved. Because he loves his family, he hesitated before declaring his determination to do it. Obviously, he had to share the details with Linda, his wife, and get her approval. But he had no doubt—nor did I—that he would accept the assignment, difficult and dangerous as it obviously was.

Jerry Thompson is an outgoing man who never met a stranger. He was born and reared on a Tennessee farm, the product of rural, middle-class upbringing. Many Klan members with whom he was to associate shared that same background. They accepted him naturally into their beer-drinking, joke-cracking, race-baiting conversations because he seemed so much like them.

He perfectly fit the Klan recruiter's image of what a Ku Klux Klan member should be like. They were at ease with him. Knowing their propensity for violence and vengeance, Thompson was never at ease with them. It is trite to call him "courageous." He is Cicero's man of courage: "Full of faith." He has faith in himself, in his family, in the bonds of friendship, and in the newspaper where he has made his career.

Still, he has about him that healthy streak of skepticism that marks every outstanding reporter I have known, assuring that while he may be betrayed, he will never be deceived.

Jerry Thompson is a big man in every way—in build and spirit and heart. He has a full, contagious laugh that adds to his powerful presence. And while he can be gruff and bluff, he has about him a sensitivity and humanity that translate into compassion for those who are powerless. There were times during his ordeal when his sense of humor and his ability to laugh at himself helped keep him stable and keen.

He is not a professional Southerner. He favors gin over Jack Daniel's, rare steak over barbecued ribs, Hemingway over Faulkner, traditional Protestantism over the Moral Majority, and one special Yankee woman over all the southern belles. At the same time, he does have some regional preferences: he thinks the soil on his Tennessee farm is the sweetest in the world, that country music is the music of the country, and that there never will be another football coach as great as Bear Bryant.

Naturally, questions can be raised about the deception involved in Jerry Thompson's assignment. He is not a racist redneck, and he posed as one. But at the same time, Klan leaders were posing publically as persons of virtue. To get behind their pious platitudes and expose what they really stood for, it was necessary for Thompson to misrepresent who he was. Had there been any other way to expose the Klan, Thompson's underground role would not have been necessary.

Thompson is a reporter with a sense of history. His re-entry to daily journalism after the Klan series was published proved that. He dug into an old and notorious murder case in which an innocent man named Leo Frank—a Jew—was convicted of killing a young Atlanta girl—Mary Phagan—in 1913.

The Frank case was tragic. The defendant was convicted in the wildest explosion of anti-Semitism in American history. When the Governor of Georgia was made aware that an injustice had been done, he commuted Frank's death sentence to life in prison. A mob soon kidnapped Frank from prison and lynched him.

Almost seventy years later Jerry Thompson headed the team of *Tennessean* journalists that reopened the case. He produced Frank's one-time office boy, Alonzo Mann, now aging and sick, who as a witness had lied under oath at Frank's trial. Mann recanted his testimony, which led to the Georgia Board of Pardons posthumously pardoning Frank.

Thompson is no poet, pundit, or prophet. He is a reporter who puts down fact after fact in one simple declaratory sentence after another. That is his strength as a storyteller. He is plain-spoken, and he writes as he speaks: plainly. Without frills. Without pretension.

There is an understated eloquence about his journalism and about this journal of his life in the Klan.

His story is as frightening today, and his reaction to his assignment as human as when he lived it nearly a decade ago.

I congratulate Rutledge Hill Press, the publishers of *My Life in the Klan*, for recognizing that even a decade after he lived it Thompson's story is still real, is still relevant.

—John Seigenthaler, Chairman, Editor, and
Publisher of *The Tennessean*, and
Editorial Director, *USA Today*

Yesterday † Today   Tomorrow † Forever

Knights of the Ku Klux Klan

National Offices · Box 624 Metairie, LA 70004 (504) 835-7959

THE KLAN OATH   TOP SECRET

I (repeat your full name) — on this date (say date) — do before God and man — most solemnly swear — that I dedicate — my life — my fortune — and my sacred honor — to the Preservation — Protection — and Advancement of the White Race — and to that great order : — the Knights of the Ku Klux Klan.

SECTION I † † † SECRECY

I swear most honestly — that I will never divulge what transpires tonight. (today)
I swear that I will forever keep secret — the signs — words — papers — and rituals of the KKK.
I sacredly vow — that I will forever keep secret — the name of any fellow Klansman.
I am willing to die before revealing such secrets.

SECTION II † † † LOYALTY

I will faithfully obey — the regulations and laws or the Knights of the KKK.
I recognise that this order is the only true Klan in existence — and that I will never associate myself — with any other "so-called" Klan organization.
I swear my undying loyalty — to the elected Grand Wizard — David Duke.

SECTION III † † † DUTY

I will respond promptly to the needs of the KKK — I will give as much of my time — and money as possible — to further its great aims.
I will fulfill all the duties of a Klansman — for at least five years.

SECTION IV † † † PROLIFERATION

I will actively work to expand the ranks — of the KKK.
I will not recommend for membership — any person whose loyalty is doubtful.

SECTION V † † † FRATERNITY

Every fellow Klansman will be as a brother to me — his welfare will come before my own.
I will never slander — defraud — deceive — or in any way wrong a fellow Klansman — or a Klansman's family — nor will I permit others — to do the same — if I can so prevent it.
I will go to the aid of any fellow Klansman who requests it — at his call I will answer — I will be truly Klannish — toward all Klansmen — in all things honorable and just.

SECTION VI † † † HONOR

I will keep secret — any secret transmitted by any other Klansman.
I will not conspire with other Klansmen to commit an illegal act of violence.
I swear that I will oppose — the enemies of our race — nation — and this order — with my life — my fortune — and my honor — and that I will oppose a serious threat — to the survival and freedom of my people — with whatever means the situation demands — If necessary — I will even sacrifice my life — in defense of fellow Klansmen — and this great order — the Knights of the KKK.
I will never judge any Klan leaders — by any newspaper account — broadcast — rumor — or any other source — other than from the authority — of this order.
I will in fact — not tolerate accusations — in my presence — against any level of Klan leadership — I recognize the duplicity of our enemies.

SECTION VII † † † DEDICATION

I believe in the Constitution of the United States — and in the great race that created it.
I will work diligently — to secure the preservation— protection — and advancement of the White Race.
I believe in complete religious freedom — and in the free practice of the Christian faith — in public institutions — but also in the separation — of church and state.
I will diligently fight against — Communism — and Zionism.
I swear my loyalty to this order forever — as the only true Klan — I shall obey its elected Grand Wizard — David Duke — and all other officers — as long as they continue with this order.
I swear I dedicate my life — from this moment forward — to fostering the welfare of the White Race — and furthering the work of America's greatest Movement — The KNIGHTS OF THE KU KLUX KLAN.

name _____   signature _J. W. Thompson_
witness _Don Black_   date _5-23-80_

Prologue

On a warm spring morning when I was ten, my father took me with him and the hand he had hired for the day into the field to clean out a fence row and put in posts for a pigpen on our small farm.

The soil was fresh, the air clear, and the smell of wild honeysuckle sweet. It felt good to be working with my dad and Willie Biggs. One of the pigs that would go in the pen would become my 4-H club project that summer.

By noon, we had worked up a heavy sweat and a healthy appetite, and we went to the house for lunch.

As we gathered in the kitchen Willie spoke quietly to my father. "It's cooler in the yard," he said. Plate in hand, he ambled toward the back door.

But Dad stopped him. "Your place is right there," he said, pointing to the chair next to mine. Willie took his place and bowed his head as my younger brother, Ronnie, said the blessing.

Midway through the meal the front screen door slammed. Neighbors never knocked so we knew it was a neighbor. We heard footsteps in the living room and then she appeared in the doorway to the kitchen.

Her eyes fixed on Willie. A strange look come over her face. She flushed. Then, without a word, she turned on her heels, went back out through the living room, and the screen door slammed again.

Willie had a strange expression on his face too.

I didn't know why they looked the way they did.

AS I SPED TOWARD Nashville on a hot, humid day in July 1979, I cursed myself for plowing those last two rows of corn and making myself late for work again. This would be the third day in a row.

I also cursed the day, more than two years earlier, that I had agreed to take the job of night city editor for the mid-state's largest daily newspaper. It seemed as if I had been in a hurry ever since. A city editor never has enough time—it's always deadline time. Or worse, past deadline.

My publisher and managing editor shared a peculiarity that I constantly seemed to have difficulty with—they desired, insisted even, that their night city editor be there for the daily news meeting that meant to start promptly at 4:00 P.M. I glanced at my watch, then my speedometer: Both were ahead of where they should have been. The meeting was scheduled to begin in ten minutes, and I knew from many past calculations that I was exactly sixteen minutes from the office. I stepped harder on the accelerator and hoped the Metro Police didn't have their usual radar trap at the forty-three-mile marker on I-24.

Things began looking up. The radar units weren't there and then, when I rushed into the office, I learned that the publisher, John Seigenthaler, had an appointment and the meeting would be starting late. What a lucky day. I had managed to finish plowing the corn and made it to work on time too.

The meeting was routine. The day city editor, the state editor, and the national wire editor pitched their respective stories for page one. But their arguments lacked some of the accustomed intensity: It was getting late and the day people wanted to go home, the night people didn't want to start too far behind.

I had just settled in at the city desk behind a large stack of copy, when Seigenthaler, who circulates through the newsroom after the daily meetings, leaned over to me. "Can I see you a minute?"

"Sure," I said, pushed back my chair and got up, trying quickly to think of a new excuse for being late again.

As we walked toward his office, he suddenly stopped at a table under the newsroom mailbox at the front of the room and sat on the tabletop. I joined him.

For what seemed like a long several minutes, he just watched as people scurried around from desk to desk, picking up copy, delivering pictures, or fumbling through morgue clips. Seigenthaler was obviously deep in thought as he looked out over the newsroom—a newsroom steeped in tradition, a newsroom where a cub reporter could get help on how to write the lead on an obit from a reporter who had won a Pulitzer; a newsroom in which other Pulitzer Prize winners, including reporters on most of the nation's great newspapers and all the major national television networks, had wet their feet in the field of journalism. Seigenthaler had been, and continues to be, a part of that tradition.

Finally, he turned to me and, in a calm, low voice, asked, "Would you be interested in trying to infiltrate the Ku Klux Klan and doing a series of stories on it?"

"Well," I began, trying hastily to appraise the possible ramifications of such an undertaking.

But he continued before I could say anything else. "I realize that it could be dangerous and that we might not be able to do it, but I think it would be a hell of a story. And it's the only way we'll ever find out what motivates people to risk their own lives in order to endanger the lives and freedoms of other people. I think we have a responsibility to our readers to let them know."

"Well," I tried again, and I still didn't have my first appraisal finished. Then, "Yes, I would be interested in such a story," I said, "but there are other things to consider. I have a brand-new baby at home, my house is still unfinished, and Linda is a relatively new wife. All these would have to be part of my decision since, I assume, it would mean leaving home for a period of time. I don't believe we could pull it off in Nashville because too many people here know me."

"That's right. It looks like David Duke has the most going for his Klan."

David Duke, just twenty-nine at the time, was the leader of the so-called Knights of the Ku Klux Klan, with headquarters in Metairie, Louisiana. He was, I knew, a tremendous self-promoter and had succeeded in getting a great deal of media attention. Indeed, he was in the news almost daily, it seemed. He had appeared on the *Tomorrow* show and *Phil Donahue*, among others, and had been the subject of numerous magazine articles, as well as at least one roman à clef. The exposure he had achieved led us to believe that his was a well-planned organization destined for national prominence, and which seemed to have attained a certain degree of respectability. I was sure this was in no small way attributable to the fact that Duke, noticeably handsome and articulate, presented a stark contrast to the rough-talking redneck Klan leaders of the past.

"So we might decide you should go to Louisiana and join up with him," Seigenthaler said. "I don't think it would take

long, maybe six weeks, or two to three months at the
most."

"I'll have to do a lot of research because I don't know a
hell of a lot about the Klan."

"Well"—now I had him doing it—"sure we'll have to do
our homework. But for the time being, let's just keep it
between the two of us, just in case we really do decide to do
it. Don't even tell Linda yet. Let's talk some more about it
tomorrow."

He walked off, and I thought he looked relieved, as if he
had unloaded a heavy burden—onto me. Several times that
night, I discovered that I was sitting like Seigenthaler, just
looking out over the city room and not really seeing anything that was going on.

Somehow, I knew Seigenthaler had made up his mind to
infiltrate the Klan before he spoke to me. Just as surely, I
knew that I would be the one to do it before I even articu-
lated my answer to him. After all, you can't work for a man
for twenty years without having some insight into what
motivates him, and you can't work in this crazy business for
twenty years and pass up a story that holds such enormous
journalistic potential.

I thought that night would never end. Fortunately, the
copy flow was heavy and it kept my mind off the Klan story.
It wasn't until the forty-mile drive home that I really started
to give it some thought, and I continued thinking for a long
time after I reached my quiet house. The prospect of getting
out of the office and working on a story again was extremely
attractive. But the prospect of going away for an extended
period, leaving behind the loving wife and kids who were all
sleeping so innocently upstairs lacked any kind of appeal.

But the need for the story was real.

Not enough was known about the fearful-sounding Ku
Klux Klan; only the bare facts were familiar: The Klan ori-
ginated in Pulaski, Tennessee, probably late 1865. Tradition has it that it was started as a joke by six Confederate
veterans as a way of cheering themselves up in that first cold

winter after the Civil War. The name itself is sort of a joke: It is a bastardized form of the greek word *kuklos*, or circle. The word Klan, consciously misspelled, was added as an afterthought.

The joke soon wore off. The original members of the Klan discovered that by marching through the streets of their hometown in sheets, they could intimidate the recently freed slaves in the area who thought that the sheeted apparitions were the spirits of the Confederate dead. The Klan developed rapidly—it became an unofficial and self-appointed police force, a way for the whites in the South to control the blacks. And where marching would not do the trick, violence did. The Klan was not the only secret white organization in the South at the time, but it most likely was the strongest and certainly the most notorious.

The original Klan was disbanded in 1869, but it did not die—it just went underground. It resurfaced officially in 1915 with all the trappings of the original Klan. The humorous names of the officers—Imperial Wizard, Grand Magi, Grand Turks, Grand Cyclops—names that were originally wisecracks, were revived, but this time in dead earnest. The Klan grew in the 1920s, declined in the 1940s, picked up again in the 1950s, and attracted the attention of the federal government. In the 1960s, FBI agents infiltrated the Klan and membership dwindled to an estimated two thousand members.

It wasn't until the early 1970s, when David Ernest Duke became the leader of the Klan, that the KKK reemerged as a dangerous force in American life.

In 1979, reports of Klan violence kept cropping up on the news wires. In May, four people had been shot in a bloody confrontation in Decatur, Alabama, between Klan members who tried to stop a black march and the marchers who vowed not to be intimidated. The Klan had recently held a rally in Pulaski, Tennessee. Crosses had been burned in Nashville where a small Klan organization was becoming active. Since all this was happening in *The Tennessean's* circulation area, Seigenthaler said he felt the paper had a responsibility to inform its readers. At the same time, we both knew that all the information we—or other papers for that matter—had been able to gather in the past had come from interviews with Klan members, and they all sounded the same. It was almost as if some public relations person had written up a standard reply for all Klan leaders. No news reporter had been able to report on the Klan from inside the organization.

It was a marvelous opportunity to try to do what could be a great story. But could I do it? Did I have the guts? Did I fully realize the danger? Would Linda agree to it? Could she handle the home front with a baby and three older children, one of whom had just become a teenager? Was it really that important? Why couldn't Seigenthaler pick another reporter, one who didn't have a family? Why me?

Four hours and six beers later, I was still sitting out on the deck and I still didn't have the answers. The sun was coming up and casting a pink glow on the hazy fog that hung in the woods behind the house, the whippoorwills had ceased their shrill, mournful whistles. It was going to be a beautiful day. Finally, I went to bed.

I hadn't been there more than a few minutes when Linda got up with the baby. He was more reliable than an alarm clock. I didn't sleep too well that morning and was awakened completely when the smell of frying bacon found its way up to me. I got dressed and went downstairs, realizing that I didn't have any more answers now than I had when I went to bed.

Joseph, the baby, dressed only in a diaper, was wide awake and reclining in his seat in the middle of the kitchen table. Linda was slicing fresh, homegrown tomatoes.

"How are you feeling?" she asked.

"Fine," I answered. "Why?"

"I just thought you might have a problem or something. Anyone who would sit out on the deck all night drinking beer when he could have been in bed with me is just naturally suspect, I guess."

"Naw, I just wasn't sleepy so I listened to the whippoorwills. But," I said as I reached for the baby, "you certainly should be suspicious of someone who had that alternative. Beer drinking never caused anything this cute and cuddly. God, he's growing like a weed, isn't he? Just look at those arms."

Linda said nothing more about my night out on the deck, but I'm sure her suspicions arose again when I left for work early.

Seigenthaler was much more specific in our meeting that day. "I'm not sure we can pull this off," he began, "but I certainly think it would be well worth the effort to try. If you've been keeping up with it, you know that the Klan is obviously growing, and as it grows, violence is growing too. Klan leaders are going on television talk shows and telling everyone how the Klan has changed, how it is nonviolent and law-abiding and gaining respectability. I'm just afraid that a lot of people are beginning to believe them."

I sat there nodding, still not sure how to respond to him.

He kept talking. "I'm convinced that if we could get inside and get close to some of the rank-and-file Klansmen, we'd find that the Klan really hasn't changed much. I think we'd find that it still thrives on fear, intimidation, and violence. If we find that this is true, we'll write it. If we find it's not true and the Klan has really changed, we'll write that too.

I started to taste those front-page headlines over *my* byline.

"I think we should try to join up with David Duke," Seigenthaler went on. "He's getting the broadcast television exposure and is obviously better prepared than most of his hosts."

It was clear that Seigenthaler had made up not only his

own mind but mine as well, although I hadn't said anything
yet.

"It may be impossible to get in," he said. "I hear they are
screening prospective members pretty closely and may even
require them to take lie detector tests. If that's the case, you
obviously can't get in. But I personally think that's bullshit.
I don't think they're being that careful. Are you willing to
try it?" He had at last asked me point-blank.

"Sure," I answered without hesitation. "I haven't discussed it with Linda, of course, but I'm sure she'll understand." So now I had finally committed myself.

Seigenthaler didn't look at all surprised. He waited for me
to do some talking.

"There are several questions I've been asking myself that
I haven't been able to answer," I told him, "like, 'Just how
dangerous will it be?' 'Do I have the guts or ability to pull it
off?'"

"Look," he said, "I admit there's going to be a certain risk
to a story like this. That's why it is imperative that we keep
it strictly between us. Don't breathe a word about it to a
living soul—not your brother or the rest of your family, not
other staff members or anybody. We can't take a chance that
a slip of the tongue could get you discovered. Obviously,
Linda will have to know what you're doing, but you don't
even have to tell her all the details."

"Don't you think the other members of the staff will ask
questions? What will we tell them when I leave? I feel sure
some of them will want to know."

"I may have to pretend to fire you," he said, "or maybe
we'll say you've been committed to a drunk farm to dry out.
At first we won't say anything. When it gets to be a problem,
I'll provide the cover."

I didn't particularly like the idea of having the word out
that I had been fired. Nor did I relish the prospect of being
labeled an alcoholic, despite the fact that several people
probably already believed it. But, God knows, with my repu-

tation for fun and games, either story, or both stories, would be believable.

"And don't try out our plan on any of your friends," he warned, without smiling. "The Klan has demonstrated it will hurt people."

"Then I guess the only remaining question I have is 'Why me?' when you've got a room full of good reporters out there?"

"Look, Thompson, we've been together a long time. I probably know you better than Linda does. Hell, if she knew you as well as I do, she'd be packed and gone before you could get home," he said chuckling. "Kidding aside, I believe you've got the sense and the guts to do it if anybody can."

That was the boss talking—stroking my ego. It felt good.

Then he continued, almost in the same breath. "And, you fit my image of a Klansman. You look like the perfect redneck."

So much for the ego. Seigenthaler has always had a knack for balancing his compliments. I came down pretty fast and started thinking about the job ahead. "All this research and preparation," I said, thinking out loud. "When do you want to get started?"

"Why don't you talk it over with Linda and we'll get started first thing Monday. Meanwhile, I'll have all the clips on the Klan sent up to me. That way they won't be signed out to you. I'll also tell the managing editor to put someone else on city desk and schedule you as being on vacation."

So it was decided. Seigenthaler believed we could do it. Although I still had serious doubts, I believed we were going to give it our best effort.

I left our meeting that day with only one nagging question left: How was I going to tell Linda that I would be leaving her all winter in an unfinished house filled with active kids and a heating system that might or might not be active?

Hell, I couldn't even tell her where I was going because I didn't know yet myself. I just hoped and prayed that telling her would be the hardest part of the assignment.

Linda is a special woman. I suspected it the first night I met her, and she has proven it time and again since.

It was in June 1975 that I first saw her, standing at the city desk in *The Tennessean* newsroom. She was asking the city editor about the workings of the scanner system we were using at the time. The city editor called me over and asked if I would show her how it worked. I quickly agreed.

Before the night was over I learned that she was the divorced mother of two daughters, the state director of a program that placed institutionalized mentally retarded patients with senior citizens for the mutual benefit of both, and a student at the University of Tennessee-Nashville, enrolled in a journalism course that would require a short internship at our newspaper. The second time I saw her was the following Tuesday night. Before the night was over, we had a date for that Saturday.

Meanwhile, on Wednesday morning, my nine-year-old son and I left for a three-day fishing trip to Panama City, Florida. It was a great way to combine my hobby with my flying lessons. The trip went fine until I came back to the dock on Friday morning. I had an urgent message to call the office. Seigenthaler was looking for me.

"When are you planning on coming home?"

"We're leaving tonight. I'll be in the office tomorrow."

"How about staying on," he said. "Remember that story we talked about last week about that fellow in south Florida?" He didn't wait for me to answer. "I received some more information yesterday, and I believe we might be on to something. The problem is someone else might be on it too. Is there any way you can go on down there today and get started on it? I'd hate like hell to get beat on it if there's anything to it."

"Well," I said, "we rode down with my flight instructor. I'm sure he'll take Todd back home to my parents' and I could rent a car and go on down to Cocoa Beach and start from there."

"That's fine. Do that. I think someone from the [Nashville] *Banner* is working on it too. Let's stay ahead of them."

The story concerned a man from the Nashville area who was allegedly acting as the agent for some Arab oil investors and who had allegedly received more than $500 million, moved to southern Florida, and suddenly died. We had information that he had faked his own death by paying off the family of a terminal cancer patient. The patient died under the Nashville man's identity, and no one in southern Florida knew the difference.

The urgency of the story and the possibility that the competition might beat me on it kept me busy for the next two days. It wasn't until shortly before midnight on Saturday that I remembered my date with Linda. I tried to call but there was no answer. I attempted again a few days later with the same results. I finally persuaded myself that she probably didn't want to talk to me anyway and I stopped trying.

That story took three weeks and all I succeeded in doing was raising a bunch of questions. We know that someone died and was cremated within hours with no family members present. The man's family, the man, and the money, if there were any, seemed to have vanished from the earth. The Florida state's attorney's office conducted an investigation, but it too was inconclusive.

Before I could get back to Tennessee, I was sent to New Orleans on another story that took another six weeks.

When I did get back to the office, there was Linda turning in a story to the city desk. I walked over to apologize, but before I could say a word, she began: "Oh, there you are. I'm a little scatterbrained sometimes, so correct me if I'm wrong. That date we made for a Saturday—did we ever agree on what month it would be?"

The next Saturday night we had our date. The following June we were married in a small country church. Linda wrote the beautiful ceremony and composed the music. Shortly afterward we started spending our weekends with axes and a chain saw, clearing a spot in thick woods on our farm for a log house we planned to build. We worked a lot, laughed a lot, and ached a lot, but we both enjoyed it. She designed the house, then we began building it—maybe some-day we'll finish.

Knowing Linda as well as I did and knowing her ability to cope with almost anything, I still didn't know exactly how to tell her about the Klan story.

I knew that from the time she was twelve years old, she had lived in the Midwest with foster parents, had been a champion debater in high school, and had been active in the civil-rights movement in the 1960s while she was a student at the University of Iowa.

For some reason I remembered that when she called her foster father, a retired high-school principal in Lone Tree, Iowa, to tell him we were getting married, he had only two questions about me, both obviously facetious: "Is he college-educated? Is he white?" After she answered both his questions in the affirmative while laughing almost to the point of breathlessness, he said, "Honey, I can't wait to meet him. Good luck. I love you."

It's funny how I relived all these things trying to figure out the best way to bring up the Klan story with Linda. I thought about our good times and our hard times; for several days I thought about everything, and I still didn't know how to broach the subject.

There was only one way: just blurt it out. We'd never had a problem communicating, with the possible exception of that first Saturday date, because we had been honest about our feelings regarding our jobs, our marriage, the kids, whatever.

I had brought home some steaks and a nice bottle of wine. A gentle breeze was blowing through the trees as the smoke from the grill rose off the sizzling steaks. The baby was asleep, Niki and Tanya (Linda's daughters from her first marriage) were watching television, Todd was spending the weekend with his grandmother, and Linda and I were sipping wine and enjoying the quiet of a country evening.

This was clearly the time.

"Linda, there's something we need to talk about."

"Finally," she said. "Maybe now I'll find out what's been on your mind. I don't know whether you've noticed it or not, but every time I've said anything to you for the last couple of days, I've had to repeat it. You weren't hearing a word I said. Just tell me this. Does it involve another woman?"

"Why hell, no," I answered, somewhat amused. "I wouldn't want to talk about that."

"Then do you have some kind of horrible terminal illness?"

"I wouldn't want to talk about that either."

"Okay. Now talk about anything else you want to," she said.

I laughed and then took a deep breath. "John has approached me about doing a story, and I have tentatively agreed to do it. It'll get me off city desk, and you know I've never been that happy with a desk job. But I need your help and thoughts before I make a final decision."

"I think that's great. I've always known you were happier covering the news than editing it. That should be a pretty easy decision to make."

"Well, it's not a routine story," I told her nervously. "There is some danger because I will have to be going deep undercover. I'll have to be away from home, possibly for several months. But it's one hell of a journalistic opportunity." Linda was still silent. I kept on prattling. "It's a story

that could say something about the world we live in, the
world our kids are going to have to grow up in. And no other
reporter has ever done it."

"Okay, okay, it sounds terrific. What is it?" she asked, her
eyes sparkling with excitement.

I swallowed. "Seigenthaler wants me to infiltrate the Ku
Klux Klan."

"Oh, shit," she said at last. "Couldn't we be talking about
another woman? I could at least compete with a woman.
But from what I know about the Klan, if they find you out
there won't be anything left to compete for."

"Well, I plan to do it in such a way that they won't find
out," I tried to assure her. "I'll spend the next several weeks
researching the Klan and preparing a fictitious background.
I'll be fully prepared before I do it, if I do it." Then, in an
attempt at levity, I offered, "Hell, I fooled *you,* didn't I?"

Linda gave me a weak smile. "I know you've given this a
lot of thought," she said, "just as I know you decided days
ago that you were going—and leaving me here all winter
with a house full of kids and a cranky boiler."

I gave her a big hug.

"Just show me how to keep that damn boiler working,"
she continued, "and fix the leak in the downstairs shower
before you leave. Todd will be a big help, and your brother
and your folks will surely help out. We might be a little
lonesome at times, but we'll keep things going here. Just
work fast and hurry home."

"I sure love you."

"I love you too, even if you are a little crazy."

I explained that the story would require a lot of thorough
preparation, so it would be awhile before I left home. And
I'd have time to fix the leaky shower. I also told her that,
even with the preparation, the story could fall through at
any point—I could be discovered, I might not get in, or several other things could go wrong. Apart from the two of us
and John Seigenthaler, no one was to know about what we
were trying to do. We'd just tell the kids, our friends, and my

folks that I was out of town on a supersecret assignment that I couldn't talk about. This was not really unlike some other assignments I had had during my years at *The Tennessean*. They would understand and not pry, I was certain.

Between the time John and I had that initial conversation and the evening I had the discussion with Linda, he and I had talked some more, several times, in fact. We brought one more person in on the planning, our managing editor, Wayne Whitt, and finally got down to the question of where we should try to carry out the plan.

Of course, we didn't know just how big the Klan was overall. William Gralnick, Southeastern director of the American Jewish Committee, an organization that has continued its efforts over the last several years to achieve an estimate of accurate Klan strength in the country, estimates the strength of all the Klan groups combined, both national and independent local groups, at twenty thousand members.

I believe that the Klan keeps a lid of secrecy on its numbers for two reasons: so the average Klansman won't know how few other members there are and, sensing the weakness of the organization, maybe abandon the Klan; and I believe they want to keep the actual numbers concealed from the Internal Revenue Service to avoid taxes on members' dues.

At the outset, the three of us agreed that David Duke's Knights of the Ku Klux Klan represented the most active and fastest growing Klan in the country and particularly in our area. There were other points, however, that we did not agree on so readily. Seigenthaler wanted me to move to Louisiana and try to join up with the Duke Klan, which had its headquarters in Metairie, a suburb of New Orleans. I wanted to be closer to home, so I suggested that I move to Alabama, where Klan activity seemed to be constantly making news. I argued that it would probably be easier to become a member there and that once I was a member I could transfer my membership to a Louisiana den. The main

objective would be to get as close as possible to the top leaders without appearing too eager or too aggressive. We finally
decided to make our first attempt in Birmingham, Alabama.
Then the real preparation began.

After weeks of rehearsing and memorizing my new background from birth to the present, my fictitious twenty-year
Army career, and my numerous associations, it was time to
make the move.

The day after Labor Day, 1979, I packed my old 1967 VW
with only the barest of essentials: a set of sheets, a pillow,
two towels, my shaving kit, and some clothes—all in one of
my brother's old Army duffel bags with THOMPSON stenciled
on the side.

As I walked to the car, carrying the baby, I tried to reas-
sure Linda that I was truly ready, that I was confident, that
I was eager to get started, and that anyway I'd be back in a
few days, after I'd found a place to live, to pick up the rest of
my stuff. We didn't really have to say good-bye now.

The two-hundred-mile drive from Nashville, "Music
City, U.S.A.," to Birmingham, "The Magic City," seemed
to take forever. It was a beautiful day and the hills of southern Tennessee had already started to take on some vivid
colors of the coming autumn. The hills gave way shortly to
endless flat fields of lush cotton and soybean in the fertile
Tennessee Valley that continues through northern Alabama. I would get to know every inch of this roadside during
the next sixteen months. I would see it go to the stark
browns and grays of winter, to the brilliant green of spring
and summer, and back again to winter.

Throughout the trip, I rehearsed my new background
over and over. It was a boring exercise, and at times I felt it
was useless, but it did keep my mind off the home and family
I was leaving behind—and off what my near future might
hold.

At about three in the afternoon, after four hours on the
road, I reached Birmingham, a clump of buildings surrounded by hills. It would be home for now, but it was not a

place I would otherwise have chosen to live. There was plenty of music back home in "Music City," but I never did find any "Magic" in Birmingham.

I spent the first night in the Holiday Inn at the airport exit on I-59. I gathered up copies of both the *Birmingham Post-Herald* and the *Birmingham News*, took a fifth of gin from my car, and retired to my room to pore over the classified ads. I had to find a place to live and, possibly, a job— preferably part-time. There were a couple of possibilities for both, but I decided not to make any phone calls until early the next morning.

Sleep did not come easily that night, despite the gin. So I decided to rehearse some more. I would invent potential questions about my past and then answer them.

My first call the next morning was to a real-estate agent who had an apartment listed near my motel. She agreed to meet me at the address in an hour and gave me specific instructions on how to find it. I inquired if the neighborhood was all-white, black, or mixed. She told me proudly that it was one of Birmingham's oldest neighborhoods and that most of the white homeowners in the area had lived there for years. I took this to mean that it was at least predominantly white. I didn't want to be applying for membership in the Klan and having to give an address in a heavily integrated neighborhood.

The real-estate agent met me at the house on Sixth Avenue South. I arrived early, telling her that a friend had dropped me off nearby. In reality, I had parked my car several blocks away because it still bore Tennessee license plates and I didn't want anyone to notice.

We were greeted at the door by Mrs. Nell Armstrong, a warm, friendly woman whose wit and sprightliness disguised the fact that she was enjoying her seventy-ninth summer. She scampered up the steps to show off the upstairs apartment that I was to call home for the better part of the next year. A spacious layout with a kitchen and bath at one end, a living room in the middle, and a large bedroom at the other end, all linked by a long hallway, it was more than adequate for my needs. But utilities were included in the $195 monthly rent, and this was the deciding factor. I wouldn't have to have power, water, and gas accounts in my name, nor would I have to take the time and go through the hassle of having them all turned on. I gave her a $100 deposit and told her that I would be moving in in about a week but would be by to drop off some belongings later.

Then I walked around until I was sure the real-estate agent was out of the area and I could return to my car undetected. My new neighborhood didn't look too bad: rows of old, large houses, all neatly kept and most with large pecan trees in the yards. It was very quiet, and no one was out— except the squirrels jumping from tree to tree through the yards.

I returned to the motel and to the classifieds to find a job. One ad caught my eye immediately. It was for a cabinetmaker's helper and I hadn't seen it in the papers I had read the day before. I learned later that afternoon that the ad was indeed running for the first time and that I was the first person to respond.

When I called, the man who answered told me that it was his son who was looking for a helper in his small, one-man cabinet shop. "I'm only here to answer the phone," he said. "David is out installing a set of cabinets. If you want to come on over, he should be back in about an hour."

I said I'd be there right away and asked for directions. The shop was in Homewood, all the way across town from where I was. I left immediately. When I finally found the shop, I introduced myself as J. W. Thompson. Although I had already said it to the real-estate agent and to Mrs. Armstrong, it still sounded strange to be introducing myself as "J.W."

Joe Skelton was a small, slim man neatly dressed in a tie and sport coat. He proudly showed me his son's craftsmanship in the few pieces of furniture and small wood products displayed in a small showroom. Then he asked about me.

When I told him that I had recently left the Army after twenty years, he began telling me about his stint in the Navy during World War II and about his other son who happened to be in the Navy at this time.

His son still hadn't returned after two hours, but another fellow had arrived seeking the same job. I could tell right away from the size of the shop that no more than one helper would be necessary. I began to get somewhat apprehensive when I learned that the other fellow, "Boot" Norris, who was much younger than I, had previously worked in a furniture factory in North Carolina and seemed to be very familiar with the cabinet business. There goes a perfect setup, I thought.

It was almost dark when David Skelton returned from the installation job. I had been waiting more than three hours and Boot had been there almost two. David was a tall, slender man in his mid-twenties with a heavy black beard and black hair. He moved and spoke in a slow, calculated manner. He met us outside the front door of the shop—he had parked and come in from the rear.

The job interview was very informal and brief. Boot, obviously more aggressive, started right in reeling off his experience in the business and talking about staining and finishing, but apparently I was more impressed than David.

When I told David that I was retired from the Army and would be willing to work only a couple of days a week and that I didn't know a damn thing about building cabinets but could drive a nail and saw a board, David immediately put me more at ease.

"You won't need much experience like that," he said with a broad grin. "I don't pay but three dollars an hour, so I don't really expect a lot. I just need someone to help in the shop and on installations. If you're willing to work part-time, I think I could probably use you both. That way we could always have someone at the shop while the other two are out installing. Why don't you come on in at eight in the

morning?" he said, turning to Boot. "And J.W., if you'll
come in Monday morning, we'll see how things work
out."

"I'll sure be here," I told him happily.

Things were really working out better and faster than I
had hoped. I had just hit town and I already had both an
apartment and a job. Since it was only Wednesday evening, I
thought I would have time the next day to get an Alabama
tag for my car and a new driver's license, and still get home
for the weekend. I was already homesick.

The tag for my car was easy enough. My sister, Kaye
Blackwell, had notarized my bill of sale for the car in Tennessee. Since our last names were different, there would be
no wondering about the notary's signature. I had simply told
Kaye that I needed the car registered to J. W. Thompson
and I would explain why later. I knew she had a thousand
questions, but she didn't ask them.

The bill of sale was all that was necessary to register the
car in Alabama, since cars produced before 1975 do not
require a title. The driver's license proved more difficult,
however. I called the examining station and was informed
that unless I had a valid license from another state, I had to
be driven to the station by a driver legally licensed in Alabama. I didn't have any idea how I would pull that off, but
I'd think of something. I have never been a more careful,
law-abiding driver than I was during that period between
when I left home without a license and the time I secured an
Alabama one.

The rest of that day and the next morning I steeped
myself in the local papers and drove around to familiarize
myself with the sights, sounds, and smells of Birmingham.
On Friday afternoon I drove home.

I called Seigenthaler from a pay phone outside Nashville
to tell him what I had accomplished. He suggested that we
meet at the office of the newspaper's lawyers (of course they
too had to be told about the plan) the following morning for

one final briefing before I left town to settle in my new home, new life-style and new identity.

It was at this meeting with the lawyers that we discussed at length what I could and could not do if I meant to stay within the law.

One thing the lawyers were adamant about was that I never, under any circumstances, go armed. They even went so far as to cite some federal cases and said they would have difficulty defending me should I be arrested with a weapon at the scene of violence.

"If you are participating with these people," said Al Knight, an expert on the First Amendment, "and someone gets hurt or killed, there is legal precedent that says that you could be charged with conspiracy to commit murder. If you're carrying a gun, there's no defense. On the other hand, if you don't have a weapon, it would be tough, but I think we could probably defend you successfully against the charge. Sounds like fun, doesn't it?"

Somehow, I failed to find any humor in that possibility, especially the part about "probably" being successful in my defense.

"Don't let anybody get you caught in some trap where people get hurt," the other lawyer, Bill Willis, cautioned. "You are still a citizen, and you have to worry about the law and about other people."

I understood.

Accompanied by Seigenthaler, I also went to the office of Dr. Otto Billig, a psychiatric expert in the field of group conduct. For years I had known Billig's reputation as one of the top psychiatrists in Nashville, but this was my first face-to-face meeting with him. Billig met us at the rear entrance of his office. He turned out to be a friendly man with a quick smile and almost white hair, and such a marked German accent that I had trouble understanding him at times. Seigenthaler, serving as both interpreter and interviewer, asked Billig to alert me to the personalities of the kind of people he thought I might encounter in the Klan. The doctor advised me to have logical, reasonable answers, not to be too anxious or overly aggressive.

"Don't push too hard. They will probably try to draw you in," Billig said. "Let them do that. If I were attempting to become a Klansman, I would not invent elaborate stories to impress them. I would deal with them as simply as possible."

After we left the doctor's office, we stopped for a beer. All the time I was mulling over what Billig had said. If he was right, this assignment could take longer than I had anticipated.

"What about Billig," I asked Seigenthaler, "do you think he knows what he's talking about?"

"Well, in the absence of any firsthand knowledge of our own, I'd have to assume he knows more than we do," Seigenthaler answered. "I would suspect that he is close to being right on the money."

The beer was good but my outlook wasn't. Seigenthaler had said from the outset that we could probably wrap up the story in three months. I had given myself six and told Linda that it would probably take that long. Now I wondered. I knew that the commitment had been made, both by me and by the paper, that I would stay as long as necessary to get the story. Now it was up to me and the people I would be dealing with.

This would be my last meeting with Seigenthaler for several weeks. My next move, the following afternoon, would be directly into my new life, new home, and then new job— all of which had a disquieting air of permanence for which I was still not totally prepared.

Before I left, we discussed again my cover story at the office and I assured Seigenthaler that Linda knew what to tell my friends or colleagues who called our home. She was to be vague and reluctant to discuss my whereabouts, almost to the point of appearing to be ashamed to talk about it.

Seigenthaler had told me that the story he would circulate

in the office would be that I had been sent, at the paper's expense, to "dry out" in an alcoholic treatment center at a location that couldn't be disclosed.

I didn't find out until after I had returned how effective this cover had been and how effective Seigenthaler had been at getting the cover story out without discussing it directly with anyone other than Whitt. I learned about it in a story that appeared as a sidebar to the series I ultimately wrote. Fellow reporter Robert Sherborne described how the cover story was launched:

> *Tennessean* Publisher John Seigenthaler stormed into the newspaper conference room, where a dozen staffers had been waiting for the afternoon news meeting to begin. Slamming his hand down on a stack of newspapers lying on the glass-topped table, he turned to Managing Editor Wayne Whitt and angrily declared:
>
> "Look, Wayne, Jerry Thompson's at it again, and I've had it with him! I'd like not to see him around here for a while. Can you see to that?"
>
> Whitt, looking exasperated, nodded his head in agreement. He would take care of it immediately.
>
> And then, in a rather subdued atmosphere, the news meeting finally began that September afternoon. Later, after the meeting broke up, one of the editors who had witnessed Seigenthaler's outburst strolled up to Whitt and casually asked, "What's the problem with Jerry?"
>
> "I think he just needs to dry out a little," Whitt replied.

AND SO IT BEGAN—the charade that, coupled with my other multiple charades, we hoped would lead me into an undercover membership in the Ku Klux Klan.

When friends and news sources, some of them developed in the early stages of my twenty-year career with *The Tennessean*, called me at the paper, they were told that I was "on leave of absence." No, no one knew when I would return. No, no one knew where I could be reached. And no, no one had heard from me lately nor did anyone expect to in the near future.

The vagueness of these replies led my friends to believe all kinds of things. Many told me after my return that they had heard that I was fired, that I was hospitalized, that I was in the process of getting a divorce and was hiding out to dodge child-support payments. A number of close family friends thought also that I was having marital problems and had merely left home and occasionally visited the children on weekends. This was particularly difficult for Linda, but she never tried to influence their thinking one way or another because, she said, "I knew they would find out eventually and then they would understand why it was so important for me to be so vague."

The most bizarre gossip about my whereabouts was spread by a nosy relative who whispered to my aunt, a terminal cancer patient on her deathbed, that I was in prison and that I was learning woodworking in a rehabilitation program there. Sad to say, my aunt died before she ever learned where I really was.

Despite the varied speculation, my cover story was obviously sufficient to allow me to conceal my whereabouts and activities for the sixteen months I was away from home.

By the time Seigenthaler brought up "my problem" at that day's afternoon news meeting, I had almost completed my first day on the job as a cabinetmaker.

It was also my first day of strenuous physical labor in more days than I—or my aching body—could readily remember. I thought I would drop in my tracks from sheer exhaustion. Unloading four-foot-by-eight-foot sheets of three-quarter-inch, industrial-grade particle board was quite a bit different from sitting behind a typewriter.

Sleep came easily that night. Much more easily than moving the next morning. After I groaned and moaned my way to the shop, and after I worked out some of the previous day's soreness by unloading sheets of plywood, the second day went much better. In fact, I was not too tired after the second day to stop for a beer on the way home.

I went to Barney's Family Tavern, just a block from where I lived. In my bib overalls, boots, work shirt, and red-and-white baseball cap with a big red *A* on the front— just like the one Alabama football coach "Bear" Bryant wears—I felt right at home.

That old luck was still holding. Most of the customers at Barney's were working people, many of them in some aspect of the construction business. I met two guys whose banter suggested that they were good friends—Don, a flooring con-

tractor, and Herb, a remodeling contractor. They immediately included me in their conversation and offered to buy
me a drink, and Herb challenged me to a game of pool. I was
in the right place. I had purposely stopped in to make some
local acquaintances because I still needed that favor—the
favor that I couldn't let my new boss, David, know about: I
had to be driven to the examining station by a driver legally
licensed to drive in Alabama. I couldn't ask David to drive
me there. He assumed that I already had a license and had
sent me earlier in the day to pick up a load of lumber in his
old Ford pickup, which we affectionately called "Old
Blue."

After a couple of beers, a few pool games which Herb
won, and a lot of conversation about building cabinets, laying floors, and remodeling houses, I explained to Don and
Herb that I had recently moved to Birmingham and had not
yet obtained a driver's license. I explained my predicament
and asked if one of them would have time to drive me out to
the Highway Patrol Station the next day.

"Aw, hell," Don said, "they tell everybody that. Don't pay
them any attention, just go out there. They'll never know
whether you drove or not."

I was no closer to solving my problem. By Friday of the
first week on the job, I had driven Old Blue several times
and had cussed her lack of brakes many more. I was getting
desperate. It was a slow morning, so I suggested to David
that I might take the afternoon off to get away to greet a
"girlfriend" I had invited to town for the weekend.

I left at eleven, hoping that I could at least make some
headway either toward getting a driver's license or toward
getting closer to someone who would invite me to join the
Klan. It would be expecting too much of my luck to hope for
both.

I had already lucked into one unexpected break which I
hoped to capitalize on. I had done my background research
on Don Black, Alabama's Grand Dragon of the Knights of
the Ku Klux Klan and had found out a lot about the man.

But it was not until I started reading the Birmingham newspapers that I discovered that he was running for mayor.

Our original plan, which, of course, had a modicum of luck built into it, was for me to hang around bars and attend Klan rallies in hope of becoming acquainted with some Klan member who would ask me to join. Now that Black was running for mayor, I could, without arousing undue suspicion, go to his headquarters, express agreement with what he was saying publicly, make a contribution, and volunteer as a campaign worker. This way I would know for sure that I would be around Klansmen.

Black, in his role as Grand Dragon, was considered to be Duke's first lieutenant and one of his most trusted confidants. From my preparation study of him, I knew that he had long been an admirer of Adolf Hitler and by the age of fifteen had read *Mein Kampf.* At his high school in Athens, Alabama, where he was known as "the weird kid," he handed out racist literature, and a police investigation had been conducted because of reports that he made threats on the life of a Jewish schoolmate. (He had once told a correspondent for *The Tennessean* that he had not made any such threats but actually had tried to make friends with the schoolmate. The girl's parents, he said, "got the crazy idea" that he was trying to strangle their daughter with piano wire. The object of Black's reputed threats is now a lawyer for the federal government; she told Seigenthaler that she still fears Don Black.) He once left high school to be a volunteer in the Georgia gubernatorial campaign for racist lawyer J. B. Stoner. During that campaign he was shot and seriously wounded by Jerry Ray, brother of James Earl Ray, confessed assassin of Dr. Martin Luther King, Jr. Jerry Ray was never prosecuted for shooting Black, and the facts surrounding that incident have been obscured with the passing of time.

Black had ideas of a military career and had completed three years of the ROTC program at the University of Alabama, when the Army investigated him. On the basis of his

background and racist attitudes, Black was barred from
completing the last year of the program that would have led
to an officer's commission. At this point, he had not yet
joined the Klan. He finished college about the time David
Duke began making news as a Klan leader. Black said he
went to Louisiana, talked with Duke, and asked how he
could help. Duke sent him back to Alabama with instructions to organize like-minded people—true believers in the
Klan movement. Black did his job well, rising to the rank of
Grand Dragon for the state and for six and one half years
had been the Klan's chief organizer in Alabama.

Now at age twenty-seven, Black was running for mayor of
Birmingham. He was not given much chance of winning,
but I felt that by volunteering to work in his campaign I
would at least be in contact with some Klansmen who might
lead me to Black. I hoped to get close to his other campaign
workers, ingratiate myself, and be "recruited" into the
Klan.

The leading contender in the race for mayor was Dr.
Richard Arrington, a very popular black member of the Birmingham City Council, son of a former sharecropper. I was
sure his candidacy was the prime topic of discussion at Black
for Mayor headquarters.

Back at my apartment, I got right on the phone to Black
headquarters. I told the man who answered that I was interested in taking an active part in the campaign and wanted to
come by and pick up some literature to distribute during the
weekend. He gave me directions to 616 St. Charles Street
and told me to ask for him—"Emmet"—when I arrived.

As I wound my way through the unfamiliar streets of west
Birmingham, I soon realized that I was in a predominantly
black neighborhood. And I was confused: Why would the
Grand Dragon of the KKK live in a black neighborhood?
Emmet had explained—or maybe he was apologizing—that
the headquarters had been moved to "Don's rented house
because the Holiday Inn kicked us out because they didn't
want to be associated with the Klan."

I turned down St. Charles Street and felt I must be nearing the headquarters. But there was not a single Don Black campaign poster to be seen. Instead, signs nailed to almost every tree urged DON BLACK GO HOME or claimed THIS COMMUNITY WANTS NO PART OF THE KKK or WE HAD A PEACEFUL NEIGHBORHOOD BEFORE DON BLACK. Black children played on the sidewalks and some rode their bikes in the street. But this was daytime; I could imagine some of the friendliness leaving as the sun disappeared behind nearby Legion Field each day.

The house was just as Emmet had described it, a small white frame with a screened-in front porch and a tall, chain link fence around the yard. When I parked my car in front of the house, some of the children interrupted their games long enough to shout, "Honky go home," and "The KKK sucks."

A strange feeling came over me. I was embarrassed and uneasy, but, most of all, overwhelmed with guilt. These kids, strangers, were associating me with the Ku Klux Klan. I didn't like that, the association. But I had to get used to it, for, as I was to learn, the Klan thrives on offending the sensitivities of others. Still, it hurt then and every other time I offended someone, but I made a great effort not to let it show.

I walked directly to the gate, let myself in, and went up to the door on the porch. Just as I knocked, the door opened and I was greeted by a smiling young man in his twenties followed by a toddler wearing only a diaper. No one ever explained who the baby was, but he seemed out of place in a house filled with racist literature and jeering black youngsters on the outside. I had the urge to pick him up and give him a hug, just as I longed to hug my own baby. For once, though, I was glad my baby was back in Tennessee. I sure didn't want him here.

"Hello, I'm J. W. Thompson," I said, extending my hand to the man. "I'm supposed to see Emmet."

"I'm Emmet," he said. "Man, it's good to see you, J. W. Come on in."

Clearly this was not a full-time home for anybody, least of all the KKK's Grand Dragon. I followed Emmet through the living room, which was furnished with one wooden chair and what appeared to be a folding card table. There were two men in the room talking. They nodded when I came in, but seemed annoyed at the intrusion. One was a large, hefty man, wearing cowboy boots, black jeans, a Western shirt, and a string tie. The shorter one was dressed in some type of industrial uniform.

Emmet didn't pause in the living room. Instead, he walked right on back to another room, also very sparsely furnished, and began talking to me about Black's campaign.

"Man, since Don went over to nigger town the other night and appeared on that radio show, the response has been fantastic. That showed that he had guts. He went right over there in their part of town and told everybody that it was the niggers was responsible for ninety percent of the crime in Birmingham and they couldn't deny it because he had the figures from the FBI."

"That's the very reason I'm here," I told him, taking the plunge for the first time. "I heard Don on the radio, and he's speaking a language that I like to hear. I just got out of the Army. I was going to stay thirty years, but the niggers are taking over the Army, so I got out at twenty and moved back South where I belong. But I can't stand the thought of living under a nigger mayor, and that's why I want to help Don." I hoped I sounded convincing.

"I believe he's got a hell of a chance." Emmet said, proceeding with his analysis of the campaign. "There's so many white candidates in the race they are going to split up the vote. The niggers are all going to vote for Arrington. If Don can get in the runoff with the nigger councilman, you'll see the biggest vote in Birmingham's history. Every white person that is registered will vote if you give them that choice. We're going to pull it off because we've got the support. There's not a white policeman who won't vote for Don just because of the way the niggers showed their ass last spring when that white officer shot that nigger girl. The people are sick and tired of their shenanigans."

Emmet was referring to an incident earlier in the year when Birmingham patrolman George Sands shot and killed Bonita Carter, a young black woman. Sands said he fired a shot at a getaway car fleeing from a robbery on Birmingham's north side. Carter was a passenger in that car and was struck and killed by the policeman's bullet. Her death sparked rioting in the neighborhood and Sands's suspension from the force. The incident was a major issue in the mayoral race, with Dr. Richard Arrington vowing not to reinstate Sands if he were elected.

"We've had more people give money to the campaign in the last three days than we have since he announced. And when people are concerned enough to give their money to a candidate, they're damn sure going to get out and vote for him."

I couldn't imagine what had happened in the last three days to make people want to give money to Don Black, but I didn't dare ask. I simply said, "I don't have a lot of money because I just got a small pension. I didn't stay long enough to get the big one, and I'm working part-time in a cabinet shop just to have something to do. But here's twenty dollars, and I'll try to give you all something every week. I'll also do whatever I can as far as passing out literature and bumper stickers. Just let me know what needs to be done."

"Man, you don't know how we appreciate it."

We walked back into the living room, where those two men were still talking. There was a large Confederate flag hanging on the front wall and several posters from Black's campaign setting out what he regarded as the issues. Emmet introduced me to the shorter fellow but just ignored the other man.

"J.W., I want you to meet Ned Coulter. Ned's an electrician and he's just like you—he heard Don on the radio and drove all the way over here to give us a campaign donation and volunteer to work to get Don elected. That right, Ned?"

"It sure is," he answered as he stuck out his hand. "I've got a wife and kids at home and it's not safe for them to go out on the streets anymore. We've got to find somebody with the guts to put the niggers back in their place, and I believe Don Black is the man that will do it."

"I'm sure he is," I answered. "I know I'm going to work like hell for him."

"Me too," Coulter said.

"By the way, Emmet," I said, as if it were an afterthought, "did I tell you on the phone the other day that I still don't have a driver's license? Well, they insist on having someone with a license drive me out to the station before they will give me a test and I don't know anyone here yet. The station is not far from here, just up on Arkadelphia Road. You don't know anyone who could drive me up there do you?"

"Do you want to go right now?"

"Sure, that would be fine. It shouldn't take but a few minutes. Can you run me over there?"

"No, we've got some other people coming over and we'll have to stay here at headquarters, but maybe Ned could. Ned do you mind going up there with him?"

"Well, I kinda hate to leave my truck," Coulter said. "It's got a lot of tools in it."

"No problem, man," Emmet assured him; "we'll keep a close eye on it. We're going to need you and J.W. both to haul people to the polls on Election Day, and I'd hate for J.W. to get put in jail for not having a driver's license."

"Okay, just watch my truck and we'll be right back."

Coulter made a last-minute check to make sure his truck was all locked up, then got in the passenger's seat of my old VW.

"I figure I might as well drive," I told him as we pulled away from the curb. "I've been driving around town for three weeks and nobody's stopped me. You don't think they'll check that close, do you? I mean as long as you tell them you drove me out."

"Naw, they'll never check. They'll probably ask me to get the car out of the parking area and drive it up to where you take the test. That's all."

As we drove along, we started talking about the campaign. The whole time I was at the headquarters, I didn't once hear the Klan mentioned. I wondered if Coulter was a Klansman but was reluctant to ask him outright.

He apparently was wondering the same thing about me and was less reluctant. "Are you a member of the Klan?" he asked.

"No, I'm not. I really haven't given it much thought."

"Them fellows back there are in the Klan and the big one was telling me all about it and wanting me to join."

I acted mildly surprised. "Emmet never mentioned the Klan to me and if he had and had asked me to join, I don't know what I would have told him."

"Well, the big one out there with me sure was trying to sign me up."

"What did you tell him?"

"I told him I'd have to think about it."

"Do you think you will join?"

"I don't think I will, but I'll support them. I've got a wife and kids and I sure wouldn't want to get out with a bunch of Klanners and get throwed in jail like a lot of them have. But I'll tell you this, something has got to be done about the niggers. They're taking over our schools, the government, and everything else. That's why I'm for Don Black."

"As I said, Emmet never mentioned the Klan to me and I'm not sure I'd join if he did," I told Coulter. I had the strong sense that he really wanted to be a member of the Klan but was too practical—and too smart—to risk the liabilities that came with the membership. Still, he would be a longtime supporter and possibly a valuable future contact for me. I tried to talk his language and play back to him what I felt he wanted to hear from me. But I was awfully new at this charade. I just hoped it would work.

"The last thing I joined was the Army," I continued, "and it took me twenty years to get out of that. I just ain't too eager to join anything right now. But I'm like you, something's got to be done about the niggers. They're even taking over the Army. That's why I got out at twenty years instead of staying for thirty."

The Highway Patrol Station was a beehive of activity. Signs directed people in all directions, one way for registration, another for administration, and another for driver's licenses. I purposely parked a long way from the entrance, hoping no one would see me getting out on the driver's side. Ned and I walked to the lobby.

A hefty corporal with red hair, whose name tag read LEE, was there, speaking very gruffly to a man who appeared to be Hispanic.

"You'd better just get out of here before you spout off too much," Lee told the man. "You are not going to take a test until you bring a birth certificate or something to prove who you are and where you came from and that's it."

Ned took a seat and I was directed to a receptionist who asked a few general questions, mainly to determine that my license was not under a revocation order from another state. I was then assigned to an examiner—Corporal Lee. I underwent a brief flash of sheer terror, thinking he might put me through the same scrutiny. I was relieved when he greeted me in a cheerful voice, took a quick glance at a photocopy of my Army "discharge," and explained the written examination. He was friendly and helpful through the whole process.

Although I was unfamiliar with Alabama's motor vehicle laws, the test was a breeze. I missed only two questions. I returned it to Corporal Lee, and he graded it and asked me to step over to a machine on the counter for an eye test. I passed again.

Once my papers had been typed up, I was given a document and told to report outside for a road test. An attractive young woman would be my road examiner. She asked me first if I had been driven to the station by a licensed driver and asked me to point him out. I introduced her to Coulter and she told him to go get the car and bring it up to the door.

When he pulled up, she told me to get behind the wheel and start the engine while she checked the signal, tail and brake lights. Then she started toward the passenger's side, stopping to talk with Coulter on the way. After examining his driver's license, she came up and opened the door but did not get in.

"I'm sorry, sir," she said, "but I can't give you a road test. Mr. Coulter's license has expired, so neither of you can legally drive."

"What can I do?" I asked pleadingly.

"Your friend'll have to go down to the courthouse and have his renewed before I can give you a test. If you'll hurry on down there and get that done and get back today, I'll hold your paperwork out. If you don't get back today, you'll have to start over."

"How can we do that if neither of us has a license?"

"Just be careful," she said. "I don't think anybody will stop you around here."

I motioned for Coulter to get into the car and off we went to the courthouse. Fortunately, there was only a short line waiting for license renewals. Coulter got in it. Soon, the necessary paperwork was filled out and he had been photographed. He stepped up to the last desk, took out his wallet, then walked back toward me—without the license.

"I still can't get it," he said.

"Why?"

"I don't have enough money. I gave Black's campaign ten dollars and I'm four seventy-five short for the license."

"Here, get back over there and get it," I said, handing him a ten-dollar bill; "we've got to get back out there."

Finally, we were on the way back and at least one of us

could legally drive. Although Coulter was the legal one, I was suddenly too anxious to take that into consideration. I was in a hurry. The examining station would be closing within minutes and I didn't want to have to go through it all again. If I made it back today, I could just pick up where I left off. If I had to come back another day, it would mean getting another licensed driver and starting the testing process again at square one. I had successfully gotten by big Corporal Lee once and I didn't want to risk it again. So, despite the fact that I didn't have a license and Coulter did, I drove. I felt I could get there quicker.

I drove closer to the building this time. The young woman saw us drive up and motioned us on over. I just knew, based on how everything else had been going, that she was going to have me drive over and give me a ticket for driving without a license.

"Did you get it taken care of?" she asked Coulter as he got out of the car.

"Sure did," he answered.

"Let me see it. I've got to be sure."

After she saw his brand-new license, she got into the car and gave me directions on where to go. Considering how I felt when she refused me the first time, I could very easily have told her where to go.

The test was soon over and I had my very own brand-new license.

On the way back to Black's headquarters, Coulter and I talked mostly about how he was unaware that his license had expired and we agreed to get together to have a beer. As I left him at his truck, he said he would repay the money he borrowed the following week. I just told him we'd get together and drink it up one night.

As I drove off, I couldn't help but think of the irony: Here I was trying to get into an organization known for extreme violence, and I was terrified to drive down the street without a valid driver's license.

I was in phone contact with Emmet at Black's campaign

headquarters almost daily after that first visit. It was still
about two weeks before the election and the campaign was
heating up.

Meanwhile, I was really beginning to enjoy the cabinet
shop, and many nights I would work late just puttering
around with all the different tools and making small items,
most of them copies of something David had already
made.

I stayed at the shop until about 10:00 P.M. one Wednesday
night, but I called Black's headquarters when I got home.
Emmet answered the phone, as he always did, with a cheerful, "This is the headquarters of your next mayor, Don
Black. May I help you?"

When I began speaking, Emmet immediately broke in.
"J.W., man, am I glad you called. You got a gun?"

"Not with me," I answered. I was proud of myself for my
rapid reply—especially since I might have been tempted to
tell him how I wouldn't dream of carrying a gun. "What's
the problem?"

"There's a carload of niggers setting outside right now.
They've been over here several times tonight and the cops
keep running them off but they just come right back.
They're just trying to raise hell. But if you can get a gun
over here, I'll put a stop to that hell raising."

"I've got a buddy that always has a gun," I lied, inventing
a story on the spot, "and he's probably over at Barney's right
now. I'll go down there and borrow it and come right on
over."

"Do that, man. The cops are getting tired of coming out
here and I'm getting tired of those smart-ass niggers. I'll just
blow some ass away if I can get a gun. I got a gun and it's
registered, but it's up in Gardendale and I can't get to it. I
believe the niggers have some guns 'cause they keep threatening to shoot the place up. If you can get the gun, hurry on
over here."

"I'll go get it right now. I'll be there as soon as I can."

I obviously didn't go looking for a gun. I felt then, and I

still feel, that if Emmet had had a gun that night there
would have been a shooting on St. Charles Street. He talked
as if he was mad and scared at the same time—a dangerous
state of mind for a man clutching a gun. I listened intently to
the news the next morning and read the *Post-Herald* to see
if he ever found a gun. There was no news of a shooting so
he evidently hadn't located one.

I talked with Emmet again the next night and made the
excuse that I couldn't find my "buddy."

"That's okay, man," he said. "The cops came back right
after I talked to you and just told the niggers they were
going to kick ass if they caught them over here again. And
the niggers knew they meant it. They didn't come back."

"Good," I said.

"Hey, you got any more bumper stickers?" he asked me.

"No, I haven't, but I'll be by tomorrow to pick some up. I
need some more posters too. I passed out what I had over in
the neighborhood where I live and I need some to put in the
windows of businesses near the shop in Homewood. I've
really been talking Don up around there, and we've got a lot
of support."

"We're picking up support every day," he said. "Come by
as early as you can because we're running low on all the
campaign stuff. We're gonna win this thing, and Don Black
is going to make one hell of a mayor. When he gets to City
Hall you're gonna see niggers running from Birmingham
like they would run from a rattlesnake."

I went by the headquarters on my way home from work. It
appeared there was still an ample supply of campaign materials, and Emmet was still making his enthusiastic predic-
tions about the outcome of the election.

He asked me where I would vote, in what precinct. He
obviously didn't know I wasn't registered. But I had gone to
the trouble to find out where the voting precinct was for my
area of town. I told him that I would vote at Holman
School.

"That's great," he said. "There's a lot of old people in that area and if you take as many of them as you can to the polls—if we can get them there—we'll have their vote."

"I'm a step ahead of you there, my friend; I've already had my landlady calling all her friends to tell them I would take any of them to the polls. She's seventy-nine and has lived there for years. She told me last night that she had ten or fifteen people that need rides. I've already told my boss that I would be doing that," I told him, completely disregarding the truth.

"That's great, J.W.," he said, draping his arm around my shoulder. "If we just had a lot more workers doing just half of what you're doing, we'd win this thing without a runoff. Keep it up, we can't let down now."

I assured him I would, as I left with another armload of literature, tee shirts, and bumper stickers.

On October 9, 1979, I was at work in the cabinet shop. I kept hearing radio reports of the heaviest voting turnout in Birmingham's history—the largest being in the predominantly black precincts. By quitting time that day, it appeared certain that Dr. Richard Arrington, the black councilman, would be in the runoff three weeks later. In fact, some stations and commentators were going out on a limb and projecting that he would lead the ballot in this mayor's race. The real contest seemed to be for the second spot on the ticket—the person who would face Arrington in the runoff.

It was interesting to note in early returns that night that the incumbent mayor, David Vann, was running well behind the leaders, and Don Black was far behind him.

By eight o'clock that night, it was over. Dr. Arrington would be in the runoff, and his opponent would be either John Katopodis or Frank Parsons. The second spot was not settled officially for several days because the vote was so close, giving Parsons such a slight edge, that Katopodis indicated he might challenge it in court. He abandoned his plans when a recount still gave Parsons the edge. So Arrington and Parsons would meet in the runoff.

When the final returns were in, Don Black had garnered only slightly more than 2 percent of the total vote, tallying only 1,700 votes to run next to last. (The bottom spot went to a black Socialist candidate.)

After the eight-o'clock announcement that Arrington was the winner, I started trying to contact Black headquarters to express my "disgust" with Arrington's win and to offer my condolences that Black didn't make a better showing. Each time I got a busy signal. I finally gave up around eleven-thirty and went to bed.

The next day at work I tried several times to reach the headquarters, but no one ever answered. I tried again that night, but still nothing. The next day I drove by the head-quarters. The house looked vacant, which was not really different from the way it had looked the other times I had seen it. I knocked on the door. No answer.

I was suddenly overcome by depression and frustration. I had been so close to the Klan. I had met and talked with real Klan members right here. I had hopes of being recruited by someone I had met and associated with right here at this house. Now they were all gone. Had my chances of becoming a member of the Klan gone with them? I wondered. I worried. At that particular moment, my outlook was bleak, hopeless.

But I wasn't about to give up. Finally, on October 11, two days after the election, I did get an answer. It was Emmet's friendly voice that greeted me when I called. "Hello, Don Black could have been your mayor. May I help you?"

"Emmet, this is J.W. I'm mad as hell about the election. Has that nigger got a chance of winning the runoff? If he does, I'm moving away from Birmingham."

"Let me tell you something, J.W., Birmingham is not going to have a nigger mayor. I know this organization that will see to that. In fact, they told me that for three thousand dollars they would see to it. You know what I mean. I don't want to say much on the phone. Three thousand is a lot of money, but I'll come up with it myself if I have to. I think, though, that if we put three thousand dollars in the Parsons campaign he'll beat Arrington. That's what I plan to do—help Parsons as much as I can."

"Well, tomorrow is payday," I told him. "I won't have much, but I'll give you whatever I can to help Parsons." I was relieved that I would not be contributing hit money.

"No, don't bring it to me. Take it directly to the Parsons headquarters downtown and tell them we're doing all we can to help."

"Okay, I'll do that, then. But I'll tell you, I'm so damn disgusted with the prospect of living under a nigger mayor that I'll probably just move somewhere else. I don't have to stay in Birmingham."

This seemed to set Emmet off. His voice got louder and he sounded mad as hell. "Let me tell you this, J.W. If Parsons don't get in, Birmingham still won't have a nigger mayor. Do you know what I mean? If I have to, I'll walk right up to his face myself and blow his ass away. You won't have to move, J.W., I'll see to that."

Emmet had frightened me the night he asked me to bring a gun to the headquarters, but when he talked like this, my fright turned to terror. Somehow, I believed that he felt strongly enough to do something that stupid, all the while rationalizing that he was doing the right thing.

I called Seigenthaler and told him about the conversation. If Emmet was for real, someone should know.

The next morning, the *Post-Herald* reported that Arrington was being given special police protection because he had received several threats. I felt a little better.

The next three weeks were probably the most frustrating of my life. I called Black headquarters each day and got no answer. Three trips to the house were equally futile. I didn't know where to turn. I was fearful that I had let my only link

to Don Black slip away, and I didn't even know who he was.
Still, afraid I would appear too eager, I never went to Parsons headquarters.

All I was doing was building cabinets, and no matter how many cabinets I built, I wasn't getting any closer to the Klan or any closer to being able to go home. At times like this I had to overcome the urge to say the hell with it and head home.

Those three weeks between the primary election and the general election seemed like an eternity. Without Emmet, I had no connection to the Klan and thus could make no progress on the story.

Finally, the general election rolled around. The race for mayor was sure to be a barn burner. Everyone I talked with had an opinion. The battle lines were clearly drawn on nothing more than black and white. The issues had somehow long since been left behind. The prospect of turning back the strongest black challenge to the city's top political post lured the white voters. And for the blacks the most important thing was backing that challenge.

The voting was again the heaviest in Birmingham's history. Outside the predominantly black areas, Arrington had little visible support, with the exception of the area around the University of Alabama-Birmingham campus, on the city's south side. Parsons had campaigned vigorously in the city's white areas, apparently conceding the black vote to Arrington.

Early returns had the race changing leads several times, depending on where the vote count was coming from. However, within an hour after the polls closed, it became apparent that Arrington would be Birmingham's first black mayor.

My landlady, Mrs. Armstrong, had left me a note on my steps the day before the election to tell me she was going into the hospital for some tests concerning her diabetes. While I was trying to plan a way to use Arrington's win most effectively to get me closer to the Klan, I gave her a call to see how she was doing.

"I was doing fine until I saw the election returns on the television," she said. "Now I'm getting sick to my stomach. I sure hope you voted for the white man."

"You can be sure that I did," I lied. "I don't know what the world's coming to. It looks like us white people are just being kicked over in the corner so we won't get in the way of the niggers."

"I know it," she said. "I've been knowing it a lot longer than you have. I've been around here for almost eighty years and I've seen what's happening to this country. I'm glad some of you younger folks are seeing it too. Maybe you'll do something about it."

Mrs. Armstrong would be a good sounding board for my newly rehearsed racist rhetoric, and I wouldn't have to be too afraid of giving myself away through a careless slipup.

Next I started trying almost desperately to reach someone with the Klan. I tried Don Black's old headquarters to see if someone was there preparing a statement on Birmingham's bleak future under a black mayor. No answer.

I called the city room of the *Birmingham Post-Herald* to see if someone there would give me Don Black's telephone number. I was told simply that the number was unlisted and no one there had it.

Rummaging through all my past notes and numbers, I found Ned Coulter's business card—the one he had given me the day he took me to get my Alabama driver's license. I called him at home.

"Ned, this is J.W. Thompson. Remember me? I'm the one you took for a driver's license." I began.

"Yeah, buddy, how's it going?" he asked.

"Well, it's pretty obvious it's not going too good for any white person living in Birmingham. Have you heard the election returns?"

"Yeah. It's a shame, ain't it?"

"It sure the hell is," I agreed. "I'm so damn disgusted I don't know what I'm going to do. I first thought I'd just pack up and leave town, but I'm so damn mad I think I'll stay just for the hell of it. That's why I'm calling you. Did you ever join up with those fellows that were trying to get you to join the Klan over at Don Black's campaign headquarters?"

"No, I talked to them some more, but I never did join. I believe in what they're trying to do," he assured me, "but I'm in a position that I just can't afford to join those folks right now."

"Well, by God, I can. I didn't think I'd ever feel this way, but I do." I didn't think I'd ever hear myself talk this way either. "I've been trying all night to get in touch with Don Black to see if he'll sign me up, but so far I haven't been able to get his number. It's unlisted."

"Wait a minute," Coulter said. "I've got his number here somewhere. Call him up right now; he'll sign you up. It's not too late to call him tonight, then call me back and tell me what he says. I'd do the same thing if I was single, like you, but I've got a wife and kids to think about first. I can't afford to get in any trouble."

Coulter's concern for his wife and kids was not shared by many other Klan members. The Klan was no longer a men-only organization. Most public Klan functions were attended by whole families; many women (called Klansladies in Klan literature), usually wives of Klansmen, were also members, and—horrifying but true—many children of Klan parents were members of the Klan Youth Corps.

After repeating Black's number back to Coulter to make sure I had it right, I made the call. Black's wife answered and told me that Black was not in town and wouldn't be back until later that night. She suggested that I might call him at work the next day and she gave me the number of the Ear, Nose, and Throat Clinic in Birmingham where he worked. She said that it wouldn't disturb him to be called at work because "people call him there all the time."

The next morning seemed to drag on and on. I didn't

want to call Black too early, but I would have to grab whatever opportunity I had to be alone with the phone. I didn't want David to know I was even talking to Don Black. Finally, at about ten David asked me to go pick up some plywood. Perfect. I only hoped I didn't seem too glad to get away from the shop.

Less than a mile from the shop, I stopped on Green Springs Highway at a convenience store that had a phone booth in a remote corner of the parking lot, and gave Black a call. The receptionist put me on hold. Soon a man came on the line with a greeting I was to hear many times after that morning, whenever I called Black at work: "May I help you?"

"Yes, Mr. Black? This is J.W. Thompson. I have never met you, but I worked in your campaign for mayor and was probably as disappointed as you were when you didn't win. Now I'm a hell of a lot more than disappointed, I'm mad, disgusted, and sick to my stomach about the prospect of living under a nigger mayor. I talked with Ned Coulter last night—in fact, he gave me your number—and told him that I'd like to talk to you about maybe joining up with your group. Would that be possible?"

"Yes, I would be glad to meet you somewhere and talk with you. Where do you live?"

"I live over close to Ned on the east side of town near the airport, but I'll meet you anywhere it's convenient for you. I'm a cabinetmaker and our shop is in Homewood, so I could meet you over on that side of town."

"Well, I'm going to be tied up tonight and tomorrow night. Why don't we try to meet the first of next week. Could you call me either here or at home Monday?"

"Sure, that will be no problem," I said. And then, to reinforce the connection, I went on. "I'll tell you, when I heard this Arrington had won, I almost packed up and left town. I may still do that, but I told Ned that I would at least talk to you first. So I'll be back in touch Monday."

"I'll be expecting to hear from you."

As soon as I finished talking with Black, I called Seigen-thaler to report on my progress. He was pleased that I had finally made contact with Black, especially after I had called so many other times to report my lack of progress. He wanted me to tell him everything about the conversation. I hadn't planned on going into such great detail. And I soon realized I had spent too much time on the phone to do my cabinetmaker's job any good, although it was still not nearly enough time for my newspaper job.

But I had a good feeling when I hopped back in Old Blue and started for the plywood company. I had actually talked to the Klan's top man in Alabama and he seemed quiet and low-key and more than willing to talk with me. Finally, some progress. At least I hoped so.

I felt good for another reason too. Since today was Friday, I could leave as soon as I got off work and head for Tennessee to spend the weekend with my family.

This would be my first trip home since I had moved down. When I left Tennessee, I didn't know for sure when I would be able to get back for a visit. I never knew. I just had to play it from day to day, and if the Klan didn't have something planned for the weekend, I would go home. Several times, however, I had anticipated going home and the Klan would schedule something at the last minute to prevent it. During the assignment, I averaged getting home twice a month.

By the time I got to United Plywood that day, it was almost noon and some of the warehouse people had already left for lunch. It took longer than usual to pick up my order and have it loaded.

As I backed into the loading ramp, I noticed an Alabama Highway Patrol car parked in front of the office. Although I had gotten my Alabama driver's license on the basis of a purely fictitious Army discharge, the license itself was valid, so seeing the car did not upset me. That is, until I walked inside and saw the large, uniformed state trooper . . . Cor-poral Lee, the same Corporal Lee who had given me the written examination for my license. Had he found out the truth through some sophisticated computer? Was he here to arrest me? My first inclination was to turn and leave. But it was too late. Both the trooper and Margaret, the woman behind the counter he was talking with, had seen me. In fact, Margaret called me to come on back where they were. "J.W., I'd like you to meet my husband, Roy," she said. "Roy, this is J.W. Thompson. He works over at Village Woodworks."

"Good to see you again, Corporal," I said offering a hand. "You're the fellow who gave me the test for my driver's license."

"Oh, yes," Lee said. "You're the Army man. I'll bet it's some switch from being a soldier to building cabinets."

"It sure is. But the more I learn, the more I enjoy it."

I saw Lee there several times over the next year and I always went to his wife Margaret to be billed out. I got to know them both much better, yet I never felt completely at ease around him. He was another victim of my deception and he was always an instant source of paranoia, no matter how fleeting.

I knew I had been gone too long when I got back to the shop. David was sitting on the saw table with nothing to do because he didn't have any plywood.

"What happened, buddy, did you get lost?" he asked.

"No, I just decided I would go out of town for the weekend and stopped and called an old girlfriend in Chattanooga to make sure she didn't make other plans. I guess we just got carried away planning all the good stuff we're gonna do this weekend."

"Sometimes I wish I was single again so I could do things like that. Boy, you've got it made."

THE TRIP HOME was especially nice. Linda could see my enthusiasm about finally making contact with Black, and we both felt that this was the most important first step in getting the story. I was confident, I told her, that it wouldn't take more than a couple of months to wind it up.

Everything went fine at home until 3:00 A.M. Monday. That's when I had to get up and start back to Alabama in order to be at work by eight. It sure was tough to leave that warm bed in the middle of the night and crawl into a cold car, to leave a place you wanted to be and head for a place you didn't.

Sipping a cup of black coffee, I took advantage of the absence of early-morning traffic and made it to Birmingham more than forty-five minutes ahead of time. Usually I would drive back on Sunday afternoons, but that day I kind of liked seeing the sun come up in a pinkish haze over the Tennessee Valley. Plus, it was something of a shock for David to see me show up at work forty-five minutes early. That alone was worth the loss of sleep.

I tried to call Black at his office three times that day before I finally reached him at home at about 5:45 P.M. He asked if it would be convenient for us to meet the next night after work. That suited me fine because this had already been a long day and I felt sure I would be turning in pretty early.

"Why don't you call me here at home about five-thirty tomorrow before you leave Homewood," Black suggested. "I don't live but about five minutes from Homewood and we'll meet somewhere over there."

I assured him that would be fine and promised to call him the next afternoon.

The next day I phoned him from the shop right at five-thirty. David was ripping some lumber on the table saw and couldn't hear me. It wouldn't have mattered though, because Black hadn't arrived home yet. I left the shop, went to a shopping center on Green Springs Highway, waited thirty minutes, and called him again from a phone booth. This time he answered.

He asked me to pick a place that would be convenient for me. I looked out of the phone booth, up Valley Avenue. A restaurant called Sambo's stood out. I suggested we meet there. I couldn't help chuckling to myself after we hung up. Here I was going to meet with the top dog of the Alabama Ku Klux Klan at a place named Sambo's—and I had picked it. I secretly hoped he would be as uncomfortable with the restaurant as I would be with him.

I arrived first and chose a booth near the front of the restaurant. I sat facing the entrance and ordered a cup of coffee from the young black waitress while I waited. I recognized him immediately when he walked into Sambo's. A tall, muscular young man of erect bearing, he stood for a moment in the doorway until he saw me. I must have been easy to spot: I was the only person in the restaurant dressed in bib overalls and a red baseball cap. I'm sure I looked like a cabinetmaker.

He walked briskly—a sort of military march-step—

toward the booth where I was sitting. "You must be J.W. Thompson," he said, extending his hand. "I'm Don Black."

His handshake was firm and his eyes—very dark eyes—were penetrating. I knew immediately there was no way this man could be stared down, no way he could be intimidated.

My main concern at this point was my performance. Could I deceive him? Could I dupe Don Black into thinking I was a retired Army sergeant, now a cabinetmaker, who shared his racist and anti-Semitic views? We'll just see, I silently told myself as I looked across the table at this well-groomed twenty-seven-year-old, who appeared to be sizing me up as we exchanged small talk about the weather.

I must say that, although I was nervous during that first meeting, I felt I held a distinct advantage, however temporary that advantage might be. I knew who Don Black was, but he didn't know J.W. Thompson.

Could this man sitting across the table from me, sipping coffee, be the man whom some suspected of threatening to strangle a Jewish classmate in high school? Was this the man who had been labeled the "weird kid" and who grew up to be a fanatic about such things as "race mixing" and "the Jewish-controlled news media"?

I learned quickly that this was indeed the man I had studied. Black wasted no time in giving me the spiel he had perfected in countless recruiting speeches during the previous six and a half years.

"White people have been too complacent and have let the country erode to the point where we no longer have a country," he told me. "The Jews are carefully brainwashing the whole nation. But they've been run out of every civilized European country and you could see that happen here."

"You might think I'm one of those white people who have been sitting on their butt and waiting for someone else to do something about the way the niggers are taking over," I told him, "and you're right." I was trying to recall and play back to him the line I had so carefully rehearsed, based on weeks of research, tedious preparation and interviews with the lawyers and the psychiatrist. "I guess the nigger mayor thing finally opened my eyes, and I know after talking with you that we've all got to get in this fight. I'm ready. I just hope it's not too late for me to do something that might help save this country."

I could tell by the look on his face that he liked that kind of talk.

Even though it was our first meeting, he had no hesitation about discussing his hatred for rival Klan leader Bill Wilkinson, Imperial Wizard of the Invisible Empire of the Ku Klux Klan. I guessed that the initial period of sizing me up must be coming to an end when Black began talking openly about Wilkinson.

I had also studied Wilkinson, and I knew he had defected from the Klan group that Duke and Black headed. Wilkinson preached that "a race war is coming" and that whites should arm themselves against such an eventuality.

There was no way then, nor is there now, to estimate the size of either group. Privately, both Black and Wilkinson imply they have followings numbering in the tens of thousands. Publicly, they never mention numbers. I'm convinced both groups have fewer members than they would like people to believe.

I knew, or at least had strong reason to believe, that Wilkinson was rough around the edges. Duke, who makes a good appearance on television, is smooth, articulate, and polished. Wilkinson thinks Duke and his followers are naive. Duke sees Wilkinson as ineffective. Wilkinson preaches vigilance and arms and violent response, if need be, to combat what he sees as the black menace. Duke, who once was convicted of inciting to riot, has counseled, both publicly and privately, avoidance of situations that could lead to arrest. "You can't do yourself, your family, or our movement any good if you are in jail," he would tell his members.

"I believe Bill Wilkinson is a federal agent," Black said to

me. "He's done more to destroy the Klan than the FBI ever
did. If he's not a federal agent, he should be." (Later, when I
joined Wilkinson's Invisible Empire, one of his Klan officers
told me, "Don Black is working for the FBI.")

My first meeting with Black had a timely element. Only
five days before, more than two dozen local Klansmen and
Nazis had engaged in a deadly shoot-out in Greensboro,
North Carolina, with members of the Communist Workers
party, who had been participating in a "death to the Klan"
rally there. When the gunfire ceased and the smoke cleared,
four people were lying dead in the street and a fifth died the
next day.

"The economy, politics, national leadership, energy, and
several other factors are going to hand us the opportunity to
reclaim our country," Black continued, talking as though he
were still running for mayor. "We must be prepared to take
advantage of that opportunity or be prepared to live under a
tyrannical dictatorship."

The waitress stopped by our table to ask if we wanted
more coffee. Black declined politely, but I asked for a refill
and sipped it as I listened to his diatribe, trying all the while
to formulate in my mind how I would broach the question of
whether I could join his organization.

I was careful to refer to it as "your group" because I
wasn't sure how open he wanted to be about the racist
organization. Trying to ingratiate myself, I began to sympa-
thize with him about his unsuccessful mayoral campaign. He
never had any illusions about winning that race, he said, to
my surprise.

"When you run for a political office, the news media cover it," he said. "I never had any thoughts about winning, but
I did have many opportunities to say things that would not
have otherwise been publicized. The one enlightening thing
about the mayor's race was that 90 percent of the white
people in Birmingham voted as a block and they did that
only because a nigger was in the race. If they would just
realize that if we stick together like the niggers and vote as a

block like that we could change a lot of things going wrong in this country. I don't know what it will take to make white people realize that we still have the majority and if we use it we can stop the federal government from shoving the niggers down our throats. Did you ever hear of a politician who didn't go after the nigger vote? They know they are all going to vote and they are all going to vote the same way. The nigger vote wouldn't be that important if the white people would just stick together the way they do.

"The Klan is the only group in the world that is looking out for white people. The niggers have the NAACP—they have CORE, the SCLC, and all kinds of groups looking out and speaking for them, but the only group for white people is the Klan."

"I'll tell you, Don," I began, "I've never had the situation pointed out to me like you have tonight. My first inclination after the nigger was elected was to move somewhere else where there's more white people. I don't have any kids in school, so I'm not worried about busing. I work in a three-man cabinet shop, so I'm not worried about affirmative action programs. But I do have to pay taxes and I'm damn sick and tired of driving my old sixty-seven Volkswagen over to Foodworld to buy some hamburger for supper and have to wait in line behind some nigger with a cart full of steaks that he pays for with food stamps, then takes them out to his Cadillac. I'm ready to join the Klan"—at last, I said it out loud—"and do all I can to help you straighten out this country before it's too late. That is, if it's not already too late."

"I'll be glad to take your application," he said. "I've got some forms out in the car."

We paid for our coffee and walked to his car in the restaurant parking lot. He opened the trunk, and I could see a clutter of posters and bumper stickers left over from the campaign, newspapers and car tools, and a two-burner hot plate. On top of the heap lay Black's white satin Klan robe. He couldn't find an application blank, but he finally pulled out three copies of *The Crusader*, the official publication of his Klan organization.

"Take these," he told me. "They've got application blanks in them. Take them home, fill one out, and I'll meet you again in a couple of days."

I had trouble containing my jubilation as I drove away that night. "I'm home free," I nearly shouted, thinking how much time I had spent fabricating my background and the twenty-year Army career and all the monotony of going over both again and again. And then the two months of living in Birmingham undercover, which mainly consisted of hard physical labor in the cabinet shop and being careful to adhere to all the elaborate precautions I had taken to establish and protect my new identity.

I was convinced I had succeeded when I left Black that night. I couldn't wait to phone my publisher and give him the good news.

Two days later, I waited for Black at Sambo's. He seemed to be in a hurry when he came in, and he refused a cup of coffee. I quickly finished mine, paid for it, and followed him out to the cold, windy parking lot.

When we got to his car, I unsnapped the bib of my overalls and took out my wallet with the filled-out application form and twenty-five dollars. Black had told me that would be my registration fee—a onetime "naturalization" charge of fifteen dollars, plus ten dollars—for my prorated dues for the remainder of 1979. I offered him the money and application. He ignored them. I suddenly felt foolish standing there with my hand extended.

Clearly, Black was suspicious, as he must be about every Klan recruit. Was he trying to detect that slightest flicker of hesitation, a momentary stumble, that one slipup, which would tip him off that I was not who or what I pretended to be?

I had known from the outset that this moment would come, sometime, someplace, but I had envisioned it in some dark Klavern meeting and had even feared that I might be asked to take a lie detector test.

During the weeks of preparation I had become J.W. Thompson, a retired Army sergeant, who was running from "the niggers up North" and a nasty divorce. Black had learned this much about my past during our first meeting, now he wanted to know more.

"Had you always lived in the North before moving to Birmingham?" he asked sharply.

"No . . ." I began, struggling suddenly to recall all the details of the story I had concocted.

But he interrupted, grilling me with his next question. "What did your father do for a living? Was he a farmer?"

"No," I responded, "he worked for a glass company. He made . . ."

Before I could answer one question completely, Black would fire off another one.

I couldn't complain. Finally, this was the opportunity I had worked toward for the four months—even I was surprised that that much time had already elapsed—since I had agreed to try to infiltrate the Klan.

The same thoughts kept racing through my mind: Look him right in the eye, stay cool, don't blow it.

I had known, of course, that Klan leaders would be cautious, that they would take precautions to try to make sure no spy got into their secret organization. I knew I was well prepared, but I had not thought, until this very moment, that there was any possibility this test would come in, of all places, the parking lot of a Birmingham restaurant.

But Black—I feel certain now that I know him much better—had planned it that way. He obviously wanted to pick a moment when I least expected he would launch a blistering barrage of questions.

He caught me off guard. I was angry with myself for not being more cynical about that first meeting. I should have known it had been too easy. I should have suspected that Klan admission couldn't possibly be as simple as that.

Piercing me again with those penetrating eyes, he asked—almost demanded, it seemed—"You say you are a retired Army man. What was your MOS?"

I had the answer to that. Establishing a military occupational specialty was part of that repeated preparation that suddenly seemed too far in the past to recall. The MOS was 058, the designation for a code interceptor.

I had obviously been too confident after our last meeting, assuming that I had been accepted. Now I was struggling to recall all those rehearsals about my career and background. Until these recollections started coming back, I would have to play it by ear. I had known all along that I would have to play it that way to a certain extent because there was no way I could possibly anticipate every question that I might be asked. I recalled my session with the psychiatrist last summer. His warnings were coming back rapidly: "Don't concoct anything too elaborate. Keep it simple. Don't appear too eager and don't volunteer any information. They are suspicious people, keep that in mind. Try not to be specific, keep it general."

"That was my last MOS," I told Black. "I started out as a mess sergeant, but then did several other things. I was in an engineering company building field stations for a while."

"What did you say your dad did for a living?" Black asked.

"He was a glassblower. He made thermometers on a contract basis for B. D. Yale. I think that was the company."

"Where were you last stationed?" He was skipping around. I felt he was trying to throw me off balance.

"Fort Devens, Massachusetts."

"Are you married?"

"No. That's another reason I came to Birmingham. I'm running from her too."

"Where did you live after moving from Kentucky?"

"My parents lived in several places in Virginia—Staunton, Norfolk, Falls Church."

And so it went, the interrogation while standing beside Black's car on November 8, 1979—a date indelibly stamped in my memory. He was calm and intense—and doggedly persistent. I was outwardly nonchalant. But I knew, inwardly, that this was my chance, perhaps my only chance, and that I could blow it if Black got too detailed in his questioning.

Black had once wanted a military career. How much did he know about the Army? He had once been in the ROTC. Would he ask me a question that any private should know but I would fumble?

"Where did you say you work?"

"Over in Homewood. I'm a cabinetmaker's helper. It's not much money, but it's something to do and it gives me beer money."

"And you are a native of where?"

"Geneva, Alabama. I lived there as a kid but we moved to Birmingham when I was little, and then we moved on to Kentucky."

I had worried about my "birthplace" of Geneva. The name of the town in southern Alabama had popped into my head during my preparation for this assignment. I once spent a few hours there in 1970 while covering George Wallace's campaign for governor.

But had Don Black ever been there? Did he know on what street the corner drugstore fronts? Did he know the name of the local high school?

I had spent two or three hours in Geneva. Maybe Black had relatives there. Knowing he was from Athens, Alabama, on the state's northern border, I deliberately picked a small, rural town on the state's southern border. Maybe he had vacationed there. Maybe . . .

There was no way to anticipate his questions, no way to know when I might slip, providing him with the only clue he would need to expose my charade.

He fixed me with what I felt were cold, calculating eyes. And then suddenly he took my money and application. Rummaging in the trunk of his car, he said abruptly, "I'll give you a receipt."

I silently breathed a sigh of relief and accepted the receipt—which had been penciled on the back of a campaign leaflet left over from Black's campaign for mayor.

"I'll be getting in touch with you in a few days," he told me. "We're going to have a meeting in a couple of weeks over in Brompton on the Atlanta highway. I'll want you there then. We like to induct four or five new members at a time. We'll go through the ceremony and you'll take about a thirty-minute oath.

"I'm glad to have you with us. It's going to take a joint effort by all of us to get done what we've got to do. We've got to stick together if we are ever going to have any power."

My knees might have been weak and shaking at that point, but I am sure my voice was strong and confident.

"I'm glad to be a part of your group," I said. "You'll be able to count on me."

I had finally made it! I was now inside the Ku Klux Klan. I hadn't even noticed till then that the night was cold and windy. But in spite of that I could feel a drop of sweat trickling down between my shoulders as I walked to my car. Now I really had something to call my publisher about.

Being so confident after my first meeting then undergoing such an intense interrogation as this one, I knew there would be many other tests I would have to undergo before this assignment was completed.

I wondered whether I could hoodwink veteran Klansmen into accepting me as a hardened racist. Could I mingle in a crowd of dozens of such people, dressed in a robe and hood? Could I picket with them, go to their Klavern meetings, listen to their speeches, maybe even torch the crosses they burn from time to time as a ritual of their bizarre faith? Could I do all this, associating with them on a daily basis, without making a mistake that would expose my identity?

The answers would be quick in coming—very soon after

my initial involvement with the Knights of the Ku Klux Klan.

From the outset of the assignment, I had lingering doubts that I would ever actually become a member of the Klan. Somehow I had felt they would be more careful, check more thoroughly, on those people seeking to join. Now that those doubts had been removed and I had paid my money, I knew I was a Klansman. I was convinced that—what was to follow—the initiation, the oath, the den assignment—would be mere formalities.

For the next two weeks, I tried to create scenarios and then rehearsed what I would do in each one. Obviously, there was no way I could possibly anticipate what circumstances I might actually face, but I tried to conjure up as many as I could.

I had enjoyed the luxury of almost three months of rehearsal time between accepting the assignment and meeting with Black. After clearing that first hurdle, the next one would be coming up much sooner. Would there be enough time? Would I be subjected to more questioning about my past when I actually attended that Klavern meeting? If so, would someone there ask me some questions that Black had not thought of?

These questions were constantly on my mind and my imagination was running rampant with all the various possibilities. Normally, when I worked in the cabinet shop, I tried only to think of the task at hand, remaining always aware that I was working with high-speed machinery that could remove a finger, a hand, or a whole arm in a split second. It would take only one careless slipup. Yet several times the next day I caught myself thinking about my meetings with Black and trying to analyze each question he asked. My probing analysis continued throughout the drive to Tennessee after work on Friday afternoon.

It was obvious that Linda did not share my enthusiasm about my finally meeting Black, paying my dues, and joining the Klan. I believe she too had had doubts that I would ever get in, and probably secretly hoped I wouldn't. Nevertheless, I tried to postpone the rehearsal during my stay at home.

Thoughts of my initiation did not settle in again until the drive back to Birmingham on Monday morning. Fortunately, it was an easy day at the shop, mostly staining and spraying and very little work with the power tools.

I had been at the cabinet shop long enough to know how to operate all the machines and long enough to become interested in seeing what I could create from a board or a pile of wood. I had begun making small items to take home. Every trip I had something new to take with me, a napkin holder, a spice cabinet, a wooden canister, a bulletin board, or a wood turning. Many nights I would stay and putter around until midnight or after before driving across town to my apartment. In many ways, my woodworking kept me from thinking of all the bad things that could happen when I attended my first Klan meeting—the many ways I could screw up and be turned away before actually being formally sworn in.

I called Black about a week after our last meeting at Sambo's. I wanted to appear interested but not too eager, so I made a special effort not to bug him on the phone.

I explained that the reason I called was that, as we ended our meeting that night, he had mentioned a rally near Florence, Alabama, "in a couple of weeks," suggesting that I might want "to come on up."

He told me the rally was still on and when I told him I would definitely come up, he gave me detailed instructions on how to find it. The rally was not too near Florence, but right in the center of a small city twenty-five miles to the east—Lexington, Alabama. I couldn't help but wonder if he had deliberately told me Florence knowing all along that it would be in Lexington. But I passed this possibility off as just another wave of instant paranoia.

Not only was Lexington east of Florence, it was only

about twenty miles south of Pulaski, Tennessee—the city that gave birth to the Ku Klux Klan in 1865.

On Saturday, November 17, 1979, less than two weeks after I gave Black my dues money in that cold, windy restaurant parking lot, I got up early. It was a bright, warm, sunny fall day. I sat at my kitchen table, sipping coffee and watching two squirrels frolic in the large pecan tree that grew beside the kitchen window. They were free and protected by law. I felt trapped and knew my only protection depended on how well I could act out the massive charade I had started several months ago. This night would be the first real test.

I was looking forward to the rally. It would be another step toward the end of the assignment. At the same time, I was apprehensive. Could I fool a true-blue Klansman into believing that I was also a racist intent on reclaiming our country for the white people? Would there be someone there from Tennessee who would readily recognize me, another newsman maybe? I had to believe that I could fool the Klansmen and I had to have faith that I wouldn't be recognized. Whatever, I had to quit thinking about it because the rally was still twelve hours away. Since even squirrel watching gets boring after so long, I got dressed and drove to the cabinet shop.

Although the shop was normally closed on Saturdays, I knew David would be there puttering around. It was obvious that he was glad to see me. He was sweeping sawdust from under the table saw when I walked in.

"Hey, buddy," was his greeting, "you decide to stay in town this weekend?"

"I'll be here all day," I answered, "but tonight I've got a date with a cute little blonde up in Huntsville. She's a hair stylist. Hell, I might even get my hair done."

"Yeah, I bet you do. You've got it made. You really make me wish I was still single."

We both chuckled.

"Well," he said, "since you're going to be here all day, it would be a good day to paint your car. If you'll go get the paint I'll work on it."

My old VW kind of resembled me—we were both bald on top. It was a good idea.

"You think it'll have time to dry?" I asked.

"I'm sure it will. Ask at the store to be sure."

The man at the store assured me his paint would be dry in four hours. We would have plenty of time.

The paint was on before 11:00 P.M., but by 4:00 P.M., it was still wet. I couldn't even open the car without getting bright red splotches all over me. How the hell would I be able to drive it to Lexington? I was near panic. David sensed my anxiety.

"Don't worry," he consoled me. "If it's not dry when you have to leave, you can take the Jeep. I can drive the truck."

I had planned to continue on north after the rally and spend Sunday at home with the family in Tennessee.

"That would be fine," I said, "but if this honey I'm going to see works out like I hope she will, I wasn't planning on leaving Huntsville until early Monday, just in time to get back to work."

"That's all right," he said. "I won't need the Jeep before then."

I was greatly relieved, since I didn't have the cash to rent a car, no credit cards, and no identification other than the Alabama driver's license based on false data. I left the shop, drove quickly to my apartment and changed clothes, and was on my way. I roared north up I-65 that afternoon in a bouncy Jeep with the canvas top flapping against its metal support rods, I couldn't think of a more appropriate vehicle to be driving to my first Klan rally—a vehicle with the word RENEGADE boldly emblazoned along each side of the hood.

When I arrived in Lexington, four hooded Klansmen stationed at the town's main intersection directed me to a parking place. The rally was being held on Lions Club property adjacent to a ball park. After parking, I started toward the group erecting the large, kerosene-soaked cross that would be lit at the end of the meeting.

There were about 150 people at the rally, including about 60 in Klan robes. David Duke would be the main speaker. Black and several others would also speak.

As I walked through the cool night, I spotted *Tennessean* photographer Nancy Warnecke sitting in her car. Nancy was part of a team of *Tennessean* staffers who conducted a separate investigation on the Klan after I went under cover. That investigation, from the outside, also involved Susan Thomas and Kirk Loggins. Since Seigenthaler felt our paths might cross, he told them about my assignment, stressing how vital it was to keep it quiet. It was nice to see a friendly face from home, but there was no attempt at any communication between us.

A jolly-looking hefty man with a red beard was pounding a stake to support the cross. When he finished, I commented that he delivered some massive blows with the sledge hammer.

"I'd do anything to keep warm," he said, extending his hand and saying his name—Don Oliver.

Then I spotted Don Black. He was surrounded by a group of newsmen, so I didn't go near. When he finally noticed me in the crowd, he nodded and smiled. He knew I was here.

A few minutes later, I saw David Duke. He was also surrounded by a crowd, but they all appeared to be Klansmen. I joined that group and managed to move close enough to shake Duke's hand and introduce myself. I told him it had been worth the trip from Birmingham just to get to meet him because I had long been one of his admirers.

"Glad to see you," he said. "I really appreciate all of you coming out on a chilly night like this."

About this time, Mike Norris, a rather rotund young man in his twenties, tested the public-address system and announced to the crowd that the rally would get under way in about ten minutes. He also reminded everyone that there were plenty of Klan materials and refreshments for sale.

When the rally began, Norris again took the microphone and urged everyone to "move on up here closer. We're all white. There's nothing to be afraid of. Move on up here."

After a lengthy prayer by a robed chaplain, the rally was under way.

Norris introduced Duke as a man of courage "who has withstood numerous life threats and physical abuse, a great leader who is running for the State Senate in Louisiana—and we're gonna help him all we can."

Duke, who looked like the proverbial Philadelphia lawyer in his fashionable business suit, pointed out a man in the crowd, also in a vested business suit, and told the group the man had "come all the way from Pittsburgh, Pennsylvania, to be with us tonight. He is organizing a Klan in Pennsylvania. Our movement is spreading. We now have Klan groups in the military and throughout the nation and world."

Duke also corrected Norris and said he was defeated in his bid for the Louisiana State Senate the year before, "but I got twenty-eight percent of the votes in a well-educated, semiliberal district of Louisiana."

While stressing that his Klan did not condone violence or breaking the law, Duke said the white majority—"and we still have a majority in the United States—must take a stand for our rights just like the blacks, the Jews, and other anti-whites." Duke never once used the word "nigger," always "blacks" or "Africans."

Referring to the recent Greensboro shoot-out, he pointed out that a witness to the shootings, Laura Blumenthal, "a Jew," had "television news film to prove that the Klansmen were fired upon first and were merely defending themselves while under the siege of gunfire. They had to get their weapons out of the trunks of their cars while they were being fired upon," he said.

Duke then asked for donations from the crowd for a defense fund for the Klansmen charged in North Carolina, while emphasizing that the "Knights of the Ku Klux Klan is in no way connected to the Greensboro Klansmen involved, but we feel it is our obligation to protect their constitutional rights to defend themselves against armed subversives."

Several robed Klansmen passed through the crowd collecting donations in plastic buckets. I chipped in a ten-dollar bill, apologizing to the bucket carrier that I was not "able to do more."

Bobby Perry, a new Klansman decked out in a brand-new robe, was called to the speakers' platform, professing to be "like Tennessee Ernie Ford, nervous as a long-tailed tomcat in a room full of rocking chairs."

"I'm ashamed of myself," Perry said, "for waiting as long as I did before deciding to take a stand for my rights and your rights. Most of you know me. I work over at Reynolds Aluminum. Years ago, when I was helping George Wallace, a nigger foreman tried to get me run off. He's been trying to get me fired ever since. Every payday you can see him going around to the other niggers and getting their money for the NAACP and their groups."

"Yeah, I've seen him do it," someone shouted from the crowd.

"Folks, if we're gonna be able to live here in north Alabama, like we've been used to, we're all gonna have to take a stand and I don't know of any better way than to join the Klan. So, take a stand and join the Klan. I wish I had done it thirty years ago."

Obviously, many of those present knew Perry personally and gave him a rousing round of applause as he left the platform.

In calling Black to the podium, Norris urged him to "warm us up with a talk like a Baptist preacher."

Black began with reports of his personal protests to the two recent "antiwhite television movies, *Freedom Road*, in which Muhammad—what's his name—Ali, was a freed slave who became a senator, and *Undercover for the KKK*, in which a football player [Don Meredith] who wasn't good enough to stay in the game played Gary Thomas Rowe, an admitted liar under indictment in Lowndes County [Alabama] for murder."

(Black and several robed Klansmen had picketed the Birmingham television stations during the telecasts of the movies. Rowe, an FBI informer, was indicted for the 1965 murder of civil rights worker Viola Liuzzo and was fighting extradition from Georgia where he had been living under another identity. Several months later the indictment was dropped altogether.)

"Rowe has successfully managed to avoid prosecution," Black said, "by staying in Georgia. And he'll keep it in court for years. There's not one bit of truth in either of those shows," Black continued, "but both are antiwhite. Just try to get an antiblack or anti-Jew show on and see how much fuss is raised. They've shown that show, ten or twelve hours of it, *Weeds* twice, about some fellow who traced his roots. And *Holocaust* was shown twice—both attempting to muster sympathy and support for the blacks and Jews. There hasn't been any shows about how the white person has been abused, pushed out of his neighborhood, his kids bused to black schools, his job promotion taken by a less-qualified black."

Black received loud applause and cheers as he left the platform.

I met him as he came off the platform and told him I'd never heard a Baptist preacher do a better job of warming people up. Several others rushed up to shake Black's hand and express their approval before he excused himself, saying he had to "get my robe on for the cross lighting," which he and Duke conducted.

Later, as Black hurried toward the towering cross, he turned to me and said, "Glad you could make it, J.W., I'll see you at the meeting."

I assumed that meant it was still on for the following Thursday night.

Up to this point, the mood of the rally crowd had been friendly and enthusiastic—even bordering, at times, on a near festive atmosphere. The one minor exception came during Duke's speech. Four teenagers, who had obviously been drinking, kept shouting "White power" and "Kill niggers" while he spoke. But then, when Bobby Perry began praising the "good work of our law-enforcement people in north Alabama," uniformed officers moved into the crowd and removed the noisy youngsters despite their assurances that "Man, I'm straight, I'm all right." However, when over the loudspeaker a voice told everyone to gather around the cross for the lighting ceremony, the mood changed to one of solemn seriousness. The folks obviously viewed this part of the rally with a special reverence. The laughing and talking that had followed the speeches diminished to whispers as we gathered in almost total silence behind the robed Klansmen circling the cross.

Black, standing with Duke inside the circle of Klan members, took one of the torches from the barrel where they had been soaking in kerosene. The other robed participants already had theirs. After igniting his torch, Black walked to the edge of the circle and held it out to one of the Klansmen in the circle. This person, in turn, offered the flame to the person on his right—a sequence repeated until the last torch was blazing brightly.

Black then led the group in a series of "salutes" in which they raised and lowered their burning torches several times before hoisting them above their heads and marching around the cross in a circle to the right.

At the end of the march, Black walked to the base of the huge cross and touched his torch to the kerosene-soaked burlap. The flames quickly darted up the cross to the cross member, becoming more brilliant with the ascent. The other robed Klansmen then moved to the base of the burning cross and deposited their still-burning torches in a pile there.

As the cross burned brighter, and after the Klan members had resumed their positions in the circle, Duke and Black went around and shook everyone's hand. Back in the center of the circle and illuminated by the flickering glow of fire-light, Duke told the crowd of the beauty and significance of the fiery cross.

"The fiery cross is a Klan symbol of the ideals of Christian civilization and in no way does it represent a desecration of the cross. It represents the truth and the light of our sacred doctrine. Let me say that the cross is an inspiration, a sym-bol of purity, of faith, hope, and love—a signal of opposition to tyranny and obedience to God."

After standing for a few moments in silent awe at the flaming spectacle before them, the people in the crowd began to turn jovial again. Some sauntered over to the sales table to make last-minute purchases of Klan souvenirs, while others went directly to their cars or trucks and began leav-ing.

As I drove home to Tennessee that night, I actually felt good. However, throughout the rally I was uncomfortable, nervous, and downright afraid. It was like hitting yourself in the head with a hammer—it feels good when you quit. I guess my mood of mild euphoria had to do with several things: going home, for one; and the fact that I had been able to talk, mingle, and associate with other Klan members without giving myself away or being discovered.

NOVEMBER 22, 1979—Thanksgiving Day. This was to be my night of initiation. Black said several others would be coming in too.

I drove directly home after work on Wednesday, had an early Thanksgiving dinner with my family and hurriedly drove back to Birmingham.

I left my apartment shortly after 6:30 P.M. The meeting was to start at 7:30. I had driven out to Brompton the week before to find out exactly where the den was and determined that it was only a thirty-minute drive from my apartment.

When I got to the white concrete-block building right off the interstate in Brompton, there were no signs of activity, no cars parked outside. I drove on through the four-way stop and turned around about a mile farther down the road. There I stopped in the parking lot of a small grocery store, where I could keep an eye on the building. I didn't want to be the first one at the meeting, mainly because I didn't want to be questioned by some suspicious stranger. I knew I would feel more comfortable and would probably be accepted without question if I arrived at the same time as Black.

I waited until 8:30 P.M. Still nothing was happening at the building, but a white Ford pickup had been driving by regularly for the past twenty minutes and its three occupants seemed to be checking me out. They were beginning to get on my nerves. The truck had passed six times and the deer rifle in the rack in the back window looked bigger each time it went by. Next time the truck passed and was out of sight, I took off and went back to my apartment.

I tried to call Black—twice from the Leeds exit and several times from home—but I never got an answer. I was pretty upset to think that I could have been back in Tennessee with my family instead of sitting in a deserted parking lot two hundred miles away. This day could be chalked up as zero accomplished toward my assignment.

However, all alone, I had time to think about some other possibilities. Here it was Thanksgiving Day. If I were really divorced and my other relatives lived in Virginia, I would have no reason to be out of town. On the other hand, if Black had any reason to suspect my concocted background, what better day than Thanksgiving to schedule a meeting? Could this just be another phase of the screening process before actually opening the Klan to me? I finally convinced myself that it was.

The next morning I called Black at work and told him I had been in Brompton, at the meeting place, but nobody ever showed up. He said he had tried to contact me earlier yesterday to tell me that the meeting had been canceled. He said he hadn't realized that the day the meeting was scheduled for was Thanksgiving.

I suspected he was lying, but I had no way to be sure. I knew I was lying when I told him I was at the shop yesterday morning just puttering around until about 11:00 A.M., when, at David's insistence, I went home with him for Thanksgiving dinner.

I didn't talk with Black again—another period of frustration and no progress—until December 4, when I contacted him at work. He said he was too busy to talk and suggested I call him back later. I called again on December 6, and we had a rather lengthy conversation.

He told me that we would probably have my initiation meeting at Brompton in a week but asked me to check with him just to "make sure our plans haven't changed again." He also said he would be out of town for the rest of this week, but "we may have something Saturday, if you want to check with me Saturday morning."

I took "something" to mean some type of Klan activity and assured him I'd call on Saturday. I was eager but consciously trying not to be overanxious.

I tried him until eleven-thirty Saturday morning—and there was no answer at his home. I called him as soon as I got home from work the following Monday to make sure things were still on for my initiation Thursday.

"As far as I know everything is okay," he said, "but let me make sure. Call me Thursday at work if you can."

I took the opportunity, the first one I'd had, to tell Black how much Duke had impressed me with his talk in Lexington last month. I said I felt Duke was "enthusiastic" and "a man full of energy."

"He sure is," Black responded. "He is a good leader."

Between that rally and this conversation with Black, I had had several strategy discussions with Seigenthaler. We decided that it might help me to get closer to Duke if I talked with Black about Duke's announced intentions to run for President and if I offered to take off at least two weeks each month to work in his campaign.

I mentioned to Black that someone had spoken of Duke's plans about the presidency and said that I would be willing to do anything I could to help him. I also wanted Black to confirm Duke's candidacy.

"He will be running in some presidential preference primaries this spring," Black said, "but only in a few states. We're not doing it to win, because we are not in a position to consider that at this point. The point is to get some delegates from the different states at the Democratic National Convention; it would be a tremendous coup for us to have delegates at the convention."

I clearly had asked what turned out to be a rather fruitful question.

Black went on: "We'd be wielding some power, plus we would have national TV exposure for the nominating speeches and seconding speeches. We could have resolutions presenting our views be placed on the Democratic platform which could prove to be embarrassing to the Democrats. For instance, a resolution condemning reverse discrimination against whites—and the Democrats will vote against it. We would have forced their hand and they would have to demonstrate to the whole country that they support reverse discrimination. So, there are a lot of things we can do with that and I think it will go a long way toward setting us up for the future elections."

I questioned him further about the logistics of a Duke campaign and asked him if there were states in which he could garner a portion of the delegates even if he didn't win the whole state.

"In most states it is just a portion," Black said. "There are very few states left with winner-take-all. In most states it is strictly whatever percentage you get. A certain percentage of the votes takes away some delegates. And, considering who the opposition is—the three main candidates in the Democratic race are Kennedy, Carter, and Jerry Brown, and all of those are very liberal—in many states, particularly in the South, I think you have a good chance of edging some of those major candidates out."

In 1978, when Duke ran for the Louisiana State Senate, his district included the Louisiana State University community and was considered a liberal district. His chief opponent was the incumbent, a conservative who was well known and well liked. Duke, the youngest candidate in the Senate races that year, never attempted to dissociate himself from the

Klan because, after all, it was the Klan that had given him name recognition. When the votes were counted, Duke had stunned many old-time political observers and had garnered nearly one-third of the votes cast.

"If he gets twenty-eight percent of the votes in the presidential preference race," Black said, "that would win a lot of delegates. In fact, that might win it for him divided four ways, because there aren't that many clear-cut contenders in this race."

After reconfirming plans for my initiation on Thursday, I told Black I would check back with him once more just to be sure.

I called his office on Thursday, but it was his day off. I tried his home repeatedly during the day and was unable to reach him. I tried again the minute I got home from work at about seven. If things were still on, I had to move fast. I had decided that I would drive directly to Brompton again, in any case. I was surprised when Black answered this time.

"Okay," he said, when I asked him about the initiation, "there is not going to be a naturalization, so we will have to wait, probably until next Thursday."

Until now, we had always talked about "initiation." This was the first time I had heard him use the word "naturalization" to describe the ceremony.

"There are not enough people to be naturalized," he continued, "we'll have to wait. We usually like to wait until we have several people at one time."

Again, he asked me to get back in touch before next week—"just to make sure." I assured him I would, and I purposefully did not call him before the day of the planned naturalization. I was afraid that if I called him too often he would begin to notice that I was too anxious. My hunch was that he had a suspicious nature, and I didn't want it to appear that I was in a big hurry, that I was working against a deadline.

At 6:00 P.M. on December 20, I called him at home. I told him that I had tried to reach him several times during the

day to find out if the ceremony was still on. I apologized for
not calling in a week and lied about "almost forgetting" that
tonight was the night of the meeting.

"We are not going to have any more meetings until after
Christmas," he said, without elaborating. "It will have to be
Thursday, the week after Christmas. Why don't you check
with me then."

During my stay at home during the holidays, I found that,
for all the people who did believe the cover story, there was
one who never did—Bob Sherborne. When I had called
home one night, Linda told me he had just left.

"What did he want? What did you tell him?" I asked,
knowing full well what he wanted. He wanted to know
about me, where I was, what I was doing.

"I told him that he already knew: the paper had sent you
off to dry out and Seigenthaler had asked me not to tell anyone where you were so they wouldn't try to contact you."

"What did he say to that?"

"He said, 'Bullshit!'" she told me. "And he also said he
would just stay here until you came home unless I would
assure him you would call him the next time you were here.
I knew he meant it, too. So I told him you would call."

When I called, he drove out to the house. I told him all
about the assignment, knowing that, without a doubt, my
secret was safe. In the long run, this proved to be one of the
smarter things I did. Many times when I was home we
would get together and I could find out what was going on
at the paper—the kinds of goings-on that the publisher
doesn't know about. And it gave Linda an added sense of
security to know he was nearby in case she needed him.

My next contact with Black was on Wednesday, January
2. He said the January 3 meeting had been rescheduled for
Thursday, January 10. I had to work very hard not to reveal
the great frustration I was feeling.

I tried to reach him the following Wednesday but was

unable to get an answer at his home several times. Finally, he answered. By this time I no longer had to identify myself; he readily recognized my voice.

"What's going on," he asked me, "you been initiated yet?" He was in a jovial mood; I didn't know what to make of it. Black asking *me* what was going on! This confirmed my suspicions that the Klan was in fact doing nothing in Birmingham.

Again, the Thursday meeting was canceled, but he said he was having a meeting that night near his home, in Bluff Park. He offered to have someone meet me at the U-Totem store at the Alford Avenue exit on I-65 south to show me the meeting place. I was to be waiting at 7:00 P.M.

I got to the meeting place at 6:50 P.M., went inside for a Coke, and returned to my car. I waited in the parking lot near a phone booth. By 7:20, no one had showed up. I tried to call Black but there was no answer. I bought a magazine and waited some more. At 8:10, after several more attempts to reach Black, I went home.

I was still so angry the next day that I didn't even try to call Black. In fact, I didn't try again until four days later, January 14. In an earlier conversation, he had told me that David Duke would be coming to north Alabama on January 15 to do several interviews with the media and attend a den meeting. I was especially interested in going to hear Duke and to personally offer him my assistance in his presidential campaign.

When Black answered, I said, "We had a little trouble getting together last Wednesday night."

"Yeah," he said, "turned out we didn't have a naturalization anyway."

He assured me that the Duke visit was still on, however, and he gave me directions to Pop's Day Care Center in Muscle Shoals. When I reached Muscle Shoals, someone could give me further instructions if I needed them. The meeting would begin at 7:30 P.M., he said, and I should allow at least two hours' driving time.

I was in Muscle Shoals in plenty of time to find the place, I thought. Then I was in Florence, then Tuscumbia, and finally back in Muscle Shoals. I stopped at a phone booth and called Pop's Day Care Center. No answer. I went back to the Omelet Shoppe, a landmark Black had mentioned, and turned off the main road. Fortunately, within two blocks, I found a firehouse. The firemen gave me clear and concise directions to the day-care center.

The center's parking lot was filled and I had to park across the street, along with several other cars. People were still arriving, and it was only 7:25. I had made it in time.

Several people with walkie-talkies were working security in the parking lots and around the building and at the entrance. When I got to the door, I introduced myself to the man—an older fellow, who just shook hands with me and said, "Glad to meetcha." I said I had come up from Birmingham and was to meet Black.

"I'll have to get Roger," he said. "You just wait right here."

He returned in a moment with a younger man who said he was "Roger Lagner, an officer here."

I said my piece again, about driving up from Birmingham and about meeting Black.

"Have you got a card?" Lagner asked. "There's always a lot of reporters in town when David Duke is here, and we have to be real careful about his security."

I explained that I didn't have a card yet, that I'd been a Klansman for only a short while and would be more than willing to wait outside until Black arrived.

"If you don't mind waiting here at the door until Don gets here to vouch for you, it'll be perfectly all right," Lagner said courteously. "You understand why we have to be so careful. After all, you're a Klansman too."

Interesting that he considered me a Klansman. But then, he had no way of knowing I had not been initiated, did not have a membership card, and had just shown up for my first bona fide Klan meeting.

It was an unseasonably warm night, and I chatted about the weather with several other Klansmen gathered at the door. One of them, a rather large fellow, even compared to me, introduced himself as Ricky Fitts. He was an independent trucker, who said he had made thirty-nine thousand dollars in 1979, working only eight months. "I didn't see any reason to work any more than I have to," he said. "Uncle Sam is going to get more out of it than you do after you make so much."

This led me to ask him about Duke.

Fitts said the main reason he was there was to "ask David Duke why the Franklin County den was closed and moved over here. Everybody says Duke is the one who authorized it," he said, "and I just want him to tell me why. Closing the Franklin County den has made it hard for many Klan members who now have to drive to Muscle Shoals in the next county to attend Klan meetings," he added.

As the general conversation continued about Duke, I asked if anyone thought he would actually run for President.

"He'll run for anything," Fitts said. "I went to the national convention down in New Orleans, and, instead of tending to Klan business, David was always too busy giving interviews and holding press conferences. He's always running for something. All he thinks about is politics. That's why the Klan is falling apart. His whole California Klan pulled out because he wouldn't help them out. He was always too busy helping David Duke. We lost two thousand members in California. They're independent now, and we're going to lose a lot more if something's not done. He's got to get more involved in Klan business instead of just having someone call him up and ask him to close a den and he authorizes it. We had a lot of good members in Franklin County, but they're not going to drive thirty miles to come over here for a meeting. And I don't blame them."

Another twenty minutes went by before Duke arrived with Willard Oliver, the Great Titan, a regional Klan offi-

cer who oversaw the operation of existing Klan chapters and
the development of new ones in northern Alabama. Both
were immaculately dressed in business suits. Duke immediately began shaking hands with all those gathered at the
door. He was friendly, outgoing, and had a firm, solid handshake. He looked each person squarely in the eye and said
with unquestionable sincerity, "Glad to see you," or,
"Thanks for coming tonight," or, "Glad you could make
it."

Fitts returned his greeting with a "Good to see you
again" then went inside.

I was still standing at the door as most of the others followed Duke inside. Black still hadn't shown up. Luckily, it
was only a few more minutes before he arrived. "Good to see
you could make it, J.W.," Black said as he approached with
outstretched hand. "Come on in."

I told him that they wouldn't let me in because I didn't
have a card, hoping that would prompt him to get my naturalization over with and issue me the proper Klan creden-
tials.

"You don't need a card," was all he said. "You're with
me."

I was relieved that Black had vouched for me. The people
I had chatted with outside were not unlike the people I had
expected to see at Klan gatherings. They all appeared to be
working people. They were open and friendly to their
friends and neighbors as they arrived at the meeting, but
withdrawn and suspicious of me. They talked about their
jobs, the weather, their hunting dogs, and the Klansmen
who had not yet arrived and speculated whether or not some
would show up at all.

Someone came along and steered the conversation away
from serious matters.

"Ja hear this one?" a newcomer asked a man standing
close by. "Why'd the good Lord make armadillos?"

"I dunno."

"So niggers could have possum on the half-shell."

Everyone burst out laughing. So I made myself laugh too.

Every time there was a lull at a meeting, I discovered, Klansmen swapped jokes. This struck me as slightly ironic, for during my time with the Klan I didn't meet anyone with a real sense of humor. They seemed to tell the same jokes over and over. And, of course, nearly all the jokes were racist.

This time, another man parried with, "You know what a real tragedy is?" He didn't wait for a reply. "That's a nigger school bus going over a cliff with two empty seats."

Again I laughed along with the crowd. I didn't want some future joke about the tragic fate of liberal newspaper reporters. Although I was doing exactly what I had set out to do months before, I was extremely nervous. I could feel a knot tightening in my stomach. Fortunately, Black was in such a big hurry to get inside and get the meeting under way that I was sure he didn't notice my nervous state. The others undoubtedly just thought I was acting normal; they had never seen me before.

I knew that quite a few people were inside from the number of cars in the parking lot when I arrived, but I wasn't really prepared to walk into a room so full of people. I counted sixty-two, sixteen of them women. I'm sure I was the only person in the room who had not officially taken the Klan oath, but only Don Black and I were aware of that fact. Once inside, I was just another Klansman. Some of the Klansmen standing near me asked me where I was from, and when I told them Birmingham, they said they appreciated my driving up to attend their meeting. If they had only known how happy I was to be there too—on the inside.

I had imagined that all Klan dens resembled the remote, concrete-block building I had seen at Brompton, but this was a modern, well-lighted, spacious room.

On the walls were crayon drawings of houses, trees, and animals, pictures by young children just beginning the life-long learning process of the realities of the world. I stood at the back, lined up against the rear wall with a number of others.

Gene Russell, the den commander, called the meeting to order and announced that a woman reporter and photographer would be allowed in to cover David Duke's speech. He started to give further instructions but was interrupted by Willard Oliver, who said that the plans had been changed, and the woman (Nancy Warnecke? I wondered) wouldn't be attending after all. "We can go on with our business as usual."

One of the first matters was a barrage of questions from Ricky Fitts and Don Oliver (whom I recognized from the Lexington rally) about the closing of the Franklin County den, to which they had belonged. Duke carefully side-stepped, passing the buck to Don Black and Willard Oliver, saying that he couldn't personally be involved in every local action at the den level "because our Klan is just too big and still growing. There's just not enough time in the day with all the other things I have to do at National Headquarters."

Black said that Willard Oliver had felt that the closing of the Franklin County den was necessary. Merging it with the Muscle Shoals den would better serve the Klan by reducing paperwork and haggling between "some officers," and would generally strengthen both groups, Black added. Willard Oliver squirmed nervously in his chair as Fitts and Don Oliver tried to pin someone down on a specific reason for closing the den. Finally, Duke said he had been unaware of the inconvenience to the Franklin County people and, if they could "come up with forty good members, the national office will issue a new charter for Franklin County. Is that fair enough?"

Fitts and Don Oliver seemed to be satisfied.

The meeting then turned to other issues.

One woman asked the Klan to get involved in a labor dispute "over at the hospital, because if they don't get that thing settled they're going to close the hospital and several of us will be without jobs." That issue was settled immediately: someone told the woman that the workers had voted only hours before to settle the dispute and assured her "everything is all right now."

One man told the group that some black women had moved into town and he claimed they were entertaining twenty to thirty white men visitors every day. "Something has got to be done about them."

At this point Duke cautioned that any forceful action taken in the name of the Klan in such a case could damage the Klan. "It would be nice," he said, "if we had the power to take care of individual situations like this, but we don't. A couple of nigger prostitutes are not our problem." Here it was. In a private Klan meeting, Duke no longer talked about "blacks" or "Africans"—now they were "niggers." "Our problem," he continued, "is much greater than individuals. We must aim at doing something about combating the problem as a whole. We've got to stick together as one front like the niggers and the Jews. Then we will have the power through political clout, and the individual situations like this local problem you have here can't exist. And besides, in order to help our movement and ourselves, we have to do it legally. You can't help the movement or yourself or your family if you're in jail."

Several people still voiced their intention to pay the women a visit. They would tell the women in no uncertain terms to leave town. Someone suggested from the floor, "If anyone goes over there, wear a ski mask or something. Don't go in your robe and put the blame on the Klan."

An old man, who had been standing beside me during the meeting, spoke up. He was not drunk but had obviously had a drink or two before he arrived. "Mr. Duke," he began, "I fought in World War Two with General George Patton, the fightingest damn soldier that ever lived. And I fought so I could come home and live in peace in our great country.

Now, I don't know where these nigger women live but I'm gonna find out. And I'll tell you this, when I do, you can come back in a week and they won't be there."

Duke, a totally different David Duke from the one I had seen in public and on television, again urged the group to use restraint and intelligence in handling problems such as this and pointed out that two of Wilkinson's Klansmen were going to go to prison for "beating up a nigger in that restaurant parking lot here just to show off and they can't do anything for anybody in prison."

Duke then launched into one of his semistandard speeches. Citing discrepancies in birth rates, he warned, "By the year 2020, we're going to find ourselves a minority in our own country. By then, we won't have any of the rights we enjoy today. Just look at how many of our rights and freedoms have been snatched away from us in the past twenty years and try to imagine what it will be like forty years down the road. It's not a pretty thought, is it?"

In affirmative action programs, he said, "whites are losing jobs to niggers who are outbreeding us at the rate of twenty-five to one, because our government rewards them by increasing their welfare payments for every little mentally retarded nigger bastard they bring into this world. That's not a dirty word," he insisted, "that's the truth, because as many as fifty percent of the nigger babies born don't have married parents—they're bastards."

The crowd was quiet and attentive. Most of the time they were simply spellbound by Duke's rhetoric, but occasionally someone would call out, "That's right," or, "That's telling it like it is."

"It's also true that they don't have the basic intelligence of whites," Duke went on. "Dr. Shockley, out in California, wrote a book more than twenty years ago that proved beyond a doubt that blacks [he slipped into his public rhetoric here] don't have the mental capacity of whites. When you find a so-called smart nigger, you can trace his roots, as Alex Haley did, and you'll find that they have some white blood in their ancestry. The government and the nigger and Jew groups have successfully kept Dr. Shockley's book from the public because they don't want this fact known."

Someone asked where he could get a copy of the book. Duke was quick to point out that this book, recorded tapes on various subjects, back copies of the Klan newspaper, *Crusader*, and various and sundry other materials could be ordered from the Klan's bookstore in Metairie, Louisiana—The Patriot Press.

At the time, Duke was also the publisher of his Klan's newspaper, *Crusader*. The paper comes out sporadically—whenever there is a development or piece of news the Klan wants to exploit—and is distributed through the mail to all members of the Knights of the Ku Klux Klan. It is also handed out free at Klan roadblocks and rallies. Few of the articles carry by-lines, and I suspect that is because Duke, the author of a number of pseudonymous books, wrote them himself. Some of these same articles hail Duke's dynamic leadership qualities. Other articles are reprinted from the national news media and highlight what Duke considers to be the government's persecution of the Klan and rejection of the "white cause." Most of the pieces, though, are devoted to the violently racist and anti-Semitic rhetoric that characterizes everything Duke says. One article in particular struck me as indicative of Duke's whole approach:

> *For some years a mimeographed sheet has been kicking around the offices of Southern attorneys. It purports to be a copy of a final examination of Howard University Law School, the celebrated black institution of higher pettifoggery, whose graduates include many distinguished lawyers as well as Justice Thurgood Marshall of the Supreme Court. Although some legal beavers have claimed the exam is a put-on, we will leave it to our readers to make the final decision as to its authenticity.*

Constitutional Law

A dude commit armed robbery. After he be arrested, the dude be hungry and ask the police to get
him some chicken wings and a RC Cola. The
police refuse and give him a baloney sandwich and
water instead. Has the dude's constitutional rights
been violated?

Domestic Relations

Sylvester have not paid his nonsupport money to
Yolanda for his and Yolanda's 14 children. This
weekend, Sylvester want to take the children to
the Coliseum to see the Jackson Five. Can Yolanda refuse to let Sylvester take the children?

Mathematics

The judge give a dude 20 years for selling smack,
with ten suspended. How much time do the dude
have to serve?

Alreatha have 100 food stamps. She steal 15 more
from Violina and send 10 to Florida. How many
food stamps do Alreatha have?

This "test" covers four columns in the *Crusader*. Although
it is so obviously a fake and is not particularly funny, I am
not sure how many of Duke's readers would see through the
sham.

Certainly none of his listeners appeared to doubt his spoken words. He told them, "Did you know that, although the
NAACP was founded many years ago, it never had a black
[he slipped again] to head it until Benjamin Hooks, who's
there now? All the other heads were Jews and it was Jew
money that kept it going and furthered its causes. And

because the NAACP is getting this money, its members are going to vote the way the Jews tell them to and they're going to do what the Jews tell them to. They don't want that money cut off."

Once Duke got off on the Jews, he became more intense and put the blacks aside. He even went to the Bible to prove that Jesus was not a Jew. "It says in the Bible," he said, "that Jesus spake unto the Jews. If he was a Jew, it would say that Jesus spake unto his people. The Jews that we know today didn't come along until more than three hundred years after Jesus. The Jews we know today were the product of race mixing in the Middle East. Egyptians were once pure white until they started mixing with the slave girls; now the whole race is dark-complexioned. The Jews of today, despite the fact that many of them have their names changed to try to disguise the fact they are Jews, all have the greasy complexion and big hook noses. They are not the Jews you read about in the Bible. It was Jew slave traders," Duke continued, "that first brought the black African slaves to this country. Many of them were glad to come because life here was much better because many of them were slaves in Africa. There are still slaves in Africa."

One person asked him to elaborate on the Jewish symbols placed on food to designate them as kosher. The man said that Dr. Edward R. Fields (secretary of the National States Rights party) had spoken to them before and told them about the symbols.

"Well," Duke said, "it's basically extortion. If you'll notice on most foods you buy in the supermarket, you find the letter K or a U with a circle around it. What happens is that the rabbi for a certain area will go to the manufacturers and tell them that for a small fee, usually a cent or few cents a package—nobody will say for sure—he will allow that manufacturer to place the rabbinical seal, the K or the U, on his product. He tells the manufacturers that Jews won't buy their product without the seal showing that it has been certified by the rabbi for Jewish consumption. Look for the seal

on the next box of Jell-O, bottle of catsup, can of coffee, or
most anything else you buy in the grocery store. However,
when Jews found out they had this power over the manufacturers, they branched out. I don't know of anyone who eats
steel wool or antifreeze, or aluminum foil, but if you'll look
you'll find seals on those things too.

That evoked laughter from most of his audience.

"What it amounts to, is that we are paying our money to
the very people who have caused and are causing our problems and trying to take our country away from us. You know
the manufacturer is going to pass that cost along to the con-
sumer, and that's us. If a Klansman goes out and gets in
trouble, you see it splashed all over the papers and on television. But you've never seen anything about the Jews
extorting money from everyone who eats in America,
because the Jews control the news media and the television
networks and they're only going to let you find out what
they want you to know."

When Duke finished speaking and fielding questions from
the floor, the audience gave him a rousing standing ova-
tion.

Willard Oliver told the group that a collection would be
taken to help defray Duke's travel expenses. As several
people passed hats through the crowd, Duke continued to
answer isolated questions and the members began talking
among themselves. After the money had been collected and
presented to Duke by Oliver, Duke asked for quiet and told
the group that he was going to leave the money in the den
for the den to use locally. "You folks have been too nice and
too helpful to me for me to take this money," Duke said. "I
want you folks to have it because I know you will put it to
good use. It is always a pleasure for me to come to northern
Alabama because the support and enthusiasm are always
high and the personal gratification I get from that is worth
more than money."

Although I was glad to have been at the meeting and glad
that Black had vouched for me, I didn't linger long mingling

with the crowd. Being as nonchalant as I could, I said good night to those near me, explaining that I had to be at work in Birmingham early the next morning, waved at Black across the room, and headed for my car.

As soon as I got outside town and drove toward Birmingham, I retrieved the tape recorder I kept in a sack under the seat and began recording everything I could recall about the meeting. I always put my "notes" on tape as soon as possible after leaving a Klan function. I became quite adept at driving along at a rather fast clip and dictating into a tape recorder at the same time.

Although I kept the recorder in the car, I never kept a recorded tape in it. As soon as I got home after each activity, whether it was a march, a rally, an aborted naturalization ceremony, or whatever, I would remove the recorded tape and replace it with a fresh one. While in Birmingham, I stored the recorded tapes in a false bottom of a golf bag I kept in plain view in my apartment. Then, before each trip to Tennessee, I would take all the tapes, packed in the bottom of a duffel bag of dirty clothes, and arrange to drop them off for Seigenthaler.

When I was in my apartment, I kept the recorder attached to the telephone. When I called a Klan contact, I recorded the conversation. When someone called me, I would activate the recorder before answering the phone.

As soon as I would get to my apartment each night, the first thing I checked was the golf bag. I had already decided that if I ever detected a recorded tape missing from my secret stash, I would casually walk to my car and drive like hell toward the Tennessee state line, leaving everything else behind. Fortunately, that never happened.

BOTH LINDA AND I had been frustrated with our jobs. I broke away by taking this assignment. She was still left with hers. As a social worker working with physically handicapped and retarded people, she had loved helping people, but now she could no longer tolerate the endless mass of red tape that made her spend almost all her time haggling with state officials over funding to keep the program going. So she decided that she, too, would find something else to do—and something that would allow her more time at home with the children.

When I called home late one night in January, she asked me how I would feel being married to a merchant. I didn't know exactly how to answer that, but before I had to she went on to explain that she had been approached by one of our friends to go into a partnership and buy a small country grocery. She sounded excited about the prospect of being her own boss, having more time at home, and especially enthusiastic about leaving her present job.

Within the next few weeks, I had to make several unscheduled trips home, many of them difficult to explain to

David. As it turned out, Boot knew how to talk about cabinets better than he knew how to build them, and David had to let him go. His departure meant that I was all the help David had. It also meant I had a full-time job. So when I had to get away, I usually concocted a story about having to meet some woman—which wasn't entirely fabricated, but also not exactly the truth. The trips were to sign notes and mortgages since the banks Linda was dealing with were reluctant to lend money to a mother of four unless her husband shared the responsibility for repayment.

Finally, the store was bought and Linda quit her job and took over running it. She was a different person almost immediately. She loved meeting the farm people, the day-to-day management chores, and making the decisions of what and how much to order from the wholesalers.

Although the little market seemed just the medicine for some of her frustrations, it only served to amplify some of mine. She didn't, in fact, have more time at home. The store required many more hours than she had anticipated. Whatever else it did, at least her former job didn't often require her to work weekends. The market did, and as a result we had even less time together.

The time we did have together, however, was pleasant. At this stage of the game we both knew that my assignment wouldn't be finished within the six months that I originally thought it would take, but we thought the additional time would be insignificant.

For a while—I don't recall exactly how long—things settled into pretty much of a routine. Of course, at this point I hadn't yet realized it was routine. I went through a period when meetings were scheduled and then canceled. My impatience mounted. I wasn't really learning much about the Klan. Still, as time passed, these periods of canceled meetings and personal frustration did offer some personal enlightenment. The events of these dead spots just pointed up to me the vast disorganization of the Knights of the Ku Klux Klan. My paranoia, however, seemed always to surface just enough to get me wondering if Black had found out who I was and if he was trying to wait me out until I disappeared and left him alone. But each time this happened, it seemed he would always come up with something to make me believe otherwise.

One time, just when I was feeling that maybe I should give up and call Seigenthaler to tell him that I didn't believe I had the patience to wait out the Klan, Black invited me to attend a meeting at the home of a doctor. I jumped at the chance. I couldn't imagine a doctor having anything to do with the KKK, so I was particularly interested in going to this meeting.

The fashionable Alabaster, Alabama, home of a prominent Birmingham-area physician hardly seemed a likely place for a "recruitment meeting" of the Knights of the Ku Klux Klan. But on an unusually warm February night, Dr. Frank Abernathy welcomed approximately sixty of us— some were Klan members but most were not—to his rambling ranch-style residence about twenty-five miles south of Birmingham. There Don Black appealed to all present to join his Klan Knights.

All during informal conversation that night at Dr. Abernathy's home, a recruit named Tim Fullerton hovered close to Black, engaging many people in conversation about Klan activity. I had heard very little, before going to the Abernathy house, about the recent police shooting of a black woman in Alabaster. But I quickly learned that the shooting, and the controversy it had generated, had brought these people to the Abernathy home to sit and listen to Don Black. And Tim Fullerton seemed to know it all.

"The way I hear it," he said to the group chatting just before Dr. Abernathy called us to order, "is that the policeman shot the nigger woman when she got out of the car with a gun."

I later learned that the woman had no gun. She had led police on a high-speed auto chase through Alabaster, and when she was finally stopped, she refused to get out of her car. An Alabaster police officer, his gun drawn, was trying to pry open the car door when his gun discharged, wounding her in the face. She was hospitalized for six days and her condition seemed to be improving. Then, suddenly, she died.

"It was a heart attack that killed her," said Fullerton to the group. "The gunshot didn't have a thing to do with it, but the jigs want to blame it on the officer."

Actually, the woman had died of suffocation when a breathing tube inserted in her trachea became clogged with mucus. But that night at Abernathy's this was not known. What was known was that black leaders in Birmingham felt the police officer had acted rashly and wanted him fired. (Fullerton told me that Abernathy had gotten involved in the controversy after these black leaders had called for the officer's job.)

"The niggers went to the City Council in Alabaster and raised hell. The next time they met, the doctor took a crowd of whites in there twice as large as the niggers had. He isn't afraid to stand up for white rights," said my fellow recruit.

When Dr. Abernathy, in slacks, sport shirt, and white shoes, called the group to order that night, Fullerton took a prominent seat in the front of the room. With his Klan tee shirt he seemed to me, as I think back on it, to be conspicuous—too conspicuous.

In introducing Black that night, Dr. Abernathy described the Klan leader: "He is a courageous man who doesn't believe that outside agitators ought to come in and stir up trouble with the police."

The woman who had been shot was from South Carolina. I wasn't sure whether the doctor thought she was the "agitator" or whether he was talking about the black leaders from Birmingham who had appeared at the Alabaster City Council meeting to protest the shooting.

Black's speech that night was almost identical to every declaration I was to hear him make during my months of association with him. At times, during telephone conversations, he would lapse into it, and run on endlessly about "the niggers being controlled by the Jews." In public, he—like both Duke and Wilkinson—was careful not to utter the word "nigger." In Klan meetings and in private conversations it was different.

"Ours is the only organization in the nation doing anything to cope with the situation the niggers are creating," Black told the audience of grim-faced men and women who packed Dr. Abernathy's comfortably furnished den and spilled out onto his sun deck overlooking a lighted swimming pool. A table in the corner of the den was covered with Klan literature and KKK application blanks.

"The Klan is the only group trying to help the police control the lawless niggers," said Black, obviously playing to the crowd.

As I sat there and listened to Dr. Abernathy and to Black, I was struck by two clear conclusions I had already drawn from my membership in the Klan:

First, there is a latent sympathy for the Klan movement among many so-called respectable citizens who shun active KKK membership. The number of Klan members in 1980 was small compared to the thousands who belonged in the 1960s and the millions who were members in the 1920s. But many people who decline to sign a membership still support the white-supremacy and anti-Semitic rhetoric of Klan leaders.

Second, Klan leaders are quick to exploit any racial incident—a police shooting, a school confrontation, or an affirmative action controversy—to try to build membership and sympathy for the Klan's regeneration. The leaders are willing to travel hundreds of miles in an effort to leech onto any bleeding racial ulcer in a community.

The undercurrent of friendly sentiment for Klan activities was a surprising—and frightening—trend I detected frequently during my involvement with the Klan. Dr. Abernathy was an obvious—but certainly not a lone—example of this sympathy. He was an affluent, in some ways influential, citizen, and a professional practitioner. He was an affable host with an outgoing demeanor and a quick smile. He had turned his plush home into a forum for an organization known for more than a century as a symbol of fear and terror.

Standing near me in the audience that night was another physician, Dr. Buford Sanders, a well-known Birmingham ear, nose, and throat specialist who employed Don Black as an audiologist and clinical technician. Dr. Abernathy introduced him as "the man Don Black works for. Dr. Sanders gives him a lot of support and guidance." Sanders declined when Abernathy asked him to speak. But he repeatedly urged Black on, in a sort of "Amen" chorus, to tell his audience about how it was the Jews who had engineered slavery in America in the early days of this country.

And Black accommodated him. "The Jews brought the niggers here," he shouted at one point, "and they have kept the niggers in their control ever since. They have used the niggers against the Christian, white population. We ought to blame the Jew for what has happened to this country. The Jew has been run out of every civilized country in Europe."

Before Black finished his speech, he asked all who were there to come back to Abernathy's in exactly two weeks for a follow-up meeting. Dr. Abernathy joined in this invitation.

Several people in the milling crowd after the formal speeches said they had been Klan members in the 1960s. One of them proudly showed his old KKK card. Several took Klan literature from the table and a few filled out application blanks.

When Dr. Abernathy opened the bar, Fullerton roamed around the room offering advice to the others, telling them why they should follow him into the Klan.

As I left, Black thanked me for joining him. "See you

Monday night at the Howard Johnson's in Hoover," he told
me. We'll get you and Fullerton through the naturalization
ceremony."

I had been astonished that such upstanding citizens as Dr.
Abernathy and Dr. Sanders had allowed themselves to be
identified with the Klan. It is impossible, of course, to know
how many well-to-do professional people support—either
personally, socially, or monetarily—the efforts of Klan leaders.

The knowledge of this kind of subtle, growing support is
what prompts the leaders of the Klan—Don Black and Bill
Wilkinson—to travel great distances to try to capitalize on
racial problems. For instance, when there was racial unrest
in Boston, Massachusetts, over busing in that city, David
Duke—then Grand Wizard of the Knights of the KKK—
went to Boston to attract attention to himself. Bill Wilkinson, the chief rival of Duke and Black, also journeyed to
Boston to try to identify the Klan with the turmoil there.
Wilkinson, who flies a private plane provided by the Klan,
also has turned up in Chattanooga, Tennessee, and Jackson,
Mississippi, and other communities where there has been
racial tension.

In the spring of 1980, my newspaper colleagues Susan
Thomas and Nancy Warnecke were developing a story on
Wilkinson when he flew suddenly one weekend to Idabel,
Oklahoma, after racial violence in that little town had left
three dead. "I'm going to Idabel to recruit new Klan members," he announced. When he got there he attracted a contingent of the state police, who shadowed him everywhere
he went. But the fact remains he was willing to fly his plane
to Oklahoma to exploit racial tragedy.

That same opportunity for exploitation had brought
Black and our small contingent of Klan members on the
short trip from Birmingham to Alabaster that night in February when Dr. Abernathy opened his home—and his bar—
to a Klan recruitment session.

But was Black really taking advantage of recruiting possibilities? Look at my case: I had been a dues-paying member of the Klan for more than three months and had been participating in Klan activities, yet I still had not been officially "naturalized" into the secret organization. Every time Black would call off the scheduled naturalization ceremony, my paranoia would suddenly resurface with a rush. I would feel frustrated, depressed, disappointed, uncomfortable, and angry all at the same time. Each time I felt sure he knew who I was and what I was doing, but I also rationalized that if he did know these things he would surely confront me, putting an end to my charade and sending me back home, back to the city desk. I worried that Black, who was a very suspicious man by nature, didn't trust me. Or was he simply not doing his job for his Klan?

After scheduled ceremonies were canceled in Brompton, Muscle Shoals, and Bluff Park, in Birmingham, I was gripped by a much more frightening scenario. On one of my many long, boring drives on the concrete ribbon of interstate highway that links Nashville to Birmingham, I conjured up this alarming possibility:

Don Black was always quick to apologize after each cancellation; each time the apology was believable and appeared to be sincere. He was just as quick to follow each apology with the promise of a new date, always in the near future, when the naturalization would be completed. But was he, I wondered, sincerely interested in bringing me into the Klan? Or was he just dangling a carrot in front of my nose to ensure that I would be around when he needed me for some entirely different purpose? Was he that smart? Was I that stupid? I didn't know. Nevertheless, I had a tendency to believe that he was using me.

I knew long before I took the assignment how well the smooth-talking Klan leaders were able to manipulate the news media and use them to their own advantage. Was Don Black doing this again?

Would I nervously—it seemed I was always nervous at a Klan function—show up for another scheduled naturalization ceremony only to find the room filled with television cameras and news reporters there for a press conference Black had called? Would I be the focus of that press conference? Would Black announce to the world that the Klan had discovered who I was and what I was trying to do? Certainly the Klan would look good and it would be more than embarrassing to both me and my newspaper. Of the many fears I had during my involvement with the Klan, this was probably the worst. (And I lived with it daily until the morning of December 7, 1980, when I, not the Klan, broke the story on the front page of *The Tennessean*.)

The fear was very much alive the cold, windy February night that I drove to the Howard Johnson Motor Lodge in the Birmingham suburb of Hoover. What better place for a press conference than a motel meeting room? I had covered many in such places. When I walked into the Malaga Room, I was surprised that only seven of us, including me and Tim Fullerton, had gathered in a room set up for fifty.

"You can see we need more people active in Birmingham," said Black's wife, Darlene. "Here's the five who always show up, no matter what is going on."

We spent a few minutes in idle chitchat before Black instructed his security officer, Ben Walker, who was wearing a small pistol on his belt, to "robe up, and we'll get under way."

Black then asked Fullerton and me to excuse ourselves briefly "while we get everything ready." The two of us went outside and walked a short distance down the corridor to begin our wait.

Fullerton had been a talkative fellow on all aspects of Klan activity two nights earlier at Dr. Abernathy's house. Now he was silent. He seemed nervous. Like me.

We waited and waited.

Suddenly, the door of the Malaga Room opened and a Klansman I knew only as "Randy" beckoned us to enter. I sensed something was wrong.

Black was standing at one end of the room, his arms

folded in front of him. "We are having trouble securing the room," he said. "There are three niggers outside trying to look in the windows. We can't get the room secure, so we'll have to put off the naturalization ceremony."

I glanced around the room. Walker had taken off his flowing white robe and was seated at the rear of the room, his pistol in his belt. Roger Patmon, the only other Klansman present, walked toward an entrance to the room that opened to a walkway outdoors. I could see the face of a young black man at the window. Patmon jerked open the door and confronted a youthful motel employee with an armful of white sheets—I'm sure the irony escaped him.

"What do you want?" demanded Patmon.

"Nothing," the young man said, walking away.

I had no idea whether the presence of this motel employee had anything to do with putting off the initiation ceremony. I hoped that was the real reason, but at the same time, all my fears lived on.

For a while I had thought I was undergoing some sort of hazing, while Black checked on the details of my background story. The story was solid enough, I felt, to pass a cursory screening, but was it obscure enough to make it impossible to refute? I certainly hoped so, because I had spent months creating it and committing it to memory.

Finally I decided that Black was not hazing me. Instead, he was Grand Dragon of a skeleton organization in the Birmingham area that encompassed only a few actual members—a reality impossible to conceal. That was obvious when, in addition to himself and his wife, he produced only three members to induct two new recruits that night at the motel.

Black suggested that, although we couldn't have the oath taking because of the "security breach," since we had the room we could have a business meeting to discuss future Klan activities. We talked about a mass rally and march in downtown Birmingham to show Klan support for the white police officer, George Sands, who had been removed from his job after he shot and killed Bonita Carter, a black woman, almost a year before. The new mayor, Dr. Richard Arrington, had said publicly that he did not want Sands reinstated on the police force. The Fraternal Order of Police had contested the mayor on the issue. Now the Klan, through Black, was threatening in press statements to come to the "aid" of the FOP and Patrolman Sands.

"If the nigger mayor doesn't put Sands back to work, we'll march on Saturday," Black told me.

Fullerton asked, "What about carrying weapons with us when we march? Won't there be trouble with the niggers when we demonstrate?"

"I'm not saying there won't be a confrontation," Black responded, "but we'll have our security there and we'll get the police tactical squad to provide security also."

I wondered then whether he knew somebody on the police tactical squad. Later I found out that he was acquainted with several squad members, but I was never able to determine the nature of his relationship with these officers.

Continuing, Black told Fullerton and me, "For those of you who haven't been with us before: We don't try to start trouble when we go out on a march. People heckle us. They call us names. But we just keep marching. We never respond to the heckling. Of course," he said, "if they start trouble, we will protect ourselves through whatever means we have to. We will be carrying placards and the staffs can be used as clubs if anybody starts anything. We make them so the cards come right off, leaving us with the staff for a club."

The meeting broke up with a round of friendly goodbyes.

"Don't worry, J.W. and Tim," Black said as we were leaving, "we will definitely get you all naturalized at the next meeting."

But I did worry. I worried through two more scheduled meetings, both canceled at the last minute, and I kept on worrying.

WHEN I NEXT SPOKE with Black, three days later, I purposely didn't mention the aborted naturalization attempt at the motel. We talked about what we would do when Arrington announced his final decision on Patrolman George Sands, which was expected the next day.

"Tomorrow will be decisive for us," Black said. "He's been talking about how it is a state law that compels reinstatement of Sands and that he has to go along with the law, regardless of his personal feelings. It sounds like he is thinking about going ahead and doing it and covering himself that way, but I really don't know what he is going to do. If he does it that way, we are going to have a problem."

Was he afraid of *not* having something to demonstrate against?

"So, in any event, either way it goes, there is going to be a lot of action. I haven't decided exactly what would be the best approach for us, whether we should go the conventional route and have a march downtown like we did last summer or think of something else to do. Something more original. I'm not sure what it would be."

Since the Klan had been very vocal on the Sands issue— urging his reinstatement—I suggested, only to hold up my end of the conversation, that we could always issue a public statement or stage a demonstration, thanking the black mayor for supporting us in the event that he put Sands back to work. This, I told him, could place Arrington in an embarrassing position.

"Yeah, we could," Black said without further elaboration. "I am concerned about the security for the march. We could just have a rally downtown or something like that. That would be a show of support for law enforcement. We could just go ahead and have a march anyway. Whatever we do, we will have to make the decision tomorrow."

I explained that I would be out of town the following day in Montgomery to measure a cabinet job, but assured him I would be back in touch before Saturday.

"Okay," he said, "either way, whatever happens will be on the news. Whatever we do, it will be announced, but you can call me Saturday or whenever you have the opportunity."

I suggested that Arrington had managed to get in a position of being "damned if he does and damned if he doesn't."

"Yeah," Black responded. "It is good to see, isn't it?" He was obviously looking forward to having a march. "We will get some good publicity on it," he said; "everybody knows about it, most everybody in the media."

I asked about the support we might expect in terms of numbers.

"Well, we will have some support," Black said. "As you know, most people will be scared. The nonmembers will be scared to participate in it because of the risks they perceive will be involved in going downtown and getting in a confrontation with a bunch of niggers. But it will be a good march."

As the confrontation between the mayor and Sands progressed, it seemed more and more maneuvers were tried in court by both sides. Sands still had the overwhelming majority of the whites in Birmingham calling for his reinstatement and he had the additional support of the FOP. The FOP was still publicly asking the Klan to stay out of the fight.

Arrington, on the other hand, had the blacks holding public meetings and issuing press releases calling for the mayor to fire Sands outright. Arrington insisted that Sands be reexamined by a city doctor before he would consider reinstatement. This further delayed his decision and gave him more time to let tensions ease.

It also kept the whole matter in limbo and neutralized the Klan's purpose for its announced march the next Saturday. Black realized that Arrington could place the Klan in the uneasy position of not having a purpose to march and rally as long as he kept them guessing what he was going to do. So Black canceled the march through announcements on the radio stations and said that, although the Klan supported Sands, he felt sure that the mayor would put him back to work and, after all, the Klan stands for "what is right."

At the same time, Black was saying privately that if Arrington put Sands back on the force "the niggers will raise Cain and our position will have more support."

The following week, on March 10, Sands was effectively put back to work, with Arrington saying he would not have city attorneys appeal the court decision placing him back on the force.

I talked to Black on March 11 and expressed my satisfaction that Sands was back at work and asked if he expected any trouble from the blacks.

"No doubt about that," Black said. "I'm sure today or tomorrow they will do something or other."

I asked what he had planned to counteract any action they might take.

"It depends on what they do," he said. "We will have to approach things differently. We won. If they stage a boycott

or something like that, we will have a counterboycott. I
think we did pretty well on this. I would say one thing: We
definitely won. But there's still a lot more to do. We have a
good start though."

The next time I talked with Black, March 17, he said,
"You know that the SCLC and a group of black organizations is planning some demonstrations on March twenty-
eighth. That will be a Friday and I will be thinking of something for Saturday following that. Either a direct counter-
demonstration or something like that. I think tomorrow they
are having a motorcade during the day in regard to this Bonita Carter thing, but there is not much we can do in response
to that on a weekday. It is impossible for us to get anybody to
turn out. I think they are supposed to be having a meeting
tonight . . . some sort of a mass meeting."

"Are we going to have a meeting or anything?" I asked.
After all, I had been a Klansman for four months and had
attended only one local meeting—the one in which my naturalization was aborted.

Two weeks after the meeting at Dr. Abernathy's, I had
asked Black about the follow-up meeting that had been
announced.

"Well," he said, "there is not going to be another meeting.
People at the hospital found out about him having us out
there and the pressure was put on him. There won't be a
meeting, but we can always count on Dr. Abernathy. He's
very supportive of our efforts."

This time he said, "Yeah, we will. I don't have a definite
time yet; it will probably be over at Ben Walker's house."

That meeting never came off, but others occurred—mostly in north Alabama. Black was spending a lot of time up
there and was saying very little about it. I suspected, but
couldn't be sure, that it either had to do with the dissension
over the closing of the Franklin County den or that he was
busy helping the Franklin County people get another den set
up.

As it turned out, I was right on both.

The next thing I learned was from a story in *The Tennessean*, which Linda saved for me between trips home: Willard Oliver, Duke's Great Titan of north Alabama, had defected to Bill Wilkinson's Invisible Empire of the KKK, claiming to have taken many members with him.

I wanted to learn as much as possible before trying to pin Black down about this. John Seigenthaler and I spoke several times to try to decide the best strategy. I never had any direct contact with other staff members working on the Klan story, it was true, but I did have the benefit of their information through Seigenthaler. We agreed that I should try to contact Don Oliver, the first person I had met at my first rally in Lexington, Alabama, in November. At the den meeting in Muscle Shoals in January it was obvious that there was a problem with Willard Oliver (no relation to Don). Don Oliver was reluctant to talk to me, a stranger, on the phone—he didn't remember me from that sole conversation with him several months before.

I asked him about the defection to Wilkinson's group.

He was noncommittal. "There is talk going on," he said.

Then, trying to make him remember me, I reminded him that I was the one who commented on his driving the stake to support the cross at Lexington with massive blows and asked, almost pleading, "You remember that, don't you?"

"Oh, yeah," he said, "I believe I do now." With that, he seemed like a different person and began to open up: "Willard has went over with Wilkinson."

"He has?" I responded, trying to act surprised.

"Yeah. He went on TV with him and all of that kind of stuff, you know. He wrote the biggest majority of the members a letter trying to get them to come over. I don't know, it is just a big mess."

I asked if he got the Franklin County den back.

"Well," Oliver answered, "that is what kinda got this rolling. We started to get it back and Willard throwed a fit."

"He took it away to start with, didn't he?" I asked.

"Yeah. He blamed that on David, and David didn't have anything to do with it. I don't know, just a bunch of stuff said, a bunch of garbage and they had a little meeting up at Russellville one night and we wasn't invited. They tried to hold a Klan Court—it was a kangaroo court—and change the reports. That is what they tried to hold up there. It was a long drawn-out bunch of garbage."

I asked how many members Willard Oliver actually succeeded in taking over to Wilkinson.

"Oh, maybe five or ten," Oliver answered. When I told him that I had heard numbers upward of seventy-five or eighty, he said, "No way. No way did he take that many people with him."

Looking back, I realized that I had mixed my signals and almost tipped my hand. Although I had tried to act surprised when Don Oliver told me of Willard's defection, I had actually learned about it from Seigenthaler in a conversation the night before. I was just lucky Don didn't catch my mix-up when I started talking knowledgeably.

It was obvious that Don Oliver was still very much in the fold of David Duke and Don Black. I expressed my alliance with both Duke and Black and accused Wilkinson of just "making a racket."

"Well," Oliver said about Wilkinson, "the only thing he is causing is people getting into jail. They just had two sent off the other day. I think they sent two to the pen. They beat up a couple of niggers. They got, I believe, six years for it. We're going to get rolling here again, that is for sure. That is what it was, it all boils down to a mess."

After this talk with Don Oliver, I immediately called Don Black, but I didn't ask him right away about the defection. He began telling me about plans for an April march. It appeared from the beginning that this one would be canceled too.

"We had a march scheduled for Saturday," Black began. "It was originally scheduled for one o'clock. The police department said we had better do it at two because the March of Dimes has something that morning and they are not going to be finished in time. Then they wanted to have it at three and we have a permit for two or three. But the March of Dimes coordinator, Andy Smith, called today and he wants us to have it some other day because he says the March of Dimes organizers called and said they have had a lot of calls from parents who won't let their kids participate at all in their Walk-a-Thon if we are there. So I am kind of debating just what to do. If it was anything else besides charity, we would go ahead and have it regardless. It might be good public relations to change the date in deference to the March of Dimes."

I suggested that if we did postpone the march, we should make our reason public.

"Yeah, we would, of course," Black said. "But I hate getting delayed on that because the weekend is significant, being the last weekend before the tax deadline." The significance, Black told me, was that people were easier to arouse to anger just before they had to pay their taxes. Taking advantage of this, Black had a pat speech in which he pointed out that the average American must work almost five months each year just to pay taxes. "Anyway, I suspect that we will postpone it until Saturday the nineteenth. This will be good public relations and we will try to get a little publicity and news coverage as to why we did it."

I then asked, for the first time in a long time, about my robe. I alternated between asking about my initiation and asking about my robe.

"I'll have it for you by the march, whenever that will be. It's being made in north Alabama."

"Speaking of north Alabama," I asked, seizing the opening, "what is going on up there? I keep hearing all kinds of tales."

"Well, Willard quit," Black said, "about a month ago. Decided he would take his ball and play with somebody else. The situation is very good. It's very solid up there right now

because he did leave and, of course, we got a little adverse
publicity when he decided to go with Wilkinson, but it
shows the kind of character he's got. After all the trouble
we've had up there with them, and he's the one who's been
right in the middle of it. Anyway, things are very solid now.
We're standing in columns that are tight, and Gene Russell
is a good commander. We banished Willard plus two others
the other day, and things are basically a lot better now. All
of these problems were raising the constant turmoil we have
had up there the past six months. Really, the last month has
resolved itself. Things are running real well up there. The
only disadvantage, like I say, is the adverse publicity, since
Wilkinson played Willard's going with him for everything it
was worth."

Russell was one of the charter members and consequently
an officer of the Klan group in north Alabama when it was
formed. He was a good-soldier type who followed his leaders
well, so when Willard Oliver left the Knights and
announced he was defecting to Wilkinson's group, Russell,
as den commander, was given more responsibility. A hefty
man with a quick smile, Russell's sincerity as an avowed
racist couldn't be questioned. He carried calling cards that
bear the inscription: "You are white today because your
ancestors practiced segregation."

I reminded Black that Wilkinson had been making many
public claims that he took over a majority of the Duke members in north Alabama and asked him if he had a specific
number of people who defected.

"Willard is the only one I know of. But the two we banished will probably go with him. I would imagine they
would. In fact, they said they would."

I asked if those two were officers, too.

"One of them was. One was the secretary, Patsy Malone.
That's part of the problem; there's been a lot of questions
about money and where the money was going and everything. She kept very ambiguous books, you know. And, Willard has had a few friends who have been the source of the

problems up there, and because they were friends of his, he wouldn't take any decisive action against them and that kinda kept everything in an uproar. I suspect some of them will go, but it won't be more than a handful of people altogether and nobody that we're going to miss."

I told Black that I had heard Wilkinson on the radio claiming to have taken in hundreds of Duke's members. I was really surprised that Black was being this candid and talkative, so I wanted to keep the roll going.

"Yeah," Black said, "what Willard said was that he had taken ninety-five percent of the membership. That's silly. First of all, everybody up there is so immune to Wilkinson because they see what he has been doing and they know where they want to be and they are not about to join Wilkinson. Second, Willard wasn't that popular. He really messed himself up in the past year as far as the general membership was concerned. Most of them were mad at him for one reason or another because he simply wasn't handling things in a professional manner. So he had very little following to begin with. But nobody—hardly anybody—would go with Wilkinson since all he ever does up there is get people arrested."

I told him I had heard about the two who were sentenced to prison recently for beating up two blacks in the parking lot of the Omelet Shoppe in Muscle Shoals.

"Yeah," Black responded, "two of them from up near Tuscumbia. They beat up a couple of niggers just to impress our people after a meeting there after a demonstration. They impressed us all right."

At this point, I again expressed my allegiance. "I am just sold on David Duke," I told Black, "and just think that he is the man that can lead the fight for our cause and I couldn't consider Wilkinson at all."

"Well, I of course agree with you wholeheartedly there," Black said. Then, back on Wilkinson: "We've had to put up with a lot from him in the past few years. Now, his whole modus operandi has been trying to get our members and not

trying to recruit his own people. For most of the past four
and a half years, almost all of his efforts have been directed
toward where we have been organizing, contacting our
people, and trying to get them to come with him. Really,
when he went up to Decatur two years ago that was the first
time and about the only time he has ever done any independent recruiting, independent of our organization. Other
than that, he has always been trying to get our people. And
he has lost everybody he has got up there. They had their
march in Tarrant the other day, and the papers said forty or
fifty, so he didn't have over sixty people there. That is pretty
poor, a pretty poor showing, considering the fact that he
brought a lot of people from north Alabama and he was
there personally. A year and a half ago, he could have gotten
one hundred fifty people easily, or two hundred, and it
shows how few people he has left. So now he is going to try
and get our people."

I couldn't help but think to myself about Black's lacka-
daisical recruiting methods. "He is going to have to get
somebody stronger than Willard Oliver to get out there and
get them," I said authoritatively.

"What's so disgusting about Willard is he has no self-
respect to go with Wilkinson," Black continued. "After all
that's happened up there, after all of the dirty little tricks
that Wilkinson has played against us . . . Willard himself
even wrote this newspaper ad on his own denouncing Wilkinson. You know we usually don't go for that, but Willard
did it on his own and now, of course, he can just conveniently ignore everything that has happened because it is a
different story now. He has his ego to think about, and he
decides to go with Wilkinson shamelessly. There's a lot to it.
There's a lot that Willard has been doing. I won't go into all
of it, but he has been a mess at times. There's been a lot
going on. You know, we should have, in hindsight, we
should have taken action a long time ago against him, but
we didn't. You know you're always kind of reluctant to do
anything."

I was astonished and elated at the depth of my exchange with the state's Grand Dragon, but I was bewildered. Why was Black going into such detail of internal strife with me, a Klansman recruit? I couldn't help but wonder if he just wanted to get it off his chest or if he would have been equally candid with any other Klansman. The only thing I knew for sure was that I didn't want him to stop now.

"You know that night up there when they were fussing about the Franklin County den," I said, "I heard that Willard was trying to put all of the blame over on David [the conversation had progressed to a first-name basis] and it was obvious to me that David didn't know what the hell he was talking about. I could see that then and I could just see the turmoil in the whole group there. They didn't look like a lot of people who believed what he was trying to do."

"That was Willard's claim," Black said. "He said that we were trying to undermine his authority. Like specifically with the Franklin County den. And he wanted to banish all of his enemies from the Klan. You know Don Oliver and his wife, Mike, the two motivating forces there in Franklin County—he wanted to banish them. He started spreading all kinds of stuff about them. We had a Klan Court and they were charged with mishandling money, among other things, but that was the worst offense. So we held a Klan Court and none of Willard's friends or Willard, who had agreed to these charges, showed up. But Mike and Don did, and they had all the records of where all the money had gone, plus the den commander had held the checkbook from the Franklin County den, which they had since it had been closed originally, and Mike and Don didn't even have that to look at, but their records coincided completely with the canceled checks. So they proved themselves innocent anyway. They had much better records than the regular den had. That pretty much stopped that, but Willard quit as a result of it because he called it a kangaroo court. The thing is, he tried to banish them without a court even. In fact, he had called the National Office and told them that they were ban-

ished—that Don and Mike were banished without even having a court. He did that on his own. So he didn't like it. He
resigned just before we had it. He had heard we were going
to have the court and he resigned."

"I don't think we're going to suffer any from his loss," I
offered, really getting into it by this point.

"No, not at all," Black said. "Like I say, we are in a lot
better shape. He was in on the beginning of the development
of the organization up in that area; that is the reason he had
the high office he had. He was at the first organizational
meeting and he contributed a lot in the first year. But after
that, he really started slowing down and people like Stanley
and Gene [Stanley McCullom and Gene Russell, the Klan
officers from north Alabama] were doing all of the work. He
was only trying to get rid of members that he considered a
threat. When any problems did come up, he wouldn't handle
them like he should. Then he would try and hinder Den
Commander Gene Russell and other officers who did try to
handle them professionally. In fact, he tried to get Gene
banished once. He didn't like the way Gene was putting too
much organization in the den. He didn't like that."

"A guy named Roger," I inquired, "he was an officer—"

"Roger Lagner," Black said before I could finish. "He is
with us completely. He resigned as an officer. He was second
to Willard, he was a Giant [regional officer]. He had a lot of
personal problems. His father was dying of cancer and he
had a heart attack and had missed a lot lately. He can't
understand Willard now. They used to be friends and he
verified everything about him. He is still working on recruiting members, but not as an officer. I was glad he resigned as
an officer, because I wanted Stanley to be the top man up
there because he is unquestionably the most qualified."

"I'm glad to hear that we are not in as bad shape as I have
been led to believe," I assured him.

"Not at all," he said. "As I say, I was very glad that Willard quit. It was the best thing that happened to us. The

only thing now is the adverse publicity we got, but it doesn't hurt us much."

My conversation with Black had been lengthy, as many of our conversations were. I liked to catch him in a talkative mood because I felt my opportunity for learning more about the Klan was enhanced as long as he was doing the talking and I was doing the listening. Since I was recording our conversations, I got so good at ejecting and flipping over a tape that I could usually do it between sentences and never lose a word. Several times we talked for more than an hour.

This conversation had been particularly fruitful because not only did I get some pretty good insight into the internal politics of the north Alabama dens, but I also gleaned a new name—Patsy Malone. I had never heard of her before, but if she was banished along with Willard Oliver, I knew she'd be interesting.

I looked her up and called her at home on April 9. I started by telling her that I had met her at the den meeting in Muscle Shoals and said how good it was to talk with her again. I was hoping her memory would be no better than mine. There's no way I could remember with whom I had a casual conversation four months ago, but I probably wouldn't deny it if someone claimed to have talked with me then. And she didn't.

I had already tried repeatedly to reach Willard Oliver but couldn't get an answer. I told her I was really calling her for Willard's number because the number he had given me wasn't getting him.

She gave me Oliver's new number and explained, volunteered even, that "he had to have it changed. We've really had a bad kangaroo court up here, two of them in fact, and some people on it had already been told how it was supposed to be, and started bothering him and he had to change his number."

I told her that I had heard of the defection to Wilkinson

and that was why I wanted to get in touch with Willard. I
also asked how many members went over to Wilkinson.

"Willard has," she said, "but no one else has defected.
They've got that rumor out. We're talking about it. We're
supposed to have a meeting this weekend. Mr. Wilkinson has
been up and talked to us, but that's as far as it went. We just
listened and asked questions. Wilkinson's group is the only
one up here doing anything. We got this feeling that all we
were doing was throwing rocks to the wind. You need to
talk to Willard. There is just some things he can tell you a
lot better than I can. We just felt like our heart was in the
right place, but that was about the only thing."

I told her I was dissatisfied with the Duke organization
and said I had paid my dues but still hadn't been naturalized
and felt they were just stalling me.

"We got that too," she said. "Not only that, I just felt like
we didn't know where the money was going. I remember
you, I think. [Her memory was apparently better than mine.
I didn't remember her.] I really hate it that things have
turned out the way they have. They had court and I wasn't
there and they said I had gone with Bill Wilkinson, which I
had not and I still haven't. But the way things are leading, I
probably will."

"I'm thinking that way myself," I volunteered.

"Willard sent out a real good letter on that stuff and he
said that Bill Wilkinson was the only man that stood behind
his people, that David Duke did not give enough leadership.
He hasn't done anything important in the state of Alabama.
It was like a kangaroo court. No one is allowed there; you
don't know who is bringing the charges against you. You
don't know who the witnesses will be, and you don't know
anything." She said she complained about the procedure
used to summon her to court and had such short notice that
she didn't go.

Then she went on to tell me that Mike and Don Oliver
wanted their own den in Franklin and gave Willard Oliver
an ultimatum on a Monday that if they didn't have their den

by Friday they would start it independently. She said Willard Oliver immediately relayed this message to Duke at National Headquarters and was told by Duke that "nobody holds a threat over my head."

"Willard took this to mean that he had the support of the National Office and suspended both Mike and Don Oliver," Malone said. She said they "kept raising a fuss" and finally got Duke to come to north Alabama and another court was held and the Olivers were reinstated. "We don't have any cooperation," she said. "Here we are fighting among ourselves and we'll never get anywhere fighting each other. I wish we would all unite—the southern groups and everybody. I don't like the splashing of guns that Wilkinson does. I asked and I questioned and questioned him and he assured us that they didn't get violent unless someone else starts it. I thought maybe I had been brainwashed against Wilkinson and maybe I should reconsider. Right now, I am just at a standstill. I want to find out what is happening, but I do wish we could get together."

Another fruitful conversation. At last I was beginning to learn about the inner workings—not to mention the factionalism—of the Klan. And it was clear to me that I would have to delve more closely into Wilkinson's operation. I realized that my initial decision to infiltrate the Duke-Black faction of the Klan movement was based largely on Duke's frequent, effective television appearances during which he gave the impression, because of access to the media, that he was the dominant Klan figure and led the most effective Klan group. But I was now becoming aware that while Duke was talking and Black following, Bill Wilkinson— their bitter rival—was beating the bushes and outorganizing them. But before I went after membership in the other group, I still wanted to be initiated into Black's organization.

ALTHOUGH I HAD attended several Klan functions, rallies, marches, and meetings, I still had not been officially "naturalized." Black kept assuring me we would have the ceremony and each time something came up to prevent it. But my Klan participation was accelerating and I was meeting more and more Klan members and learning more about Klan activities, so I kept suppressing the urge to rush him.

On a warm, bright, sunny Saturday morning, April 19, we had a different kind of protest scheduled. The National Alliance Against Racist and Political Oppression, in conjunction with the NAACP and the Southern Christian Leadership Conference, had announced plans to put the Klan "on trial" in an effort to expose violence and terrorist activity by Klan members.

It seemed that everytime we had a weekend function planned, the weather was always beautiful, making me wish even more that I were home in Tennessee instead of in Birmingham. The pecan tree was fully leaved out, the dog-

woods and azaleas were in full bloom, and I couldn't help
but think of all the things I could be enjoying if only I were
home. Instead, I was preparing to attend a meeting in the
Birmingham City Council Chambers. And, as usual before
every Klan activity, I was jittery.

I arrived at City Hall shortly before 10:00 A.M. Several
Klan members, some I had never seen before, were already
gathered on the front steps. They were easy to identify as
members of the Klan because they were dressed in the black
jeans and vests that constitute the Klan security uniform or
wore Klan belt buckles or Klan pins. Black had told me not
to wear anything that would readily identify me as a Klan
member because "we might have to slip into the meeting."
Clearly, not everyone got the word.

While we waited outside, a young man, with a shock of
sandy hair protruding from beneath his black cowboy hat,
joined our group. He wore black jeans and a belt with KKK
tooled in the leather buckle. Although he seemed to be
acquainted with most of those present, he went from man to
man, shaking hands with the fervor of a small-town politician running for constable.

"Hi, I'm Bill Riccio," he said, extending his hand. "I'm
glad you could take the time to be with us today."

"I'm J. W. Thompson," I answered, taking his hand. "I've
always got the time to do something worthwhile."

"That's the spirit, my friend," he said, giving me a slap on
the shoulder and moving on to the next man on the steps.

Among those I had met before were Black, Ben Walker,
his security force lieutenant, Stanley McCullom and Gene
Russell, and some local Klansmen who were members of
Black's Knights. I learned that Riccio and several others I
had not previously met were members of Bill Wilkinson's
Invisible Empire. Since that was a rival organization, I was
somewhat surprised to see them joining us for a protest.
When I asked about this later, Black explained that,
although "we view the Klan from different perspectives, we

sometimes have a common cause, especially when the niggers and Communists try to lump us all together and blame us all for everything that has ever happened."

Right before we entered the council chambers as a group, Black sent McCullom to call all the local television stations to "let them know we are here." We entered the room quietly and took seats on two rows of benches in the rear of the room. We weren't wearing robes, but everyone there knew we were Klansmen. Within minutes, four Birmingham policemen, one black, entered the room and took up positions at each corner.

The meeting was just getting under way, with one of the organizers explaining the purpose, when Ben Walker unfurled a Confederate flag that he had concealed under his shirt. Several Klansmen draped it across their knees throughout the meeting.

Anne Braden of the Southern Organizing Committee and a nationally recognized civil rights activist, outlined a series of incidents of Klan violence and intimidation throughout the country. "People think the Klan's white-supremacy philosophy reaches no farther than the South," she said. "There have been incidents in recent years of Klan terrorism from California to Rhode Island. There is something people can do about it, but they have to know what kind of organization the Klan really is. That is what this hearing, and I hope others, will be for."

This was to be a "People's hearing on the terrorist activities of the Klan," said Grover Smith, Alabama field director for the National Association for the Advancement of Colored People, who chaired the meeting. Referring to the Klan, he said, "These people are a threat to the total community. We are going to issue a report of our findings from the persons who have come here to testify. Everyone who will testify here today has had a direct connection with the Klan and some of them have been brutalized and intimidated. . . ."

Some members of our group clapped vigorously at this

statement. I didn't and Don Black, who sat beside me, didn't.

"This is a terrorist group," Smith continued, "and we feel that if this continues it could have a chilling effect on society."

The organizers of the meeting were visibly disappointed at the small turnout. Several council members and city department heads had been invited and several had committed to attend, Smith said, but a section in the front of the room reserved for the special guests remained vacant.

"Unfortunately, there don't appear to be too many people interested in learning about Klan terrorism, even if it's in their own backyards," Smith said.

This time, we all clapped.

One of the first "witnesses" was G. T. Miller, an eighty-one-year-old feedstore operator from Luverne, Alabama, and a former member of the local Klan faction in his small hometown. Miller was not in the least visibly shaken when a roar of applause went up from the Klan section when he talked about being beaten and shot by what he termed "two-faced Christians who belonged to the Klan." His voice cracking and choking back tears, and occasionally wiping a few away he couldn't choke back, Miller told a tale of terror during and after his active association with the Klan.

"They tore my butt up once," he said.

More clapping from our group.

"Wanted me to beat up this colored fellow," he continued. "I couldn't do it, so they took turns beating me up."

More clapping.

He said his troubles with the Klan began in the 1930s when he joined the local group out of curiosity because he wanted to know more about the organization. "But as quick as I found out what they stood for, I come out of it."

He said his most serious troubles began after he left the Klan. He was harassed, threatened, and shot once. His feed mill and grocery businesses were boycotted by his neighbors because he refused to fire a black employee, but he said he expected that kind of treatment because his "customers were afraid of having their barns burned down."

"Another time," he continued, "the Kluxers got after me and this other man. He took off running and I told him, 'For God's sake, don't run, they'll shoot you.' I knew because they'd pasted my backside with buckshot before."

More cheers and clapping from our section. I still can't describe the embarrassment and humiliation I felt as I sat there that morning as a member of a group of ignorant, insensitive, rude, and unfeeling human beings. I couldn't make myself clap along with them, and I was just glad that Don Black wasn't joining in.

Miller paused at the outburst and wiped away the tears with a wrinkled old hand before continuing. "I told him I'd see if I could outtalk them. So we talked and argued and cussed one another for everything except something good. Finally they let us go. But I say now that if ever another one bothers me again, there's going to be a dead Ku Kluxer or a dead Miller, one. It don't matter to me because once you get to be eighty-one years old, you ain't got much longer to live anyway."

We clapped again.

The next witness, a black man, Willie James Williams, a real honest-to-goodness retired Army sergeant who headed the NAACP in Sylacauga, Alabama, told of having his home shot into with a deer rifle while his wife and children were inside.

More clapping. They clapped again when Williams told of how the police didn't come to investigate the shooting because someone else had had a television set stolen and all the officers were "tied up" on that investigation.

After about two hours of having the Klan depicted as a bunch of lawless, violent hoodlums, Black leaned over to me and said, "We're leaving. As we leave we'll shout, 'Smash Communist treason.' Pass the word."

When the word had been passed to all, and when Black was certain all the television cameras were rolling, we rose together and began filing out. Black started the chant at the top of his lungs. The sheer volume of his voice surprised the hell out of me and I'm sure I jumped off the floor. I suspect it surprised the rest of the people in the room too.

By the time he had started the chant the second time, I had begun shouting too. Walker and some of the others carried the Confederate flag aloft as we left the room, and, as Black had planned, the television cameras were taking it all in.

"That didn't come off as strong as I hoped it would," Black said outside the chambers. If it had been any stronger, I couldn't have stood it, I thought, but I didn't say a word.

Several of the Klansmen left. I stayed with Black, who was obviously waiting for some of the television people to approach him. He wasn't disappointed. Two local stations did taped interviews with him.

While we waited, we walked over and looked out a window, just the two of us, and discussed the possibility of asking for the use of the Council chambers to allow the Klan to refute some of the charges made against it.

"The Wilkinson people were clapping for all the wrong things," Black confided. "I can't understand those folks sometimes. All they are doing is making sure people never forget the Klan's violent reputation of the past. Violence and guns should be the last resort, not a way of life."

This made me feel better, hearing some words of reason coming from the state's top Klan official.

During the coming months, however, I learned it was dangerous to be lulled into thinking words coming from a Klan official were reasonable. I also learned that the statements Black made that morning about guns were either designed to be misleading or his philosophy changed drastically during the next year.

I left the City Hall as Black began his second television interview. Outside, several members of our group were still hanging around. Bill Riccio was making the rounds again, shaking hands and telling everyone what a success our presence had been.

I thought at the time that Riccio was too nice, too friendly, and even a little too enthusiastic to be real. Later our paths would cross again. I would meet him, march with him, listen to his fiery speeches about blacks as "ape niggers." I would hear him threaten to kill people and I would learn that law-enforcement authorities viewed him as the most militant and most dangerous of any member of the Alabama Klan. I would also learn that he was Wilkinson's State Chaplain of the Invisible Empire of Alabama. Indeed, I would get to know Mr. Riccio much better.

After he left, I walked up to Ben Walker to assure him I would be at our next meeting. He was standing beside an old blue van talking to the men inside. The two Klansmen inside, both members of Wilkinson's group, were eating chicken from a nearby fast-food outlet.

"These fellows slipped off and got something to eat," Walker said to me as I walked up.

"I see that," I responded.

"I'll tell you," said the one behind the steering wheel, "nigger hatin' makes you hungry."

Black had been talking about some kind of public meeting like a rally or downtown march ever since our meeting at City Hall. I think he was pleased with the publicity our presence there had brought the Klan, and him personally, since he was the official Klan spokesman.

However, definite plans for some other activity to focus attention on the Klan had not progressed past the talking stage until one afternoon in early May. I had just switched off the radial arm saw when I heard the word Klan on the radio in the shop. Maybe the story would be repeated on the next newscast thirty minutes later, I thought. I would make every effort to be near the radio and not near the noisy machinery, just in case. The story was repeated, and it was also in the afternoon papers. But it didn't concern "my" Klan, it involved the Wilkinson Klan.

I knew immediately that Black would be fit to be tied when he heard that Wilkinson's State Chaplain Bill Riccio, and his Grand Dragon, Roger Handley, were planning a protest at the federal prison at Talladega, Alabama. The prison was being used as a holding facility for several hundred Cuban refugees—Cubans just fifty-five miles from Birmingham!

Knowing how hard Black tried to stay a jump ahead of the Wilkinson Klan, especially anywhere near Birmingham, I was right on the money about how he would feel when he heard of the rival Klan's plans.

"It just burns me up that they beat us to the Talladega thing," Black told me that night. "We should have been right on top of that."

This indicated to me that Black was unaware that the Cubans were being held at Talladega until that day. His ignorance of this fact probably upset him as much as Wilkinson's beating him to the punch.

"We've got to come up with something else," Black continued, somewhat desperately, "but I don't know yet what it will be. Be sure to check with me every day; maybe we'll come up with something by the weekend."

I tried to reach him the following day, but never made contact. I also tried for more than an hour on Friday night. Each time his line was busy. I finally decided to try him early on Saturday morning. I reached him then.

"I talked to David [Duke] late last night," Black said, with a hint of joviality in his voice, "and he had a better idea."

"Is that right?" I answered, assuming he meant Duke's idea was better than Wilkinson's.

"Yeah. How would you like to go to Florida?" he asked.

"I'd love it," I answered, knowing full well that I would

much prefer to go home, but the opportunity to be with both Black and David Duke had to take precedence. "When did you have in mind?"

"Well, a bunch of us are leaving from Woodrow Wilson Park [in downtown Birmingham] in about forty-five minutes. We're planning to take several cars, but if you come on down we'll probably have room for you in one of them."

"Gosh, Don, I couldn't possibly make it by then. I'm just getting up and I have to run by the shop for a few minutes. Why don't I just come on down alone and meet you there."

I had plenty of time to get downtown to meet him, but from the outset, I had tried to avoid being isolated with any Klansmen for any period of time. I didn't want them asking me about my past, the Army, my family, or anything else that might result in that one slipup that could lead to the discovery of the truth, so I knew I didn't want to be in a car full of people and give them five hours to question me on the way to Florida.

"All right," he said, "we're going to Fort Walton Beach for a big rally. David has lined up people from all over the South to be there to protest the invasion of the Cubans. We're going to stage a demonstration at the holding facility they have set up at Eglin Air Force Base and then rally tonight in Fort Walton. We're scheduled to be at the air base at three-thirty and the rally will start—it will be on the road you come in on—at seven."

"That's fine," I answered. "I'll have plenty of time. Sounds like it'll be fun."

"It will be. I'm sure glad you're going to be able to make it, J.W. We'd like to make a real good showing. I'm sure David has notified a lot of news people and we'll probably get a lot of good coverage. I'll see you this afternoon."

As soon as I hung up, I was almost sorry I had even made the call. No prospects now for a beautiful weekend at home. As I dialed Seigenthaler to tell him about the change in plans, I half hoped he wouldn't want me to go, though I knew all the time he would.

"Why don't you hurry and maybe you can catch up with the motorcade?" Seigenthaler said. "Meanwhile, I'll call Jimmy Ellis and get him on the way."

Ellis, *The Tennessean*'s chief photographer, was usually at every public function I participated in. (Nancy Warnecke, who had photographed my first rally in Lexington, had left the paper for a year's study at Harvard on a Nieman Fellowship.) I was tempted each time to have a beer and chat with a friend, but neither of us had ever made any attempt to communicate.

Over the months, Seigenthaler and I had come to end most of our telephone conversations the same way, a closing with a repetitive ring: "Be careful," Seigenthaler said, "and call me. Dammit, Thompson, don't keep me hanging. I want to know what's going on, and I want to hear from you every day."

"Sure, John, don't worry, I'll call you."

My next call was to Linda. "Honey, I'm not going to be able to make it home today."

"What's the problem?" she asked.

"They've changed their plans and we're having a big rally in Florida tonight. I've got to go down there."

"I bet you hate that," she said with a hint of sarcasm in her voice.

"I don't want to go, but—"

"I'm sure you don't," she interrupted. There it was again.

"I've got to go. Seigenthaler is sending Ellis down from Nashville and I've got to be there."

"Well, have fun."

"You know it won't be a fun trip. These things never are. But since it'll be too late to drive home tonight after the rally, I may just stay over and go deep-sea fishing tomorrow."

No response.

"Is everything all right there?" I asked.

"We're all fine," she answered somewhat tersely.

"Look, I've got to go. I'll call you tomorrow. I love you."

"Like I said, have fun," was all she said. Click.

Another call I wished I hadn't made. The whole conversation was totally out of character for Linda. She was usually understanding, supportive, and loving. This time she was none of those. Maybe she was tired, I thought. Maybe the baby kept her up last night, maybe there was some problem at the store—she'd had two coolers go out the week before. Maybe the dogs had peed on her roses again. Hell, it could be anything. She'll be all right tomorrow, I reasoned.

For several weeks, David, my boss, and I had been talking about driving down to Florida for a fishing trip. This would be a good opportunity to kill two birds with one stone. Besides, it would save some future weekend for me to go home. I called him, and he said he'd be ready within the hour.

David had no idea I was a member of the Klan, and I had no intention of letting him find out. Not that it would have made any difference in my job or our personal relationship, I just didn't want him—or anyone else I dealt with privately—to know it. When I picked him up at the shop, I had already decided I would take him directly to the motel and make some excuse about having to see an old girlfriend. David might not believe such a cock-and-bull story, but he'd never question it. I knew him that well. And I could always tell him the truth later.

We stopped in Alabaster, picked up a six-pack, then turned onto I-65 and headed south toward Montgomery. It was a comfortable drive. The sun was shining and it wasn't too hot. I was glad I had someone to talk to.

Along the way, I laid the groundwork for my "old girlfriend" story and, just as I thought, David didn't question it.

It was almost 3:00 P.M. when we neared Fort Walton
Beach. I would have time to make it to the protest at Eglin
Air Force Base, but I couldn't dally. About five miles north
of the beach, I rounded a curve and noticed the traffic slowing down to a crawl. Then I spotted a large crowd of people
up ahead, many of them in Klan robes.

Oh, hell, something must have gone wrong, I thought to
myself. This isn't Eglin.

I drove by a line of about seventy-five Klan members,
men, women, and children, all holding up placards denouncing the Cuban refugees in some way or another.

David said, "Look at those idiots. Can't they find something better to do?"

This was the first time I had ever heard him express an
opinion, or anything close to one, about the Klan. I suddenly
didn't know what to do. There were too many Klan members and others milling around, the traffic was too slow, and
many people were shouting jeers and insults from their vehicles. Anything could happen at any minute. I had to make a
decision and I had to make it fast. I either had to tip my hand
to David or try to rush him on to the motel and race
back.

I saw Jimmy Ellis as we went by. That made me think of
another way to see what was going on.

"Hey, I think I recognized somebody I know back there,"
I said excitedly. "I'm going to turn around and go back."

"Aw, man, let's go on and leave them people alone,"
David urged. "They're crazy."

"Naw, let's go back. They're not that bad," I assured him
as I wheeled the car around in front of a small drive-in market.

We had to park a short distance away. As we walked
toward the crowd I could hear Don Black shouting various
chants on his portable electric megaphone.

As we entered the fringe of the gathering, I said to David,
"Why don't you wait here and let me go up and say hello to
the fellow I know?"

That apparently suited David fine. He stopped in his tracks.

I walked to the front of the line and directly up to Don Black.

"Hey, J.W., glad to see you could make it," Black said, extending his hand. "They wouldn't let us on the Air Force base, so we decided to have our protest down here until it's time for the rally. This is where the rally will be too. We're probably attracting a lot more attention than we would have on the base, anyway. Go over and get you a sign and get in line."

I walked over to a stack of signs and took the top one. It said, DON'T MAKE FT. WALTON A HAVANA. I stood between two women, one of whom I had met before—Mrs. Don Oliver— and joined right in with the chants.

Almost every car, whether it was occupied by blacks or whites, slowed as it passed to view the spectacle I was a part of. Many people made obscene gestures and shouted and jeered at the Klan members. We didn't respond.

Jimmy Ellis was busy photographing me and others and, occasionally, a passing car protesting our presence. I saw the bright lights of a television camera crew to my extreme left. The cameraman was coming right down the line of Klan protesters right toward me. Suddenly, a wave of sheer terror swept over me. The cameraman was Jon Smith, of Nashville, who works for CBS in Atlanta, an old and close friend. He would surely recognize me, shake my hand, and call me by name. Don Black was standing only a few feet away. I had to act fast.

I broke ranks and stepped out of the line, walking toward the highway, looking into the distance as if I had detected some sort of disturbance or something. I just "happened" to walk directly toward Jimmy Ellis. He looked puzzled when he saw me coming and outright startled when I spoke to him without ever changing my gaze from down the highway.

"Get to Jon Smith," I uttered under my breath. "Jon Smith, on your right."

I hoped and silently prayed that no one in the Klan realized what I had just done. I had talked to a newsman, something strictly forbidden for a Klansman to do. Was I detected? If so, would they connect me with *The Tennessean*? Had I just blown my whole cover, the cover I had spent months rehearsing and living? And what would happen if I had?

When Smith came by my spot in the line, he photographed me with the same professional-looking expression everyone else saw. He did not, however, use the news film until after our story appeared in *The Tennessean* on December 7, seven months later.

After about two hours in the protest line out front, our group moved into a fenced-off area behind a small store. A huge, diesel-fuel-soaked cross had already been erected. As we moved to the rally site, I went back to where David stood and asked him to join us.

"What in the hell is going on?" he asked. "Are you in the Klan?"

Suddenly, he was brimming with questions. And I wanted to avoid the answers.

"David," I began, "I'm sure you are a little confused by all this. I'm sure I would be if the circumstances were reversed. But if you just won't mention to anyone what you've seen tonight, there'll come a day when I can explain everything to you. I'll just have to ask you to trust me for the time being."

"Don't worry," he assured me, "I won't ever tell anyone I went to a Klan rally. My folks would have a fit if they knew."

Several local Klansmen spoke at the rally that evening, all telling their audience how awful it was to be living in the same community with "Castro's criminals." Others blamed the entire problem on President Jimmy Carter. Still others just took a scatter shot at the federal government for allowing the Cubans to come ashore in the first place.

When Black spoke, he said essentially the same thing only

more elaborately. He blamed the government, and specifically Jimmy Carter, for allowing the Cubans to come to the
United States, he blamed the government for "using our tax
money to feed and house the scum that Castro wanted to get
rid of, allowing them to live better than you and me." And
he blamed the government for its announced plans to relo-
cate the refugees and find them employment. "The next
thing you know," he shouted with the fiery zeal of a Funda-
mentalist preacher, "the government will tell you you'll
have to leave your job so a Cuban criminal can have it.
Folks, that's what they call affirmative action. We've seen
what happens when a black wants your job, or some other
minority wants your job. Now we're going to see what happens when a Cuban wants it. I'm sure Mr. Carter will have
them all registered to vote before November."

When Duke took the podium, he echoed briefly the same
speeches we had already heard about the Cuban refugees
and then went into his more or less "standard" speech, lam-
basting the Jews and blacks.

"Good white people, we still have a majority in this country but we're losing it fast. We must stand up for the white
people and we must do it now. The African population in
this country is outbreeding the white people by twenty-five
to one. We're being overrun by mentally retarded little African bastards. Now, folks, I didn't say that to be talking ugly.
The fact is that the majority of the Africans born in this
country are illegitimate and—look it up in your dictio-
nary—the correct term for this is 'bastard.'"

"Hey, we've got one of them nigger bastards here tonight," a gruff voice shouted from the crowd. Duke ignored
it.

There was a black television newsman in the crowd that
night—probably the most courageous newsman I've ever
come in contact with. He was from WSB-TV, Atlanta, and
his cameraman was white. As the various speakers shouted
their onslaught of racism and hatred from the speakers' platform, the black newsman circulated through the crowd,

interviewing people about why they had come to the rally.

"Would you tell me why you came here tonight?" he asked, holding the microphone in front of a man standing near me.

"I'll talk to that fellow," the man replied, pointing to the white cameraman, "but I ain't gonna talk to no nigger."

"That's all right. Let's move on," he said to his cameraman, who was ready to rush to his defense.

Then he came to me. I have since wished I had thought of something brilliant, maybe even patriotic, to say. I might have mimicked some of the other brilliant replies I had heard that night, like: "I luv my cuntry," or "I'm tard of the niggers, Cubans, Vietnamese, and ever'body else coming over here and takin' our jobs and getting food stamps and welfare," or, "I'm here 'cause I'm white and 'cause I hate niggers."

Instead, I fulfilled a secret, longtime desire to give the answer that I'd been given so many times during my career as a journalist.

"No comment." Besides, I didn't want to be seen on TV just now.

Between the time the speakers finished and the cross-lighting ceremony began, I exploited the hell out of David. I introduced him to Don Black, David Duke, Ben Walker, Don Oliver, and several others. Each time I was meticulous in making sure they understood he was "my boss." I even told Black later that David was so impressed with the speeches and the rally that he would probably be our next convert. "I'll sign him up, 'most any day now," I said, and Black was pleased.

After the official ceremony was completed and the cross was still burning brightly, Duke continued his speech.

"We oughta burn the Cubans on that cross," someone shouted.

"Naw, we oughta burn Jimmy Carter," someone else responded.

"Hell, no," another called out emphatically. "We ain't

got no Cubans here and we ain't got Jimmy Carter here. But
we have got us a nigger. Let's burn him."

About this time, other shouts, loud shouts, could be heard
from five young black men in Air Force fatigues, standing
outside the fenced field: "You crazy, honky motherfuckers."
"You goddamn idiots." "Come on down here and we'll build
a fire under your honky asses."

The invitation was unnecessary. Within seconds, almost
two hundred people were running toward them. The
onslaught of humanity flattened the fence in the area where
they stood. Several sheriff's deputies rushed in. Somehow,
before the Klansmen reached them, the men managed to get
back into their car and were surrounded by a cordon of huge
deputies carrying riot sticks, who escorted them to the highway, where they sped away.

The rally was over.

The commercial fishing docks were a beehive of activity
early Sunday morning. Deckhands rushed around loading
bait and ice onto the dozen or so boats still in harbor; some
had left as early as 2:00 A.M. A slight mist rose from the
water as David and I sleepily stumbled aboard the *New
Florida Girl.* The boat's huge diesel engines were already
running. At 6:55, Captain Mike Marler came aboard,
checked the bait and ice, and walked directly to the wheel-
house. At 7:00 A.M., the lines had been cast off and the huge
boat was easing out of its slip.

As the boat headed south out of the ship channel at Des-
tin, Florida, the dark murky waters of the Gulf changed to a
bright blue-green. David and I sat on the west side of the
boat in the shade and watched small flying fish jump from
the water in the boat's wake and glide for yards before set-
tling back into the water. We drank coffee and talked of all
the fish we were planning to catch and how much more fun
it was to be fishing than making cabinets. Not once did we
mention the Klan or what had gone on the day before.

After about two hours, the boat started slowing and

circling. The deckhands had already put the bait out on the rail and had positioned the large rods with electric reels at their respective positions.

David had become quiet during the last hour. He sat staring out over the water. I was sure he was trying to figure out how to tell me that his business didn't need a Klansman, in fact, couldn't stand a Klansman. I got up and walked around the boat and talked to the other people.

As we circled, Captain Marler had his eyes glued to the Fathometer, looking for the fuzzy lines that would indicate fish below. I went back to where David was sitting and informed him we were almost ready to begin fishing.

"Okay," was all he said.

I couldn't blame him for wanting to get rid of me. If I had had a business that depended on customers from all cultures, all colors, all religions, I wouldn't have a Klansman working for me. I was mad at myself for letting him find out. I'd just have to find another job.

Finally, the boat stopped. Captain Marler rang a bell signifying it was time to lower our lines to try for a big red snapper or grouper.

"Come on, David," I urged, "it's time to get 'em."

He stood up slowly, picked up his rod and reel, lowered his line, and then turned to me. "Buddy," he said, "I don't feel too good."

No sooner did his line touch bottom than a fish almost snatched his rig. He reeled in a large snapper, the first fish of the day.

Then he threw up.

And I was relieved.

I went on to catch thirty-five red snappers and a ten-pound scamp. I couldn't wait to phone Linda and tell her of my good fortune.

Back at the docks, I left David to oversee the cleaning and icing down of our catch, and I phoned Linda. I knew she would still be at the store.

"Hi, darling," I began, "you won't believe the day I've

had. I caught thirty-five snappers and a big scamp for Todd.
I wish you had been with me."

"You won't believe the day I've had either," she said. "I
wish I had been anywhere but here."

"I can't wait for you to see the fish. They're beauties."

"I don't want to see the fish, or anything else. You can
take the fish and stuff them."

"What the hell's wrong with you?"

"Everything. Joe just pulled a bottle of juice off the shelf
and broke it. While I was trying to get him out of the broken
glass, the damn minnow tank ran over, I've got Joe in my
arms and I'm standing here right now ass-deep in minnow
water and prune juice. I don't even have time to talk."

"I'm sorry I bothered you. I just wanted to tell you I love
you."

"Well, that's fine, but I've gotta go now. Bye."

Dammit, for almost four years now, I thought she was
different, I said to myself as I walked back toward the ice-
house where David was packing the fish. I bet she thinks I'm
enjoying this damn assignment. Having fun. Hell, I'd much
rather be home, but she knew when she married me that I
was a newspaperman, and she should have known that there
would be times when I'd have to be away on a story. She was
beginning to sound just like other women: blind, selfish, and
inconsiderate. If she didn't have time to talk to me, damned
if I would inconvenience her again for a while.

"Partner, you still look a little puny," I said to David. "I
don't think you're up to that drive home. Let's stay over
another night and go home the first thing in the morning."

"I don't know about that," he said. "I'm feeling better.
Maybe we'd better go on; we've got a set of cabinets due out
Wednesday."

"Naw, I can tell you feel too bad. We'll finish the cabinets
tomorrow afternoon and Tuesday. We'll have plenty of
time."

"Well, maybe you're right," he said.

The next morning David was up 6:00 A.M. feeling chipper

and ready to hit the road. We got back to the shop about 1:00 P.M. We'd been there about ten minutes when the phone rang.

"It's for you, J.W.," David said, and then almost in a whisper, "It's a woman."

I couldn't imagine any woman who would call me at the shop, unless it was someone with the Klan.

I was wrong. It was Linda, the only time she ever called me at the shop. "Are you all right?" she asked.

"Sure, I'm fine, why?"

"Well, I was just lying here for a few minutes to rest before going back to the store, and you know those roses you gave me on our honeymoon, the ones I pressed and framed along with the note you wrote me?"

"Yeah."

"Well for no reason at all, the frame fell off the wall and broke all to hell. I just knew something had happened to you. Are you sure you're all right?"

"Sure, honey, I'm fine. Are you sure you're all right?"

"Oh, Jerry, it seems my whole life is coming apart at the seams. Nothing is going right here at home, at the store, or anywhere. I miss you, I need you, and even if I haven't acted like it the last few days, I really do love you. I guess when the roses fell off the wall, I just panicked. I'm sorry I bothered you at work."

"It was no bother, believe me. I love you and I'll be with you just as soon as I possibly can. I promise."

David had walked to the service station next door to get a Coke while I was on the phone. I was glad he didn't hear my conversation.

"David, that was my dearest girlfriend up in Chattanooga," I told him when he returned. "She made me an offer I couldn't refuse. I told her neither one of us felt up to working this afternoon and that I would be right on up there. I'll be back the first thing in the morning. Is that all right."

"Yeah, that's fine," he said. "I think I'll just lock up and go home. We'll get an early start tomorrow."

WHEW! I hadn't told Linda I was coming home, but I knew I was going, even before I hung up the phone. I drove hard for four hours directly to the market, where I knew Linda would be.

"What are you doing here, stranger?" Linda said, genuinely surprised to see me walk in the door.

"You sounded like you were in dire need of a big hug," I answered, "and I just wanted to make damn sure I was the one to give it to you."

I know the old farmer waiting to pay for his chewing tobacco wondered what was going on as we smooched like teenagers behind the counter, but at that moment he was the furthest thing from our minds.

I rushed home to prepare some fresh red snapper. When Linda got there and the whole family was at dinner, her feelings about my catch had obviously changed since the night before.

After the children left the table—rushing away as usual to avoid the inevitable cleanup following a big fish fry—Linda stared down at her plate and I knew we were about to have one of our serious talks.

"Honey, I'm sorry I've been in such a foul mood the past few days," she began, "but nothing seems to be going right. I'm coming apart. I just can't take it anymore."

"I know it's tough, Linda," I responded, "but it can't be much longer before I'll be through. It seems that I've just now shifted into high gear. I'm really making some progress. I've been accepted in the Klan, they trust me, they ask me to participate with them. Hell, this is the point I've been trying to reach ever since I went down there a few months ago."

"That's just it, Jerry. You look at it as just a few months, but to us—and I mean the kids and your folks too—it seems like you've been gone forever. You told me the assignment would take three—six months at the most. Do you realize you've been gone more than that already?"

"Sure, it's taking longer than I thought it would, but I can't rush those people, Linda, without putting myself in one hell of a precarious position."

"I know that, but do you realize that Joe is walking and talking, and you may have missed the cutest part of his life? When he was first learning to walk, he fell more than any kid I ever saw. But every time, he would just get up and try again. He was so damned determined. I couldn't help but cry as I watched him. I just know that someday he'll find something that he's so interested in doing that he will leave his family, his home, or anything else he cares for, to do it. He's just that damned determined."

"Well, that's certainly the nicest and most subtle way I've ever been called selfish."

"Jerry, I didn't mean to imply that you were selfish, but maybe I did too. I've given it a lot of thought—it seems I have a lot of time to think lately—and I haven't decided which one of us is selfish. Am I selfish for wanting you here at home to help with the kids, the house, the garden, the horses, or just the everyday things like taking the garbage out or doing the grocery shopping once in a while, or running Todd to ball practice, or just being here to give me a

hug like today? (By the way, I really needed that.) Or are
you selfish for putting our needs and wants aside and continuing to do what you want to do? I don't feel good. I'm
always tired, I'm irritable with the kids and everybody else.
Sometimes, I just don't feel like living. Jerry, please come
home."

"Linda, you know I can't do that right now. Maybe I am
kinda like Joe. I've been down so damn many times in the
last few months, but I've kept getting up again. Joe is not
going to quit walking and go back to crawling because it's
been too damn hard to get where he is. And I can't quit
either for the same reason. I've got to go on just a little
longer. I'm making progress now and things will speed up,
I'm sure. Honey, I truly believe what I'm doing right now is
helping us all. You haven't met these people, haven't seen
how they act, talk. You haven't seen how they're teaching
their kids to hate just as they do. Believe me, their kids need
a helluva lot more help than ours do."

"All kids, all people, need help, but I'm not sure their kids
need more help than ours. Let me show you something." She
got up and took a single sheet of paper out of a cabinet drawer. She handed it to me.

It was a hand-drawn picture of a robed and hooded Klansman holding a burning torch. At the bottom of the page
were the words: *We know who you are. KKK.*

"Where did this come from?" I asked.

"Todd said he found it under a rock over behind the barn.
He conveniently had three witnesses when he found it, the
girls and Richard [my nephew]."

From the very outset, Linda and I had attempted to shield
the children from knowing exactly what I was doing. We
told them only that it was a secret assignment for the paper
and admonished them not to talk to anyone about it. They
were to tell prying friends and relatives they didn't know
where I was or what I was doing and let them believe what
they pleased.

In retrospect, I'm not sure this was the best way to deal with it.

We are fortunate to have curious, inquisitive children and equally fortunate that, although they are too smart not to find out what I was doing and who I was doing it with, not one of them mentioned it to a soul. Speculation on what I was doing was running rampant among friends and relatives, especially relatives. Some would get the kids alone and pump them for information. But the kids always said, "I don't know."

There were rumors in our small farming community that Linda and I were having marital problems and that I had left home, returning only on occasional weekends to see the children.

"It's obvious Todd put it there and then took the other kids back to support the story he was going to make up about it," I said.

"I know that, Jerry, but it's just another way he is asking for help. He's tried to talk you into coming home and that didn't work. He cried and begged you to come home and that didn't work. He threatened to run away from home himself if you didn't come home and that didn't work. When he brought this in the other day, I told him that it was just a prank someone had thought up and that it wouldn't scare anybody, especially his daddy. He insisted that I show it to you anyway. Jerry, he's going through one of the most difficult periods in his life right now. His voice is changing, his life is changing, his body is changing, and all these things frighten him and make him terribly insecure. He needs you. Can't you see that?"

"I see that, honey, but Todd's a tough little boy. Hell, he's already gone through more troubles and tests than many adults. He'll be all right."

Sure Todd was a tough little boy. He had to be. The circumstances in his life, totally beyond his control, had forced

him almost to skip childhood and go directly to being an
adult. He was certainly called upon to bear burdens that
adults would struggle under. Maybe this was a burden I was
putting on him that I could control. Did I have the right to
do that? Could he take yet one more load? I wondered.

Linda went to bed. I stayed downstairs and tried to jot
down some of the highlights of the Florida trip, but my
thoughts kept going to Todd, the girls, the baby. I kept
thinking of that picture he had "found" in the field. But I
also recalled some of the periods in his life, our lives, that
had served to toughen him to the realities of our world.

The girls, Tanya, nine, and Niki, eleven, seemed nonchalant about my absence and shrugged off the many questions
about my whereabouts with the same attitude. Todd, however, who had just become a teenager shortly before I left,
would have been going through a very difficult stage in his
life even without the additional complications of the inces-
sant questions and my not being home. He had already gone
through much more than any little boy deserves. (True, he's
only a few inches shy of six feet and weighs two hundred
pounds, but he's still my little boy.)

When Todd was only four, his mother and I had serious
problems, and by the time he was five, divorce and custody
proceedings were filed and he and I had moved out. I
enrolled him in school in an adjoining county, settled into
the new routine and seemed perfectly happy. Then I was
hauled into court by his mother for a hearing to determine if
I should pay her expenses while the divorce was pending.
When the case was called, the judge dismissed it because she
wasn't there to present her side. I thought this somewhat
strange. As I left the courthouse, I was met by my brother,
Ronnie.

"Now I want you to stay cool," he began, "and don't do
anything stupid."

"What's the problem?" I urged, almost frantic.

"While you were in court, she stole Todd out of school. The kindergarten teacher called me at home and said his mother came in, grabbed Todd, ran out to the car, and took off. Todd was screaming at the top of his lungs."

Staying cool and not doing something stupid that day was the hardest thing I had ever done. While fighting the urge to do physical harm to someone, including myself, and the urge to just break down and cry and accept defeat, I thought about what to do. I had two choices: I could simply give up and try to explain to Todd in his later years that I did it for his own good, or I could continue the fight for custody and, regardless of the eventual outcome, explain to him later that I did it for his own good.

I quickly persuaded myself that we would both be stronger in the long run if we didn't give up. I went directly to my lawyer's office. The lawyer quickly drew up papers to have Todd returned to my custody while being very careful not to offer me too much hope that the judge would go along with it. We had to wait all afternoon, until after the regular court docket had been disposed of, and then try to persuade the judge to hear our case.

The judge agreed to hear our plea in chambers after warning that it was rare indeed that he would issue a custody order without a full hearing in court. After the lawyer presented our case, the judge turned his chair to the wall, obviously trying to decide what to do. There was a resounding silence while he thought it over. I'm sure he could hear my heart pounding. I could.

Finally, he turned back around and said, "I don't usually do this, but I'm going to issue a change of custody in this case because I feel this woman used the court to make sure she knew where Mr. Thompson was while she took the child out of school. Because of this, I'm going to grant Mr. Thompson temporary custody until this matter can be heard in court."

By this time it was dark outside. While we were waiting

all afternoon, I found out that my wife had moved out of the house and into an apartment on the other side of town. That's where Todd would be.

The lawyer hand-carried the court order to the sheriff's department and asked for a deputy to serve it and retrieve my son. I rode with him.

When we arrived at the apartment, the deputy asked me to wait in the car to avoid a confrontation. After he entered the apartment, I could hear my wife screaming, then Todd crying, and I asked myself: Why does Todd have to go through all of this? Have I done the right thing?

Todd was still crying as the deputy brought him down the steps, but calmed down immediately when he saw me coming toward them. He clung to me and sobbed, "Daddy, Daddy," over and over again. I held him close so he wouldn't see the tears streaming down my cheeks.

"Everything's all right," I assured him. "We're going home." Home at that time was the guest bedroom in my brother's house in a subdivision in a small town thirty miles south of Nashville. Todd went to sleep on the drive home.

When I pulled into the drive, there must have been twenty neighbors from blocks around gathered on the patio. They had heard that Todd had been taken from school and that I was trying to get him back. They had been there for hours waiting to find out what happened.

There was not a sound as I got out of the car. But when I went around to the other side and got Todd out, there was a cheer that could be heard for blocks around. Then there was hugging and kissing and laughter and tears.

The little girl across the street handed Todd a crumpled sheet of construction paper on which she had written, *"Welcum home Tod."* Obviously she had had more confidence in the day's outcome than I had.

Almost two years, many days in Circuit Court, and the longest day I ever spent in the Tennessee Court of Appeals later, I was awarded full legal custody of my son. I just hoped and prayed that the bitter injuries we both suffered during the lengthy ordeal would soon heal without leaving permanent scars.

Soon afterward, Todd and I moved to the farm we still live on and he started going to the same school I had attended as a child and even had some of the same teachers.

Todd visited his mother regularly, she and I got along better, and he knew he had a mother and a father who loved him, even if they didn't live together anymore.

Todd and I spent many hours together fishing and just walking over the farm. We shared the miracle of the birth of a new calf and later the birth of a baby colt from his own mare. We were more than father and son, we were the best of buddies. Things went along smoothly, seemingly getting better every day for almost three years before tragedy struck again.

Todd and I were in Florida on what had become our annual Thanksgiving fishing trip. At 5:00 A.M. on Thanksgiving Day, we were awakened by a banging on our trailer door. It was Curt Cox, the man who ran the dock we fished out of.

"Jerry," he began, "someone from Tennessee just called and left a number you're supposed to call back right away. She said it was an emergency. Sounded like she was crying."

"I'll be right down as soon as I get dressed."

A million things, all bad, ran through my mind as I hurriedly pulled on my clothes. Had something happened to my parents, my brothers, my sister? Linda and I had been dating for several months, could something have happened to her or her daughters? My grandmother had been sick. That was it. It was my grandmother, I was convinced.

It wasn't yet daylight when Todd and I jumped into the car and headed down the road to the dock.

Mr. Cox handed me the number; it was my former sister-in-law's. I knew right away it didn't concern my grandmother. Whatever the news was, I felt it best if Todd wasn't in the room when I got it. He went out and I made the call.

I was right. Before I went out to find him, I said to Mr. Cox, "How am I going to tell that little fellow out there that his mother is going to die, probably before we can get home?" The man she had been dating had shot her in the head. She was in the hospital on machines.

Todd didn't say a word when I called him to the car. Then I told him. "Todd, your mother has been shot."

He immediately burst into tears and cried uncontrollably for several minutes, finally managing to ask:

"Is she dead?"

"No, but she's hurt real bad. She's in the hospital and everything that can be done is being done. We're going home right now."

We drove home in less than eight hours without ever mentioning his mother again. But there were times we would go for miles and miles without saying anything. It was awfully hard to find anything to be thankful for on that Thanksgiving Day.

She died the next morning without regaining consciousness.

That seemed so long ago yet so recent. Had Todd ever recovered from the blow? He had never discussed his mother and had only recently put her picture out on his desk.

I kept recalling a tearful conversation I'd had with him one Sunday morning about two months before. That seemed like a long time ago too, but the memory was vivid and, I believe, will continue to be over the years to come.

I had slept late on a Sunday morning and when I came downstairs, I was surprised not to see Todd in the living room with the girls and the baby.

"He's still up in his room," Linda told me, her voice only slightly above a whisper. "I think I've heard him crying a couple of times. Maybe you should go see what's wrong."

I knocked gently on his door. He was sitting on the side of his bed and his eyes were red and swollen.

"What's wrong, son?" I asked, sitting in his desk chair.

"Daddy, I can't take it anymore," he said, tears rushing down his cheeks.

"Can't take what anymore?"

"Living here with these people and you gone. I'm not even kin to these people, and when you're not here they treat me like a stepchild, and that's what I am. Linda is always taking up for the girls. She doesn't care anything about me."

"I can't believe that, Todd. I remember Linda telling you before we got married how she had always wanted a son and how much she loved you. She might ask you to do things you don't want to do, but I can't believe she would mistreat you. I know her too well."

"You don't have to believe me. I'm just telling you I'm not living here anymore. Ever since Joe was born, she's had her own son. She doesn't need me anymore."

"Son, she does need you. I need you. We all need each other. I realize it's tough being the man of the house, but it's tough on me too being away from all the people I really love. It won't be much longer before I'm back home for good and everything will be better then."

"That's what you said when you left last summer, and that's what you said Christmas, and that's what you're saying now. What am I supposed to believe?"

"I know what you're saying is the truth, son, but things have kinda gotten out of my control. I can't rush these silly people and risk their finding out who I am and what I'm doing. All I can promise you is that I'll be home as soon as I possibly can."

"Look, Daddy," Todd said, "my real mother is dead. And if you keep messing with the Klan, they're going to kill you. You're all I've got, Daddy, and if something happens to you, what am I going to do?"

I felt guilty as hell. I knew that Todd was being honest

enough to put forth a blatant reality—a real possibility that
I had consciously tried to avoid. Maybe he was being more
realistic than I was. I put my arms around him and, in the
most convincing tone of voice I could muster, told him,
"Son, the Klan is not going to do anything to me. They're
not that bad."

"Huh. I don't guess they killed five people over in Greensboro, or shot four people in Decatur. Don't try to tell me the
Klan's not bad."

He was certainly keeping up with the news. I didn't know
whether to be glad or sorry, though. "I'm not telling you
they're not bad," I said, "I'm just telling you they're not
going to hurt me. It's because of things like Greensboro and
Decatur that I've got to go back and find out as much as I
can about these people. I'll be all right."

"Well, I'm just telling you this: If you go back, I'm going
to run away from home. I can't stay here any longer where
nobody cares about me."

"Someday, I'm sure you'll understand why I have to go
back. I don't like to beg, but I'm begging you to try to understand and try to bear with me. I apologize for forcing you to
grow up too fast and I apologize for maybe not growing fast
enough myself. I love you, I love you very much. It doesn't
matter what you do now, or whenever, that won't change.
Now why don't we both go and wash the tears off our faces
and go down for lunch?"

"I'm not hungry."

I went downstairs alone. I wasn't any too hungry either.

Three times on the drive to Birmingham before dawn the
next day I pulled off the interstate to turn around and go
back home. And three times I talked myself into going on.

In my first phone conversation with Black after getting
back to Birmingham, the first one since the Florida rally, he
told me of plans to form a new Klan den in Brookside, a
small Birmingham suburb on the city's western edge. He

was almost boastful when talking about the prospective members of the new den—most of them, he said, were defections from Wilkinson's Klan.

He invited me to attend an organizational meeting of the new den the following Saturday night. I figured that if there was a new den forming, there would be new members to be naturalized. This might be my chance finally to take the formal oath of a Klansman. I of course accepted the invitation. Black explained that Brookside was difficult to find and asked me to meet him at a truck stop in Forestdale. "You can ride with me from there and maybe together we can find it," he said.

We met at the truck stop at six-thirty the following Saturday. He was right about how hard it was to find Brookside. We got lost, or at least took the wrong road, twice before Black finally decided we were at the right place. It was a small frame house set on the side of a hill. The road curved around the yard of the house. I doubted we were at the right place, because directly across from the drive that Black was already pulled into was another drive leading down to another small frame house with several blacks milling around in the front yard.

"This is the place," Black said, as a short, young man dressed in the garb of a Klan security officer came out the back door and started toward the car. I introduced myself to the young man and he responded, "Glad you could come out, J.W.," but he never did tell me who he was.

Inside, about fifteen men and women were sitting around. I had seen a couple of the men at the courthouse the month before when we disrupted the mock Klan trial. I knew at that time they were with the Wilkinson group and I suspected several of the others were also defections, as Black was going out of his way to accommodate them.

Some asked Black about the possibility of being arrested while participating with his Knights because they were on probation from earlier arrests. He told them that he was well aware that an arrest could result in the revocation of their probation and assured them, "In our group, if anyone is arrested we try to make sure it is me and the officers and not the members. We try to avoid arrest altogether, but in that event, I'll be the first one to go."

After Black addressed the prospective members on meeting procedures, order of business at meetings, educational sessions, rally speakers, and various other Klan matters, he scheduled two naturalization ceremonies for the new den— one for the "secret member" and the other for the rest of the new members. I had never heard of a secret member before that time and I was curious.

After the meeting finally broke up and several of us were standing outside, I went over to one of the men I had met inside and asked just what a secret member was. I had picked him out because he acted less like a Klansman than any others I had met up to that point—or afterward, for that matter. He was quiet, unassuming, seemingly secure, and always smiling and friendly. His wife, who was in the latter stages of pregnancy at the time, was also at that meeting.

"A secret member is usually somebody with money," he said to me. "Only the top officers know who they are, but the secret members provide money to get new dens going until they get on their feet and start raising money on their own. I've never met one, but I'm told they are doctors and lawyers and people like that."

I've never known one either, but I certainly have met some people I suspect.

On the drive back that night, Black initiated the conversation about my naturalization and leveled with me about the one that was aborted back in February at the Howard Johnson's.

"We could have secured the room that night," he said. "It wasn't that. While you all [Fullerton and I] were waiting outside, we decided that we had serious doubts about Fullerton. He knew too many people he shouldn't have known, he was talking to too many people and spending too much money. I found out that his father once worked for the Birmingham Police Department and that he had done some undercover work for the police before going to California. He never bothered to tell me about these things. He was just too eager, too cooperative, and too knowledgeable, so we thought we had better wait him out. I hear now that he may have gone over to Wilkinson. We'll just let Wilkinson have him.

"Now we'll get you naturalized right away. If we can't do it when we have the naturalization over here at the Brookside den, I'll have you over to my apartment and we'll do it there."

I felt somewhat relieved that night. Apparently, Black had never suspected my undercover role. In fact, I had been a Klansman ever since that November night he took my money in Sambo's parking lot. Since that night, I had been involved in many Klan activities, even though I had not taken the formal oath. Each time—too many times to recall right off—my naturalization had been scheduled, something had come up to prevent it. Although I had grown accustomed to getting all prepared for the ceremony so many times only to have it rescheduled, I still didn't want to miss a chance at it. As I left Black that night, I told him I would call him the next week so we could try again to have my naturalization ceremony. Since he brought the subject up initially, I felt pretty safe in keeping it alive. I wanted to push him, but I didn't want him to realize I was pushing.

I talked with him a couple of times during the next week and each time I brought up my naturalization and each time I said, as he suggested, we could do it at his place. I guess he finally got tired of putting me off, so he set yet another date.

"Call me Friday," he said. "It may be possible that we could get together over here Friday night and get you naturalized."

I knew I would make the call on Friday, but I never really expected it to amount to anything. There would be another excuse, I was sure.

I wasn't really ready for it when I called him on the latest designated date—May 23, 1980—and he told me to come on over. I thought of a thousand reasons why he might still cancel it.

It was just one minute before 7:00 P.M. when I knocked on the door of his apartment that night at 1325-A in the Chestnut Tree complex in Birmingham's Bluff Park section. The Grand Dragon himself opened the door and welcomed me in to be naturalized.

Black and I were alone in his apartment that night and he anointed me "Klansman." He invited me to have a seat in his comfortable furnished living room, warning me about a broken leg on one of the chairs.

I had known him at times to be cold, reticent, and suspicious, but this night he was friendly and outgoing and introduced me to his wife's cat, Loki—named, he said, for a Norse god of olden times. The cat was pregnant and due to give birth almost any day. He remarked that it should have been named for a goddess. That was the nearest thing to a joke I had yet heard him utter.

Darlene was shopping, he said. I had no idea who else would attend my naturalization. As it turned out, nobody else would. Even that was no real surprise. In the months since I had paid Don Black my initiation fee, he had never been able to produce more than a handful of members at any meeting in Birmingham.

Gradually, I had come to the conclusion that he had only a skeleton organization in his hometown. Apparently, I was right. Later, when he left the post of Grand Dragon to become national Grand Wizard, he moved the National Headquarters to Tuscumbia, Alabama, in the north, where he had the strongest concentration of members.

Now, in the quiet apartment—quiet except for the television tuned to a fifties-style sock hop—he seemed to be stalling. Was he going to postpone the ceremony yet again? For fifteen minutes we engaged in small talk—the weather, the cat, the presidential primaries, and his concerns that the "niggers and the Jews" were gaining more control every day Jimmy Carter was in office. Small talk, indeed.

Suddenly, his mood changed, he became solemn and serious. "Let's get on with the ritual," he said. "It looks like Darlene is running late. I was hoping she would get back in time to participate in the ceremony."

He stood, walked to another room, leaving me watching the sock hop. Within a few minutes he was back in his long white satin robe. He turned off the TV, lowered the lights, lit candles, and placed them on the dining-room table. He brought a glass of water from the kitchen, made a couple of trips to another room to assemble a lot of documents, then escorted me into the dining room and told me to stand directly before him.

His eyes sought contact with mine. I tried not to blink.

"Raise your left hand," he instructed, "it is nearest to your heart."

I raised my left hand. I couldn't help but feel the nervousness building within me.

"It usually takes four officers of the Klan to do this," he said. "But as Grand Dragon, I am empowered to do it alone."

At last, through this so-called secret "sacred" ceremony, I was to become a Klansman by "oath" as well as by dues, initiation fee, and participation. This was another big step in my life in the Klan.

Black, twenty-seven, is six feet three inches tall. He regularly practices karate and stands with a rigid, almost military bearing. He was an imposing figure indeed that night in the flickering candlelight.

He began by congratulating me on my "courageous" decision to join the Klan.

Courage? Hell, my heart was in my throat struggling to thump its way past my Adam's apple.

The Klan, he told me—as if I didn't already know—was an organization dedicated to white supremacy. "It is a Klansman's nature to assist those who aspire to things noble in thought and conduct and to extend a helping hand to those worthy," he said, reading from his official KKK documents. "Your desire to become a Klansman is sincerely respected and has been considered in the light of honor and justice," he went on.

Suddenly I felt giddy and was afraid I might giggle. But Black was painfully serious, completely wrapped up in what he was saying—that's what was making me feel giddy.

"You may now come forward and advance to the next step of knightly honor," he intoned. "However, if you are of faint heart, advance no further, for this is no light honor. You are about to take a vow of blood and honor."

When he mentioned blood, the urge to giggle suddenly left me.

The "next step" in the ritual was a series of ten questions which I would have to answer. "Our requirements of thought are simple, but they are also sacred. We require as an absolute necessity, an honest answer to the following questions:

"Are you a white American citizen and not a Jew?"

I said I was a white citizen and not a Jew.

"Is the motive prompting your ambition to be a Klansman sincere and unselfish?"

I said it was.

"Have you ever been rejected upon application for membership in the Knights of the Ku Klux Klan?"

I had not.

"Do you believe in the Constitution of the United States and will you, without reservation, take an oath to defend and preserve it?"

This is hardly the way I would demonstrate my patriotism, but I said yes on both counts.

"Are you in favor of a white man's government in this country?"

"Certainly," I said as emphatically as I could.

"Do you believe in the right of self-preservation for our people against the exercise of unlawful and unjust actions coming from any level of government?"

I wasn't particularly concerned at that point about unlawful and unjust actions from the government, but I had a growing concern about self-preservation. I answered that I did.

"Do you believe in religious freedom, including the right for the people to practice the Christian faith anywhere they assemble, including prayers in schools and public places?"

I didn't feel religious, but I said I did.

"Will you faithfully obey our Klan constitution and laws, and conform willingly to our laws and regulations?"

I said I would.

"Are you willing to dedicate your life to the protection, preservation, and advancement of the white race?"

I answered that I was willing.

Black then detailed what he said were the "distinguishing marks of a Klansman" and told me I was seeking to develop them. "They are not found in the fineness of his clothes or his social or financial standing, but are spiritual and racial: namely, a compassionate heart, a prudent tongue, a courageous will bonded to racial purity, all devoted to our race, our country, our families, Klan, and each other, these are the distinguishing marks of a Klansman . . . and you claim these marks!"

He warned me then never to betray the Klan. "If you should ever prove yourself a traitor, you will be immediately banished in disgrace without fear or favor. Your conscience will torment you and direful things will befall you."

I was not especially concerned about my conscience, but the threat of "direful things" made me shiver.

"Do you understand all this?" he asked.

I said I did.

"Then," he continued, "with heart and soul, I welcome you and open the way for you to obtain the most noble achievement on earth, that of a Klansman. Be faithful and true until death and all will be well with our people and we will reach our destiny."

The recital went on: If I had any doubts about my qualifications or sincerity in becoming a Klansman, he invited me to expose them at this point. I didn't have any doubts about either.

"I congratulate you on your courageous decisions to forsake the world of selfishness, of fraternal and racial alienation, and to join our racial community, the Invisible Empire. The prime purpose of our movement is to advance our great race, to practice Klannishness, to protect our homes and families, and to resurrect our country from the fires of racial degradation and degeneration and to make our people the sole master of their destiny," he read from the official Klan handbook.

"If you have any doubt as to your ability to qualify as a citizen of the Knights of the Ku Klux Klan, you may now have the opportunity to retire from this place with the goodwill of the Klan to attend you, for I warn you, if you falter or fail at this time or in the future as a Klansman, you will be banished from citizenship in the Invisible Empire without fear or favor."

All I could think of was that "direful."

"This is a serious undertaking. I am not here to make sport of you, nor to indulge in silly frivolity. Be assured that he who puts his hands to the robe of the Klan and looks back is not fit for citizenship in our racial community or the fellowship of fellow Klansmen. Do you wish to retire?"

"I will stay," I answered, but I didn't add that I wasn't sure for how long.

We then had a prayer, almost a rhyming prayer that echoed many of the Klan's goals and purposes, a prayer that asked for guidance in achieving them, and a prayer that I've never heard since. I have also made a search through Klan literature for a copy of it, but to no avail.

After the prayer, he droned on about the "honor and dedication" required of a Klansman. Reading from his ritual program, he told me the oath I was about to take would be lifelong and it would be one that I would defend to death if necessary. He was deadly serious. "If you wish to stay, you will take the oath; if you wish to retire, you can leave now."

This time, he didn't say anything about the Klan giving me its blessing or offering its understanding. I knew this would be my last opportunity to leave.

I stayed.

"Keep your left hand raised and repeat after me," he said.

And I repeated the oath:

"I, J. W. Thompson, on this date, May 23, 1980, do before God and man most solemnly swear that I dedicate my life, my fortune, and my sacred honor to the preservation, protection, and advancement of the white race and to that great order, the Knights of the Ku Klux Klan . . ."

"For the next seven sections you will keep your hand raised," he said. "I will read each section and then ask, 'Do you so swear?'"

Then he began reading from the printed oath (which is labeled TOP SECRET and reproduced here):

SECTION I † † † † SECRECY

I swear most honestly — that I will never divulge what transpires tonight. (today)

I swear that I will forever keep secret — the signs — words — papers — and rituals of the KKK

I sacredly vow — that I will forever keep secret — the name of any fellow Klansman.

I am willing to die before revealing such secrets.

"Do you so swear?" he asked.
"I do."

SECTION II † † † † LOYALTY

I will faithfully obey — the regulations and laws or the Knights of the KKK.

I recognise that this order is the only true Klan in existence — and that I will never associate myself — with any other "so-called" Klan organization.

I swear my undying loyalty — to the elected Grand Wizard — David Duke.

"Do you so swear?" he asked.
"I do."

SECTION III † † † † DUTY

I will respond promptly to the needs of the KKK — I will give as much of my time — and money as possible — to further its great aims.

I will fulfill all the duties of a Klansman — for at least five years.

"Do you so swear?" he asked.
"I do."

SECTION IV † † † † PROLIFERATION

I will actively work to expand the ranks — of the KKK.

I will not recommend for membership — any person whose loyalty is doubtful.

"Do you so swear?" he asked.
"I do."

SECTION V † † † † FRATERNITY

Every fellow Klansman will be as a brother to me — his welfare will come before my own.

I will never slander — defraud — deceive — or in any way wrong a fellow Klansman — or a Klansman's family — nor will I permit others — to do the same — if I can so prevent it.

I will go to the aid of any fellow Klansman who requests it — at his call I will answer — I will be truly Klannish — toward all Klansmen — in all things honorable and just.

"Do you so swear?" he asked.
"I do."

SECTION VI † † † † HONOR

I will keep secret — any secret transmitted by any other Klansman.

I will not conspire with other Klansmen to commit an illegal act of violence.

I swear that I will oppose — the enemies of our race — nation — and this order — with my life — my fortune — and my honor — and that I will oppose a serious threat — to the survival and freedom of my people — with whatever means the situation demands — If necessary — I will even sacrifice my life — in defense of fellow Klansmen — and this great order — the Knights of the KKK.

I will never judge any Klan leaders — by any newspaper account — broadcast — rumor — or any other source — other than from the authority — of this order.

I will in fact — not tolerate accusations — in my presence — against any level of Klan leadership — I recognize the duplicity of our enemies.

"Do you so swear?" he asked.
"I do."

SECTION VII † † † † DEDICATION

I believe in the Constitution of the United States — and in the great race that created it.

I will work diligently — to secure the preservation— protection — and advancement of the White Race.

I believe in complete religious freedom — and in the free practice of the Christian faith — in public institutions — but also in the separation — of church and state.

I will diligently fight against — Communism — and Zionism.

I swear my loyalty to this order forever — as the only true Klan — I shall obey its elected Grand Wizard — David Duke — and all other officers — as long as they continue with this order.

I swear I dedicate my life — from this moment forward — to fostering the welfare of the White Race — and furthering the work of America's greatest Movement — The KNIGHTS OF THE KU KLUX KLAN.

"Do you so swear?" he asked.
"I do."

We had been at it for about forty minutes now and were nearing the end. He had me repeat the "dedication" clause:

"I swear I dedicate my life—from this moment forward—to fostering the welfare of the White Race—and furthering the work of America's greatest Movement—THE KNIGHTS OF THE KU KLUX KLAN."

He then held up the small glass of water and read further from his papers: "With this life-giving fluid, more precious than and far more significant than all the sacred oils of the ancients, I set you apart from the men of your daily associations. . . . As a Klansman, may your character be as pure, your life purpose as powerful, and your Klannishness as real as this simple water."

Holding the small glass of water aloft, he continued: "Mortal man cannot assume a more binding oath: character and courage alone will enable you to keep it. Always remember that to keep this oath means to you honor, happiness, and life. But to violate it means disgrace, dishonor, and death. May happiness, honor, and life be yours."

He then asked me to kneel and, with the water glass in hand, he said, "I dedicate you in body [placing a few drops of water on my shoulder], in mind [placing a few drops on my head], in spirit [waving his hand in a circular motion above my head], and in life. . . ."

Then he proclaimed me a Klan Knight.

Without a doubt, that was the strangest moment of my twenty-year career as a journalist.

Black then instructed me in his Klan's secret handshake: the forefinger and middle finger of one's right hand extended up the wrist of the person with whom he shakes hands. Then he told me: "AKIA stands for 'A Klansman I am.'"

Shaking his hand with the secret handshake, I repeated the initials, "AKIA."

Solemnly, he presented me with my Klan citizenship certificate, suitable for framing, and a copy of my "blood oath."

(After my mother read the oath when we published it in *The Tennessean,* her only comment was: "I hope you had your fingers crossed.")

I had come a long way in the Klan, I told myself as I drove away from Black's apartment that night. But, at the same time, I knew I still had a long way to go.

The oath I took with Black and the oath I later took when I joined Wilkinson's Invisible Empire were almost identical. In fact, the ritual leading up to the oath Black administered and the Knights of the Ku Klux Klan handbook I was given later made numerous references to the "Invisible Empire." At first I wasn't sure whose group I was joining. I was confused about the names of the two groups and the top officers. Wilkinson is Imperial Wizard of his group and Duke held the title of Grand Wizard.

The Tennessean team that did the Klan stories while I was undercover did a lot to clear up my confusion. From their profiles of Wilkinson and Duke, I learned more about those men than I could have in Alabama.

Born in Galvez, Louisiana, Bill Wilkinson graduated from high school at sixteen, and joined the Navy. He was shipped to California, where, he says, he became "nauseated" at the sight of "coloreds and whites dating." After he left the Navy in 1968, he and his wife, Barbara Jean, moved back to Louisiana.

When he was interviewed by *The Tennessean* reporters, he told them: "I guess the thing that set me off again was that, back in Denham Springs, my kids were in school, and I didn't think my boys were learning everything they should. The people at the school said it was because the colored kids were slow learners, so they had to hold the white kids back too. I can't tell you how mad that made me. I was furious."

At the same time, a few miles from Wilkinson's home, there was a growing Klan organization headed by David Duke, a Louisiana State University graduate eight years his junior. Duke impressed Wilkinson with his talk of "genetic inferiority" of blacks and the historic threat of the Jewish "hybrid race."

Both young men were ambitious, both smart, both aggressive. Although they got along at first, it was probably inevitable that once their personalities and ambitions rubbed against each other, sparks would fly.

Neither will talk publicly about their eventual split, but privately, under probing, bits and pieces emerge—but only bits and pieces. Wilkinson's friends say the break occurred when he arranged a giant rally at Walker, Louisiana, in 1975 and Duke pocketed some five thousand dollars raised at the gathering. Duke emphatically denies this. He told one of the reporters that only six hundred was raised—the largest amount he ever attracted at a Klan function—and that he put it all in the Klan's coffers.

Duke's backers contend that the split came when Wilkinson tried to "steal away" the Denham Springs branch of the Klan. Duke says that in 1976 his "figurehead" Grand Wizard, Jerry Dutton, now a New Orleans printing craftsman, pilfered his membership lists and Klan handbooks and literature and turned everything over to Wilkinson.

Immediately after a showdown meeting at the Klan headquarters in Denham Springs one day in August 1975, both Duke and Wilkinson rushed to the courthouse and filed separate corporate charters. Wilkinson registered as the "Invisible Empire, Knights of the Ku Klux Klan," and Duke filed under the name "Knights of the Ku Klux Klan, realm of Louisiana."

After the showdown and subsequent split, Wilkinson began laying the groundwork for his own national Klan organization with the help of several Duke defectors, eventually including Dutton, who for a time worked as editor of Wilkinson's Klan newspaper.

It is easy to believe Duke's contention that Wilkinson obtained, and converted to his own use, the handbooks, membership lists, and other Klan literature. After becoming a member of both factions, taking the oath in each, and acquiring the handbook of each, I can attest that the similarities are much more than coincidental.

Duke obviously rewrote his Klan oath, deleting all references to the Invisible Empire, but he did not delete the phrase from his Klan rituals and Klan handbook.

Instead, he added a section to the handbook under the heading OTHER KLANS and in so doing, obviously stroked his own ego, while, at the same time and without mentioning him by name, took several hardy jabs at Wilkinson's character and intellect.

Under the section on OTHER KLANS, Duke wrote:

> The Knights of the Ku Klux Klan under the able leadership of David Ernest Duke is the traditional Klan organization. Its roots go back to the original Klan birthplace of Pulaski, Tennessee, in 1865. It is the only Klan organization that uses the same basic titles, ranks, and ritual of the original Ku Klux Klan. Many so-called Klans use titles and rituals that were formulated in 1915 rather than 1865. They go by various names. There is no other organization that goes by the original and simple name, "Knights of the Ku Klux Klan," with no other prefixes!
>
> Many of these other, so-called Klans are run by ignorant, self-serving men who understand little of true Klan history and still less of the Klan philosophy to which we have dedicated our lives. For instance, some are anti-Catholic. The original Ku Klux Klan was never anti-Catholic. How asinine it is for White Christian people to fight against each other in the face of the world anti-Christian, communist threat!
>
> Some of these so-called Klans are set up by the FBI

front men who work hard to destroy the Klan image by ridiculous and ignorant statements, violent acts, and by channeling potential patriots into ineffective, pitiful little "Klan" groups. All this is documented by sworn testimony before the United States Congress.

The Knights of the Ku Klux Klan is the only true Klan organization in the United States. It is the largest, the most active, and the only Klan organization that can trace its roots directly back to Reconstruction. In addition, it is the only "Klan" that still basically uses the original Klan rituals, insignias, and organizational structure.

A few years ago, in the darkness of the new Federal "Reconstruction," White people seemed to lose heart and the Klan sunk [sic] to its lowest level of activity since Reconstruction. A brilliant young leader, David Ernest Duke breathed the breath of life into our suffering movement. Through sacrifice, hard work, by taking great risks, and through an unequaled dexterity of mind, he brought the Ku Klux Klan moving forward again, and at an even greater pace it moves forward now. It is impossible to talk about a rebirth of the Ku Klux Klan unless one speaks about David Duke.

Duke, a prolific writer whose books range from a manual for black militants, under the pen name of Muhammad X, to an explicit how-to sex manual under another pseudonym, goes on and on in that particular section of his handbook extolling the attributes of "his" Klan and of David Duke. He challenges his members to name a Klan leader "who can speak, write, and lead better than David Duke."

At the time he wrote the new section, he probably did

have the "largest, the most active" Klan following in the nation.

However, I am convinced, after participating in and belonging to both groups, that Wilkinson's group is the larger, more active, and by far, the more militant, Klan group. And he has taken his lead with a plan, a blueprint for action, probably drawn up originally by Duke and acquired through whatever means.

Regardless of what they call their groups, both Wilkinson and Duke have done much to bring a lot of visibility to their respective "invisible" empires.

This visibility is never more evident than when a car approaches an intersection in broad daylight to find both streets lined with robed Klansmen handing out literature and collecting money in plastic buckets: a Klan roadblock. Such roadblocks, while illegal in some cities, including Nashville, is one of the most popular ways for the Klan to raise money in Alabama, where other groups sometimes use the same procedure.

Black called me at my apartment one Thursday night in July to ask me to participate in a roadblock the following Saturday in Center Point, a suburb near where I lived. He instructed me to meet Roger Patmon in a park there to get further instructions.

I called Linda and told her I would be late getting home.

As I approached the park, I spotted Patmon's pickup truck. It was hard to miss, since a large Confederate flag was attached to the bed of the truck and blowing in the breeze. I pulled over alongside his truck. I was somewhat surprised that he remembered me from that first aborted naturalization attempt at the Howard Johnson's. He was alone when I arrived but a couple I had never met arrived shortly. Patmon had a rifle, a pistol, and a shotgun on the front seat of his truck. He told me another group of Klansmen was conducting a roadblock at the other end of the county. I knew ours was about to get under way because all the others started getting into their robes. Although Black had been telling me for months that my robe was "on the way," I still didn't have it. Before we ventured onto the busy highway, Patmon gave me some basic instructions:

"Never reach into a car for a donation; let them hand it out the window. Someone could wait until you leaned in the window and then drive off.

"If niggers, or anybody, comes by and shouts at you or cusses you, just ignore it. But if somebody should try to run over you, or if anybody takes a shot at you—and we have had both to happen—we'll have people on the perimeters that will see to it they won't get away.

"Don't be too aggressive and don't try to force your literature on anybody or throw it in their cars. If they want it, or want to put a donation in your bucket, they'll stop and wait for you.

"And mainly, just keep alert."

We then moved to a restaurant at one corner of the intersection. Suddenly two vans pulled into the same lot and two van loads of sheriff's deputies, all in uniform, got out. I expected soon to be riding in one of those vans myself—on the way to the county jail.

"Oh, shit, I bet they are going to mess us up," Patmon said, when he spotted them.

Two of the deputies walked toward where we were standing at the rear of Patmon's truck. It was already hot that morning, but the presence of the deputies made it seem even hotter.

"How are you fellers, today?" one of the deputies asked as he approached Patmon.

"Fine," he answered, "how about yourself?"

"Aw, we're all right," the deputy said. "Do you all plan to put up a roadblock here today?"

"Yeah," Patmon answered, "we was just ready to get out there."

"Do you all have a permit?"

"No, we didn't have time to go down and get one."

"Well, we ain't got one either," the deputy said, "but we don't have but one roadblock a year, that's when we raise money for the Boys and Girls Ranch. We sure would appreciate it if you fellers would let us have this intersection today. You all could go over to Highway Seventy-nine. That's a pretty good place; it just ain't as good as this one."

"Since it's for the boys and girls, we'll go somewhere else," Patmon said. "I just hope you all have a good day."

"Like I said, we sure do appreciate that," the deputy said. "Good luck to you. If we can ever help you out, just give us a call."

We decided to move to the intersection suggested by the deputy. As I got back into my car to follow Patmon and the others to the new location, I noticed that I wasn't quite so hot anymore.

When we arrived at the intersection, I got a handful of *Crusaders*, was handed a yellow plastic bucket, and then positioned myself on the center line of the side road coming into the intersection.

I was shocked to find as many as half the people passing stopped to give money and accept literature. Most contributions were coins—quarters or half-dollars—but many were dollar bills, and one person tossed in a ten. And the cars and trucks, driven by whites, included Fords, Chevys, and Toyotas—as well as Cadillacs and Lincolns.

The Klan is not gaining members by the thousands, but I saw an alarming number of indications that there is growing street support for the Klan.

On the other hand, blacks are concerned, harassed, and angered by the new presence of the Klan. During my time participating at Klan roadblocks, blacks who drove by let it be known that this type of Klan activity was an affront and an insult. Frequently, they shouted at us. Once a car carrying a group of blacks circled the block three times to pass by and hoot at me, each time roaring by a little closer to my toes. I was scared out of my wits.

On one occasion, a pastry truck, driven by a white man with a black helper on the passenger side, stopped at my post. The white driver was obviously going to drop a donation in my bucket. After dropping two one-dollar bills in the bucket, the driver asked me for some Klan literature.

"I'm glad to help you fellers any way I can," the driver said. "Somebody's got to do something about the niggers. I keep telling my boy, John, here that a nigger will do all right as long as he keeps in his place, works hard, and stays away from our white women. Ain't that right?"

Luckily, the light changed and he drove off before I had to answer him.

During that whole episode I'm sure I was more uncomfortable than John. John just sat stone-faced, staring straight ahead, never changing his expression. I've often envied his self-control just as I've often wondered if the contempt I'm sure he felt at that moment was more for me and my white-robed colleagues or more for the man he had to work with every day.

AT HOME the atmosphere was becoming more strained. Both Linda and I made a conscious effort not to discuss my assignment or even speculate about its possible end.

Since Klan activity had begun to accelerate somewhat, I never knew for sure when I would have a chance to go home. Most Klan activities, aside from den meetings, were held on weekends. And on the weekends that I didn't get home, I spent most of my non-Klan-related energy in the cabinet shop. I thoroughly enjoyed taking a few boards and making something useful or pleasing to look at out of them. I began to notice that we were having a lot more time for puttering around the shop during the week also. It seemed that the cabinet business had suddenly gone to hell. There was hardly a day when I didn't see in the classified section of the *Birmingham News* that another cabinet shop had placed all its tools up for sale.

I didn't fully realize the magnitude of the construction slump until one Friday afternoon when David informed me that he didn't have the money to pay me. He hadn't taken in the meager $120 that I had coming for that week. I understood and appreciated his honesty. To make matters worse, one of David's longtime friends, Chris Smith, left school at the University of Alabama-Birmingham and came to David for a job. David explained everything to Chris, but he said the three of us would hold out as long as we could. Things were better the next week, and we made about $40 each.

I could see that the cabinet shop wouldn't last much longer—just when I was beginning really to enjoy it. David had long ago begun letting me go out and take measurements, bid on jobs, and give estimates on new countertops or repairs. I was a part of this business. Besides, I couldn't let it fold. I needed it much worse than it needed me. The Klan identified me with Village Woodworks. That's where Don Black, Ben Walker, and others called me when they needed me. All good Klansmen had a steady job, and this one was mine. It gave me credibility and showed stability. I had been here for almost a year now.

David, Chris, and I kept thinking and talking of ways to make money, to keep the business going. Several months before, we were building at least two sets of cabinets a week and turning down some of the least attractive jobs. Now, if we got one set of cabinets, it was a good month.

Since we weren't building cabinets, we began building more furniture—just whatever we felt like building and anything we could build from the scrap wood we had left over from cabinet jobs.

We partitioned off a portion of the shop and made a "showroom" up front to display our latest creations. We didn't buy one line of advertising, but somehow people started coming in off the street to browse around and usually buy something from the "showroom."

Then came the break I needed to preserve my cover. We found out that a semiannual furniture show would be held in mid-July in the Merchandise Mart in Atlanta. Chris talked his father into putting up the entry fee for the show. I called my office, and Wayne Whitt arranged for me to get enough expense money to chip in on the wood we'd need to build our show entries and pay my expenses for a week in Atlanta. David would supply tools, shop, and expertise.

When we backed our small rental truck into the loading dock at the Merchandise Mart, in the shadow of the towering Peachtree Plaza Hotel, I felt somewhat intimidated, to say the least. Massive tractor-trailer rigs with the names of well-known, well-advertised furniture companies emblazoned on the sides were *already* unloading and others were awaiting their turn at the docks.

Our booth was on the sixth floor, which was as open as an aircraft hangar and was rampant with activity.

Despite the fact that we were exhibiting along with almost six hundred other furniture manufacturers, to an audience of almost two thousand buyers who had paid to get in, our booth stood out.

We tried our damnedest to arrange seven pieces of furniture in a sixteen-by-twenty-foot booth to make it appear full and to cover as much of the dull-gray concrete floor as we could, but we weren't too successful. The other exhibitors had carpenter crews, plush carpeting, elaborate lighting and drapes. And all had brochures. The best we could do in this area was to explain that our brochures "didn't get back from the printer in time for the show." The others also had huge order books. We slipped out to the nearest Woolworth's and bought an order book. I immediately tore out about the first third and threw it away. If I happened to write an order, I didn't want our first customer to faint when he saw his invoice numbered 001.

David and Chris headed back to Birmingham in the rented truck, leaving me alone with our furniture in Atlanta.

"If you sell all the samples," David said as he left, "you won't need a truck. Otherwise, we'll come back with the pickup. Let us hear from you."

Just like Seigenthaler, I thought. Maybe both of them were expecting too much.

The week wore on. The buyers (you could always tell them by their freshly pressed fashionable suits, white shoes, and, almost always, an obviously snobbish attitude) would saunter into my booth, give our furniture a quick once-over, maybe open a drawer or slam a door before mumbling something under their breath and walking out. I tried on many occasions to tell them about the construction of the furniture—three coats of hand-rubbed clear lacquer . . . None seemed interested.

Each day I would call David to tell him that I hadn't had a nibble, much less a bona fide bite.

Then, on the fourth day, I could see someone examining our furniture from across the floor. It was a man dressed in a sport shirt, open at the collar, and a pair of plain, light green slacks. I went over to talk with him. He asked me about the furniture.

"My partners and I made it. We have a place over in Birmingham."

"I'm really impressed with the quality and the design. Who's your designer?"

"We kind of design it as we go," I answered. "If the board fits, use it—that's our motto."

"Could you make this stuff in unfinished?"

"Sure. In fact, we could make it a lot quicker if we didn't finish it. You see, we put on . . ." By God, I finally got to tell somebody how we did it.

"How many of these could you make in unfinished?" he asked, pointing to our design of an Early American hutch.

"As many as you need," I answered cockily.

"How long would it take for delivery?"

"How soon do you need them?" Still cocky.

"I'm not just fooling around," he said somewhat sternly. "I'm serious about buying some of your line."

"Just tell me what you want and how many. I'll be glad to write it up."

"How big is your operation?"

Maybe he is serious, I thought. "Right now, there's only

three of us, but we're willing to expand to whatever extent necessary to supply you. We were strictly in the cabinet business, but that kind of slowed down so we decided to build furniture. This is our first time outside Birmingham. You can probably tell."

"My name is Jack Crowley. I'm a factory rep and I cover six states in the South. I'll take on your line and you pay me seven percent of the total order. I can tell you right now what I'll be needing. Can you be in production in thirty days?"

"Hell, we can be shipping in thirty days," I said, some of the cockiness returning.

"Okay, I'll need about five hundred of these and two hundred fifty of these, and an unlimited supply of bookcases, probably by the truckload. I can almost guarantee you that I'll move more than four hundred thousand dollars of your product before this time next year, but I'll pace it so you'll have time to gear up for it. Can I realistically expect you to start shipping in the next thirty days?"

"You sure can. I'll call my partners right now and tell them to start gearing up. What do you want first?"

"Let's start with the bookcases. Build about ten of each size and then build about five of the hutches for samples."

"We'll whip those out next week."

"Good," he said. "One of my good customers owns five Unpainted Furniture Stores in Alabama and Tennessee. He and I'll come by your factory about the middle of the week and we'll just write up his first order right there on the spot. He'll keep you busy and keep the cash flow going until you expand enough to get in full production."

"That'll be fine. We'll be looking for you." I couldn't wait to call David.

"If you fellows can gear up fast enough, that four hundred thousand figure might be grossly understated. See you next week."

"Factory"? Four hundred thousand "understated"? "Expansion"? "Production"? "Shipping"? "Factory"? That's

the one that kept pounding in my mind. How in hell were
we going to make a small, one-room shop, centered around a
single table saw, look like a factory? And to a man who
owned a chain of furniture stores and a man whose job took
him to factories and stores in six states?

We'd manage some way. We'd have to now.

My hand was trembling as I dialed. I didn't know whether to be overjoyed or fearful. Had I violated the unpardon-
able caution that I'd heard all my life in the country—
letting my alligator mouth overload my hummingbird ass?

"Yes, operator, I'll pay for the call," David said.

"David," I began with a sense of urgency that he obviously detected.

"Yeah, buddy, what is it?"

"David, we're gonna need a bigger truck."

He was ecstatic. I told him about Crowley and he relayed
each sentence, each phrase, to Chris, who was whooping in
the background.

"They'll be at our factory sometime next week," I said.

"You didn't tell him we had a factory, did you?" David
asked in astonishment.

"No. He told me."

"J.W., I hope you haven't put out more bullshit than we
can shovel."

"Don't worry, partner," I assured him, "from now on the
shop is the 'factory.' It's just a matter of semantics."

"Are you sober?" he asked.

"Sure, but I may not be for long. This damn place closes
down in about two hours and then they're having a cocktail
party for the exhibitors. Hell, they might even have one for
manufacturing executives. If they do, that's the one I'm
going to."

"Don't go anywhere," David said, "until Chris and I get
there. We're coming to help you celebrate."

It was a good night. The apprehensions didn't set in until
the next day.

We hastily gathered the wood and got some bookcases and

a hutch in "production" before Crowley and his customer paid their visit to our "factory." It was clear that we didn't fool them, but they were understanding and willing to give us a chance.

As Crowley had promised, they gave us an initial order for five hutches and twenty bookcases. For the next two weeks, all three of us worked long hours to deliver that first order on time and to make sure it was perfect. Before we had finished unloading the first order, we had another, even bigger than the first. Meanwhile, Crowley was phoning in additional orders, almost daily, from the various states he covered. The furniture factory was booming—and taking in more orders than it could possibly produce.

During this initial flurry of activity, I had somewhat neglected the Klan. I had kept in contact with Black, but I was not spending as much time as before. Fortunately, the Klan was not doing much during this period, mainly because there were no current events or major causes that the Klan could benefit from.

Seigenthaler and I had already been planning my move into Wilkinson's Klan. Luck had so far played a big part in the assignment: I was lucky to get into the Klan in the first place; I was lucky to find a job that allowed me the necessary freedom to participate in Klan activities and lucky to have a boss who was not too inquisitive; I was lucky not to have been discovered from within the Klan; and now the booming furniture business would provide me with another lucky break.

David owned a plot of land in Cullman, Alabama, where he had planned for several years to build a house. I suggested that he find a shop in Cullman for the "factory" expansion. I pointed out that when the business grew, the shop rent and the additional labor required would be much more affordable in Cullman, and it would also be convenient to his land. And I volunteered to move to Cullman to oversee the renting of space and setting up the shop.

Once I was certain about the move, I called Betty Mize,

Wilkinson's state treasurer in Birmingham, whose name I had seen in the paper, and expressed my disgust with the lack of activity in Black's group. I told her I would like to talk to someone in the Invisible Empire about possibly joining up with them. She said she would contact the Empire's Kleagle, or organizer, Roland Torbert, and have him contact me.

I was surprised when my phone rang less than ten minutes later and it was Torbert.

"Mr. Torbert, I wasn't really expecting to hear from you so soon. I called Mrs. Mize because I had read in the paper that she was with you folks and she's the only one I could think of to call. I talked to Don Black earlier tonight and was just sort of disgusted. We haven't done a damn thing in three weeks and don't have any plans to do anything in the near future. When he recruited me, he impressed on me the urgency for white people to get off their ass and do something about the way the whites are being treated in this country. That's why I joined."

"Well," Torbert said, "we are doing something. I signed up twenty people last week in Tarrant City, and we have more joining every day. At least every two weeks, we're having a rally, a march, or a protest. We want the people to know that we are looking out for the white people."

I got myself revved up. "As I told Black when I first met him, the only other thing I ever joined was the Army and it was because I felt I could do something there. I feel like I did do something. But I don't feel that I've really done anything in the Klan. I like Don Black and David Duke, I think they're both smart men, but I'm just a little disappointed that we're not doing more than we are when there's so much that needs to be done."

"I don't think we'll disappoint you in that area," he said. "I'll be glad to sign you up with us. We are always looking for good members willing to work."

This was easy, I thought. "Well, like I said, I didn't really expect to hear from you so soon and I just called Mrs. Mize because I was disgusted. I'm not sure that I would just up and leave Black and Duke because I do believe they are sincere. But I would like to sit down and talk with you about your group because I think, from what I've heard and what I've read, that Mr. Wilkinson is quite a bit more active than either one of them."

As hard as it was not to rush out and meet Torbert that night to sign up with Wilkinson, I deliberately put him off, remembering that Dr. Billig had told me months ago, "Don't be too eager. Let them pull you in rather than you pushing your way in."

"I'm going to be out of town tomorrow and the next day," he said, "but why don't you call me the first of the week and we'll get together and have a cup of coffee and I'll point out what we're doing and what we plan to do? I think when you compare us with them, you'll see right off which group is doing the most."

"I'll call you Monday, about this time," I told him.

"That's fine, Mr. Thompson. I'll be looking forward to hearing from you. It's been a pleasure talking to you. Have a good weekend."

"Let me ask you something else," I said, almost forgetting to lay the groundwork I had gone to so much trouble to plan. "I'm in the furniture business and we're setting up a factory in Cullman. I'll be moving there in a couple of weeks. You all have a Klavern up there, don't you?"

"Oh, yes. That's one of our strongest areas. Terry Tucker is our EC [Exalted Cyclops] up there and Terry's a good man. Yes sir, Cullman is kinda our flagship Klavern." Which, of course, I knew.

"Well, I mentioned to Black that I was moving and he said we only had about two members up there but said we would concentrate on getting a good, active den going when I got up there," I lied.

"I'll be surprised if he has anyone in Cullman," Torbert said. "I'll tell you, Terry is so active up there that if anyone wants to join the Klan he's going to join ours, and I think you will see what I'm talking about when you get up there."

On Monday I tried several times to reach Torbert, each time getting an explanation that he wasn't home, he was out of town, or "he probably won't be home for several days."

I also tried calling Don Black, but got either a busy or no answer.

The next morning I learned the possible reason why both of them had been unavailable: *The Tennessean*, in a front-page copyrighted story by Susan Thomas and Bob Dunnavant, detailed a complex scam that pitted con man against con man—a scam that effectively destroyed David Duke as a Klan leader and catapulted Wilkinson to a pinnacle of popularity among his followers.

It seemed that Wilkinson, through a long series of telephone conversations, which he had carefully tape-recorded, had led Duke to believe that he would pay him the hefty sum of thirty-five thousand dollars for his membership list and the names of subscribers to the *Crusader*. Duke, obviously lured by the prospect of the windfall, agreed to meet Wilkinson at an abandoned farmhouse off Highway 31 in the middle of a pasture, near Hanceville, Alabama, to consummate the deal.

Duke arrived shortly after midnight Sunday night, accompanied by Don Black and carrying a plastic garbage bag containing, he claimed, the names and addresses of three thousand members of the Knights of the Ku Klux Klan.

They were amiably greeted by Wilkinson and some of his most trusted top aides, Torbert included. After some small talk, they got down to business. Duke and Black must have been unaware that they were playing right into Wilkinson's hand—playing indeed to an audience he had handpicked and stationed in a darkened back room of the farmhouse, an audience of news people who would videotape and record the entire transaction. The prearranged cue for the newsmen to make their presence known was the moment it was Wilkinson's turn to sign the contract and turn over the money.

Duke was ashen as he was surrounded by rolling cameras and running tape recorders. Wilkinson, starring in his elaborately planned production, announced: "You've gotten about as much of anybody's money as you will get."

"Well, obviously you're a dishonorable liar all the way through," Duke countered.

"I did lie to you when I told you I was going to buy your Klan because I had no intention of doing that, but I sure did want everybody to know where you stood and how low you really are," Wilkinson replied. "I never thought I'd see the day I'd be buying your Ku Klux Klan."

"You're not. My official endorsement is what you were buying. That's how it works," Duke said.

If such a deal had been made, it would have joined the nation's two largest Klan groups—Duke's Knights of the Ku Klux Klan and Wilkinson's Invisible Empire. But Wilkinson had carefully orchestrated the event and the news coverage for the maximum benefit of his own efforts to recruit as many members as he could from the Duke organization.

"I'm sorry that we had to do this," he said. "I'm really surprised that this ever could take place because I can't believe you would go through with it—taking money to sell your endorsement and quit the Klan."

"He set me up," Duke said in a telephone interview from his home in New Orleans the following day. "I was never going to sell my Klan. I was going to sell my endorsement. Wilkinson did this just to discredit me. It's disgusting, just like his low dealing. He's low, really low."

Wilkinson boasted that the late-night meeting was a "success" and that he staged it only to "tell the world about David Duke." He said he had arranged the meeting after Duke contacted him on several occasions since January about the possibility of buying the rival Klan membership lists. "At first I thought we were going to talk about Klan unity, but he made overtures for selling his organization to me that made me sick to my stomach," Wilkinson said.

"A lie," Duke said in a later interview. "I have been considering resigning from the Klan, and I was looking for ways to stop the infighting within the Klan by talking to Wilkinson," Duke said. "That's the only reason I ever talked with him. Obviously, I made a mistake."

This final clash between the two Klan wizards should not be too surprising—it may even have been inevitable—considering their bitter split in 1975. Since then, Wilkinson, the ex-sailor, who preaches open armed militancy against blacks and Jews, has called Duke such names as "egghead" and "Judas." And he has ridiculed Duke's Klan tactics, saying, "You don't fight wars with words and books. You fight them with bullets and bombs." Duke, who denounces violence, had described Wilkinson as a "traitor" who was no threat to his organization.

The story of the aborted "unity attempt" or "sellout"—depending on which Klan spokesman was describing it—dominated the national news for the next several days.

Two days after the initial story broke, Duke announced he would resign from the Klan, as he had planned even before his ill-fated meeting with Wilkinson, and would name a temporary successor to take the helm of his battered and demoralized Klan organization. It was widely speculated that Black would be his choice. "It's an impossible situation," Duke said. "I'm resigning because I don't think the Klan can succeed at this point because of its violent image and because of people like Bill Wilkinson. He's low and dishonorable. People see Wilkinson and believe all Klansmen are like that—bad and violent. All the good in the world I have done and could do doesn't make any difference because most people don't differentiate between Klans. They think we're all like that, and that's disgusting."

Then Wilkinson responded to Duke's resignation announcement: "It was the only thing he could do in light of Sunday night. His problem is that he can't deny what happened. He was going to sell his people out. They know what kind of person he really is now, so he didn't have any choice but to get out."

Meanwhile, Black remained elusive and unavailable for comment for the next several days. I tried several times to reach him at home in the evenings and each time the phone went unanswered. I tried on Thursday to reach him at the Ear, Nose, and Throat Clinic and the receptionist said, "He no longer works here."

That same night I got a surprise call from Roger Patmon, who surfaced from time to time at Klan functions but not as often as some of the others.

"J.W.," he began, "we're having an emergency meeting tomorrow night over at my brother's house at Robbins Cross Roads. You've met my brother Arlen, haven't you?"

"No, I don't believe I have," I answered. "What's going on anyway?"

"We can't talk about anything on the phone," he said. "I'm going to let Ben tell you how to get there, and it's terribly important that we get everybody we can to come to the meeting. Ben and I are trying to call everyone we can, but if you see anybody or talk to anybody, tell them how important it is for them to be there. Don has called an emergency meeting."

Walker then got on the phone and gave me detailed instructions on how to reach Robbins Cross Roads and told me the actual meeting place would be on Bippy Brickyard Road, but that he would meet me at a small store at Robbins Cross Roads and "you can follow me down to Arlen's. Otherwise, you wouldn't ever find it."

He was certainly right about that too. Walker was waiting at the market when I arrived after driving solid for more than forty-five minutes from my apartment on Birmingham's east side. He motioned for me to follow him, and it seemed like another ten miles down a narrow, winding, dark road before we came to a clearing and Arlen's house.

More than twenty people—men, women, and children—

many of whom I had never seen before, were milling about the yard. Patmon and Walker had done their telephone roundup well.

We were there for about twenty minutes before Black arrived. I mingled with the crowd, introducing myself to those I didn't know and making small talk with those I did. Not once, however, did I hear a mention of the sellout attempt, of Duke, or of Wilkinson. It seemed everyone wanted to talk about something else—the weather, Arlen's garden, his goats, his tractor, anything but the Klan and the turmoil it was going through.

When Black arrived he talked with several people, but he appeared nervous and fidgety, which was unlike the calm, authoritative air he usually displayed in the company of Klan members. Finally, he suggested to Patmon that the meeting be called to order. When Patmon announced that it was time to start, almost instant silence prevailed and everyone—there were nearly fifty people by now—gathered in a large circle in the backyard.

Black stepped to the center of the circle, still appearing uneasy. (I could certainly empathize with him, but I hoped my appearance and feelings weren't as obvious as his.) "I guess you all have heard about what's been going on and what's been all over the news this week," Black began, shuffling his feet and looking down at the ground. "Well, it's nothing like you've heard. What you've been hearing is just another low-down media stunt by Bill Wilkinson. It's just another low-down stunt that shows he's more interested in Bill Wilkinson than he is about what's happening to this country.

"I've been in contact with David every day this week. I was so disgusted at first that I thought seriously about leaving the Klan also. But after talking with David and after giving it some deep thought, I decided that we had too many good, dedicated people in our organization to abandon them. So I've decided to remain with the Klan."

At this, Patmon started clapping, and others joined in.

"To give you some insight on what really happened last weekend, I'll tell you what took place and how it came about. Wilkinson contacted David several months ago and proposed that our groups get together in the interest of Klan unity. David had been giving some serious thought for a long time about starting an organization to be known as the National Association for the Advancement of White People, so the discussion progressed between him and Wilkinson.

"Wilkinson offered David some money to get the organization going and agreed to write a letter to all Klansmen in both groups pointing out that the move was the biggest step toward Klan unity in the last fifty years and, at the same time, acknowledging that David has been an excellent leader sincerely interested in advancing the cause of white rights.

"In return, David was to resign from the leadership of the Knights of the Ku Klux Klan and devote his full attention to the formation and operation of the NAAWP. It was that simple. David certainly didn't intend to sell out his membership as Wilkinson and the media have said.

"It was probably the greatest opportunity we've ever had to become a powerful, viable force in this country—a group strong enough to be a political force, to be recognized by politicians. But Wilkinson, through his own selfish stupidity, destroyed that opportunity and saw to it that true Klan unity will probably never be achieved because nobody will ever trust him again. I don't see how his own members can have any trust for anybody so low down that he would sacrifice our whole movement and everything we've been working toward for so long, purely for his own little personal ego trip. I can't tell you how much contempt I have for that man."

I wondered whether this comment was going to elicit more applause or some other show of support. But the crowd just remained silent.

"Anyway, as I told you, I had been thinking about leaving the Klan, but after thinking it over I've decided to stay—that is, if you people want me to stay."

Now they cheered him a bit and did some clapping.

"Here's what David suggested: Before his resignation becomes effective he will appoint me, temporarily, as Grand Wizard. I will serve in that position until we can hold an election that will be open for nominations of anyone else you might want in that position. I believe that we can get the nominations out and all the ballots back in approximately thirty days. Also, since David is leaving the Klan, I think we ought to move our National Headquarters to north Alabama, probably Tuscumbia, where we have the largest concentration of membership. We will, however, open a permanent public relations office in Birmingham.

"So I guess what I'm asking you folks tonight is whether that would be agreeable with you. If so, then we will petition the rest of the membership on the same things I've pointed out here tonight."

The support was overwhelming for Black's proposal, with one member after another praising Black, cursing Wilkinson, and even some offering mild criticism of Duke's recent leadership.

Black's mood of uneasiness and uncertainty was quickly replaced by the fiery zeal of a circus barker as he continued to outline plans for a total reorganization of the Knights. The spring returned to his step and the volume of his voice increased as he gestured with his hands and, occasionally, a clenched fist.

"We're the only real Klan," he shouted, "and we've always been the only real Klan. We will not be destroyed, or even slightly deterred, by some low-down, selfish creep. This is a new beginning and we will move forward with the ideals set forth by David Duke, the greatest Klan leader this country has ever known."

Vigorous applause and shouts of support greeted him. Then Black asked for questions.

The first one came from Patmon, who was obviously pol-
iticking for Black's old job as Grand Dragon for Alabama.
"What about Grand Dragon?" Patmon asked. "Who's going
to take your place?"

"We'll put that up for nominations also," Black said, "and
let the membership throughout the state vote on that too."

After several other questions, I asked one myself: "Don,
you know how I admire David Duke and I think most of us
here do. Would there by any objection to us participating in
both the Klan and the NAAWP?"

"There would certainly be no objection," Black answered, "but we have a big job ahead of us that is going to
take all the time, energy, and money we can afford right
now. David is aware of how difficult it is to start a new
national organization and he's prepared to work hard at it
and I'm sure he wouldn't want any of us to give anything
less than everything we have to offer to the Klan. After all,
we all know the Klan is David's first love. I think for the
time being we all should devote all our efforts toward building the Klan into even a greater organization. Then, maybe
at some later date, we can all join forces and really get something accomplished."

I took this detailed explanation to mean simply that Black
didn't want us dividing our loyalties between the two
groups—and to the Klan, I found, loyalty is interpreted in
terms of money. He didn't want anyone there sending any
money to Duke; if they had any extra cash they should put it
in his floundering Klan organization.

Before the meeting broke up, Black reminded the group
that a rally was scheduled the following night in Collinwood, Tennessee, and urged all who could to attend. "If
we've ever needed to make a really impressive showing, we
need to now. Every one of you who possibly can, come on up
to Collinwood tomorrow night, and bring everyone you can
with you. In light of what's happened in the last few days,
the news media is going to be covering everything the Klan
does, and we need to show the public as well as other Klan

members that we're not even down, much less out."

When the formal meeting was over, hardly anybody was in any hurry to leave. Most of them stayed around to talk about the future or to tell Black personally how satisfied they were that he decided to remain as their leader.

As a small group of us stood around Black, I had another question. "Don, how are all of these changes going to affect the robe you ordered for me from National Headquarters?" I asked.

"Well, I don't think we're going to be getting much from National Headquarters until we get a new headquarters established in Tuscumbia. Several members have ordered robes, and I guess we'll have to get a supplier locally."

"You haven't got your robe yet, J.W.?" Ben Walker asked. "We'll solve that right now. Randall here has got an extra one that he's outgrown. It should just fit you; if you want it."

"Hell, yes," I said, "then I'll have it for the rally tomorrow night," hating to admit that a robe that once fit Randall Cooper, who weighed near three hundred pounds, would "just fit" me.

Cooper agreed to sell me the robe for twenty dollars. However, it was not complete—he had lost the hood. Walker assured me that he could have a hood made for me within the next week. The robe was closer to a tent than a sheet, but, unfortunately, it did "just fit."

Right after that meeting, I headed home to Nashville. If the rally the following night was going to be in Tennessee, there was no reason not to go home. On the way, I stopped and called Seigenthaler to tell him about the rally, since this was the first I had heard about it and Jimmy Ellis needed as much notice as possible.

I was somewhat apprehensive about attending a rally so close to home, and I thought of a thousand possible ways I might be discovered as I drove down the Natchez Trace Parkway late the next afternoon.

* * *

Several hundred vehicles moved at snail's pace through the small town's narrow streets, several hundred people had already gathered on the vacant field where the rally would be held, and at least that many more were searching for parking spaces or walking toward the field. With all these people, all this interest, there was no way that I wouldn't be recognized.

My first inclination was to turn around and go back to Nashville. But I had a freshly laundered white robe neatly folded on the front seat—the robe that for more than one hundred years had been one of the nation's foremost symbols of hatred and intimidation. Without consciously admitting it, I wanted to see if clothing myself in this garb of racism would alter my personality as much as I had seen it do to other men and women I had met in the Klan. I had to know what it felt like to openly, notoriously, and publicly offend the sensitivities of other people. And I am certain, still, that I did just that to some of those people who were standing in the shadows of the small service station across the street from the rally site viewing the spectacle from afar.

However, I didn't let either urge—the one to turn around and go home or the one to don the robe—interfere with my carefully conditioned sense of caution. In recent months, caution had become a way of life. So I parked the car and, without the robe, went through the crowd to see if I recognized anyone who might expose my true identity. Other than Klan members, the only person I recognized was Jimmy Ellis, and, as usual, we didn't even subtly acknowledge each other's presence.

After the rally speakers started their fiery racist harangues, I returned to the car to dress suitably for the occasion. I stood beside the car pulling on the robe, snapping each snap down the front, tying the sash on the left—it was always tied on the left—then checking the various adjustments in the reflection of the window glass. Yes, I knew the feelings of the people standing silently near the service station because I too had experienced them. Now, however, I was experiencing another feeling—one of pure childish silliness. How in the world, I thought, could anyone feel comfortable, important, or purposeful in anything that looked so damned ridiculous?

One of the first people I saw as I walked back toward the rally was Randall Cooper, whose robe I had bought the night before.

"Hey, the robe fits good, don't it?" he asked.

"Yeah, it worked out pretty good," I answered, an embarrassing admission in the face of the mass of humanity doing the questioning.

"You got a gun?" he asked.

"Hell, no, I don't have a gun," I answered. "Why? Do you think I'll need one?"

"Oh, no, I just wondered. A lot of the others have guns and I was just wondering."

Cooper never failed to ask, "Have you got a gun?"

I had been warned repeatedly by Seigenthaler, the newspaper's attorneys, and by my own logical reasoning never to carry a gun or go armed. Only once during my affiliation with the Klan did I violate that admonition. It was about two weeks later, at a rally in Athens, Alabama, Don Black's hometown, after a downpour. The rally was late getting under way, with the organizers obviously waiting for a larger crowd to gather. I was walking around the muddy field dressed in my robe. I didn't notice the police car as it drove off the road onto the field, but Dennis Thomas, a captain on the security force, did. He rushed up and shoved a large revolver right at me.

"Here, hide this," he commanded. "John Law is here. I'll have to see what they want."

Suddenly I found myself standing there, holding a huge pistol, then hurriedly concealing it under my robe. As Thomas talked with the police officers, I tried my best to act nonchalant and confident, but, believe me, it was purely an act. Fortunately, the police car didn't stay long.

I felt silly every time I put the robe on, but never sillier than this first night in Collinwood, as I walked back through the crowd toward the flatbed truck that was the speakers' platform.

As Black, dressed in a dark business suit and tie—he wore his robe only for naturalization ceremonies and cross lightings, never when he spoke at rallies or during protest marches—spewed forth his vehement racist rhetoric, he was flanked on either side by grim-faced, robed Klansmen whose eyes kept scanning the crowd with the intensity of Secret Service men around a President. Roger Patmon, arms folded, stood on Black's left and Stanley McCullom, in a similar stance, was on his right. Several others, with their backs to the truck, surrounded the platform on the ground, departing from their statuelike appearance only to applaud vigorously the highlights of Black's speech.

As Black concluded his talk, he invited all those present to stay around for the cross-lighting ceremony. I knew I couldn't participate in the ceremony because I didn't have a hood. But it had been a good rally from my perspective: Ellis had taken several pictures of me dressed in the robe with other Klan members who were also hoodless during the rally. The complete uniform was necessary only for the ceremony. Yet Black, who always donned his robe for the cross lighting, never wore a hood for the ritual.

I walked toward the huge burlap-wrapped, diesel-fuel-soaked cross towering in a remote area of the field behind the speakers' platform. I couldn't help thinking how lucky I had been, yet again, so close to home among several hundred people without being recognized as Jerry Thompson, reporter. But before I had finished thinking about how lucky I was, the streak continued.

One of the men I had met at the emergency meeting the night before—I never did find out his name—slapped me on

the back and said, "Boy, I'm glad you were able to make it
up here tonight. This is one of the best rallies we've had all
summer. Just look at all these people. Come on, let's get a
torch."

"I'm going to have to watch from the crowd. I don't have
my hood with me," I explained.

"I'll fix that. You just wait right here."

In what seemed like no time at all, the fellow returned,
saying, "My wife's got a bad leg and she wasn't going to
participate in the cross lighting anyway. Here, you can wear
her hood. Like Don said last night, we need to make a real
good showing."

I put the hood on and the fellow made a slight adjustment
to it to make sure the crease was perfectly centered. At the
same time, it dawned on me that I had never participated in
a cross lighting before and therefore was not familiar with
the proper ritual. I would have to pay especially close attention to avoid being the only one out of step. I naturally
reached for my fuel-soaked torch with my right hand, but
before anyone else noticed, I transferred it to the proper
hand.

Stanley McCullom lit Black's torch with a cigarette light-
er. Then Black used his burning torch to light Stanley's.
Next, while Black stood at the base of the cross with his
torch burning brightly, Stanley walked to the circle of robed
Klan members and lit the torch of a member and then the
entire circle was lighted from torch to torch, in a counter-
clockwise direction.

Once everyone's torch was blazing, Black began the
ritual with the words I had heard several times before, but
never with the flaming torch high above my head. ". . . Be-
hold the fiery cross still brilliant: all the troubles throughout
history have failed to quench its hallowed flame . . ." And
on it went.

After we all marched around the huge cross and "saluted"
it with flaming torches raised, Black placed the flame of his
torch at the base of the huge cross. The small trickle of

flame grew in intensity as it scampered to the top like a frightened squirrel. Then Black stepped back and the rest of us deposited our torches at the base of the cross. Within seconds, the entire cross was aflame. We had resumed our places back in the circle when I noticed Jimmy Ellis inside it with Black and McCullom, firing away with two cameras. I wondered how long he had been there, but I didn't find out for several months. Ellis had moved in close as we moved toward the base of the cross, and when we took our places back in the circle he was inside it. Normally, no one other than those high-ranking Klan officers were ever inside the sacred circle, but no one asked Ellis to leave so he took advantage of the situation and snapped away. The color picture he took that night, showing me holding a burning torch above my head and other Klansmen in the background also with torches raised, was the front-page picture that accompanied the first story of my Klan series, and is now on the jacket of this book. There I was in all my splendor, a borrowed hood, and a tent-sized robe that "just fit."

I looked solemn. I felt silly.

BACK IN BIRMINGHAM on Monday, I resumed my efforts to reach Torbert. I felt this was the perfect time to express further my disgust with the Knights of the Ku Klux Klan and even push a little, if I had to, to become a member of the Invisible Empire. I felt the time was right because the Duke-Wilkinson aborted sellout deal was still very much in the news, and I felt Torbert would never question my sincerity about what I would describe as a growing disappointment with David Duke. I would try to make him feel I was personally hurt by Duke's actions. It was late Tuesday afternoon before I made contact.

Although I was lying through my teeth and, up to this point, had been playing hard to get, I wanted Torbert to think I was so disgusted that I was ready to make the move to Wilkinson's Klan at the first opportunity. I hoped he would feel a certain sense of urgency to get me signed up before I could change my mind. If he did, I thought, he might be a little lax in his background investigation. I knew from my past dealings with Black's Klan that both groups were eager to raid members from the rival group. I could only hope that Torbert was as competitive as Black when it came to luring a member away. So I tried hard to persuade him I was ready to move.

"Mr. Torbert," I began, "I tried all last week to get in touch with you. I've never felt so betrayed in my life. As much as I admired the man, I've had it with David Duke."

"Well, Mr. Thompson, it was because of all that mess that I was so out of touch last week. I went down to Louisiana with the Imperial Wizard for a few days. We were pretty busy."

"When I couldn't reach you, I went to an emergency meeting last Friday night that Black called to explain everything," I told him, without adding that I attended the Collinwood rally the next night. "According to Black, the news media got their stories all screwed up. He said Duke never intended to sell his membership but would have agreed to attempt to merge our group with Mr. Wilkinson's. Black said the money, the thirty-five thousand dollars, we kept hearing mentioned was not solicited by Duke, but simply offered by Mr. Wilkinson to help him get the National Association for the Advancement of White People started. According to Don, he was just as surprised as anyone else when the incident was reported as a sellout attempt. I just can't believe Black would have a part in anything like that."

"Mr. Thompson, I'm not going to spread rumors or talk about another Klansman, no matter whose group they are with. You and me both took an oath and said we wouldn't do that. But Bill knew David was only interested in the money and that's why he wanted some witnesses outside the Klan to see what went on. I'll tell you, there were several people that didn't agree with him on this, but he convinced us. Those fellers, Duke and Black, came in just as friendly as could be, carrying that garbage can full of names of their members. That alone would have violated the security of the Invisible Empire because we never have all of our members' names in one place.

"They continued to be friendly," Torbert went on, "right up to the point the news people came out. Now the news did screw up one thing: They said that the contract was left unsigned, and that's not right. Duke and Black signed the contract agreeing to everything, then they left in such a damn hurry they didn't even take it with them. Bill still has the contract with their names on it. After they signed it and the newsmen came out of the back room with their lights on and their cameras running, you should have seen their faces. One of them asked Duke what was going on and all he said was 'Klan Unity.' That man was so white, you could have cut his throat and he wouldn't have bled a drop."

"Mr. Torbert, I read the papers and watched television and got one story, then I listened to Black's explanation and got another one, now I've heard even another version from you. I'll tell you this, and I'll tell Mr. Wilkinson too, for that matter, I think whatever happened was a dirty trick, but I'm not sure which side played dirtier. I figure that if the deal was to come down like Duke and Black said it was planned, we would have had a joint meeting between you folks and our group and it would have all been done aboveboard. Just because Duke and Black agreed to meet at midnight at a lonely farmhouse out in the middle of a field makes me immediately suspicious of them."

"Well, I'm telling you just like it happened," Torbert said, "and I was right there. I agree that it was a little dirty, but that's the only way Bill could do what he wanted to do. I told Bill that's what I thought as we drove back that night, and I also told him that I understood why it had to be done that way. But I also told him that if anyone ever put me in that kind of position and embarrassed me in front of all those newsmen, I would kill them, no matter who it was."

I couldn't help but think further down the road, of the stories I planned to write. Would they upset Torbert, or any other Klan member, to the point of wanting to kill someone—namely me? I couldn't think of that right now, however. I just said, "Well, if I could have found you last week right after I heard about the whole thing, I would have rushed right out to wherever you were to sign up with you folks. But after thinking about it a few days, I just decided I would get out of the Klan altogether. But I changed my mind again after hearing Black try to cover up for Duke. I don't know how sneaky they actually were, but I do know they are not telling their members the truth about the whole thing. And, after giving it some more thought, I figured that anyone who could put Duke in such a position had to be a smart man. So, if you folks are still looking for good members, I'm still ready to sign up with you."

"You bet we are, Mr. Thompson. I'd like to meet you somewhere tonight, but I've got some people I've got to see out in Tarrant City then I've got to be out of town until the weekend. I got so far behind last week fooling with all this mess that it will take me several weeks to catch up."

"Well, as I told you the last time I talked with you, we're building a factory up in Cullman and I'll be moving up there tomorrow or the next day. But I'll be glad to drive back down and meet with you any time you say," I said, hoping he wasn't trying to give me a runaround or put me off.

"If you're gonna be in Cullman," he said "that won't be necessary. Why don't I just call Terry Tucker and tell him you will be contacting him when you get up there so he'll be expecting you?"

"That will be fine. I'll call him tomorrow as soon as I get moved in."

"Okay, he'll be waiting to hear from you. I get up to Cullman quite a bit, and I'll be looking forward to seeing you the next time I'm up there."

"All right, sir, I'll be there."

I didn't bother to tell him that I didn't even have a place to move into in Cullman. But by this time tomorrow night I would have.

I told David that I was moving to Cullman the following

day and would appreciate his telling any callers that I had gone up there to set up the other factory and would then be "on the road" selling furniture.

"I'll be in and out of the shop," I told him, "but I won't be able to be there on a regular basis. Maybe someday all this shit will make sense, but right now, I'd be very grateful if you would tell Chris, your father, your wife, and anyone else the same thing."

"That won't be any problem," he assured me. "You know, Chris and I were talking the other day about you. If somebody came up to us and asked us what we knew about J. W. Thompson, we couldn't really tell them a damn thing. All I know is that you've been in the Army, you came down here from somewhere in Virginia, you make a lot of long-distance phone calls and get a lot of calls, you've got a girl-friend in Chattanooga and a brother named Ronnie and I have no idea where he lives, and that's it. I told Chris that if you got your arm cut off in the table saw, I wouldn't know whom to call or how to reach them."

"David, I realize all those things and all I can tell you is that it's no accident that you don't know more about me. But right now I can't tell you any more. I can tell you that I'm not a criminal on the lam and that I'll never do anything to hurt you or Village Woodworks. I can promise that some-day we'll sit down with a jug of Jack Daniel's and I'll tell you more than you ever wanted to know about J. W. Thompson."

"Well, as I said, I'll do anything you want me to. There's no problem with that. But if you get in trouble—here or in Cullman or anywhere—just call me and I'll come to you and do anything you want me to. I haven't shot a gun in several years, but I used to be pretty good at it."

I was truly touched. "I sure hope like hell that I'll never get into a spot where I would need a good shot, but, believe me, I sure appreciate the offer."

I was up early the next morning assembling my belongings in cardboard boxes. I knew I was moving today, I just didn't know exactly where. Once the packing was done and the boxes were placed in the back of the pickup truck I had just traded my VW for in Nashville, I headed for Cullman.

I stopped at Jack's Truck Stop, at the first Cullman exit heading north from Birmingham. I got a copy of the local paper from the rack out front and went inside to order lunch. By the time I had finished eating, I had marked three possible apartments in the classifieds. I called my first choice from a phone booth outside the restaurant and told the woman I would be right over.

I pulled up at a modern, rambling brick house on the corner of South Second and Hickory streets. Mrs. G. Bice—I never did find out what the "G" stood for—met me at the door. She was much more inquisitive and had more rules than Mrs. Armstrong, my Birmingham landlady.

As she showed me through the neat apartment, converted from half of a two-car garage, she said, "Now, Mr. Thompson, you live alone. That's fine. This is a nice quiet neighborhood and I don't know anything about you, but I want you to know what I expect. I don't want any wild drinking parties, any wild women. Although I personally don't drink, I don't have anything against someone else taking a drink as long as they do it responsibly and don't let it get out of hand. We don't have much of that here in Cullman because the whole county is still dry."

I confidenly assured her that I would have no trouble complying with her rules because, I explained, I would be on the road a lot selling furniture. But just the thought of doing what she told me not to was appealing. I gave her a deposit on the apartment, left some of my boxes, and told her I wouldn't actually be moving in until early the following week. I stopped to call the phone company and ordered my phone service, then I headed back to Birmingham.

It was getting darker, with threatening clouds and gusty winds coming from the west, as I drove back south. I thought of all the crazy, stupid things I had done in the past year, including my taking this assignment in the first place,

but I couldn't think of any single day that I had screwed up
as much as this one—I had just rented an apartment that
was located a minimum of forty-one miles from the nearest
beer store.

Later that night, I was lying on my bed in Birmingham,
watching television, when Mrs. Armstrong called out, "Mr.
Thompson, Mr. Thompson, could you come down here for a
minute?"

"Sure!" I shouted as I started for the door, thinking something had happened to her.

She was waiting at the foot of the steps that led up to my
apartment when I opened the door. "Mr. Thompson, are
you watching television?"

"As a matter of fact, I was," I answered, somewhat puzzled. "Why?"

"Did you see on the TV that they had spotted a tornado
coming right at us? It's over Center Point right now."

"No, I didn't. I must be watching a different channel."

"Well, we've got no time to waste," she said urgently.
"You come on down to the basement and we'll stay down
there until it blows over."

There was no tactful way I could refuse, so I told her I
would be right down. I was glad later, because in the many
months I had lived there I had really never gotten to know
the woman I paid my rent to each month. I had already
given her notice that I was leaving, but hadn't told her
exactly when, since I had found out only a few hours earlier.

She was rocking back and forth nervously in an old rocking chair as I descended the dark stairs to the basement.

"Oh, Mr. Thompson, I'm glad you're down here," she
said in a voice that was higher pitched than usual. "I've
been in this world for eighty years and I've never lived
through a tornado and I sure don't want to tonight."

"Well, I haven't either," I responded, "but if we have one
tonight, I sure as hell want to live through it."

"Oh, you know what I mean," she said, smiling and apparently more comfortable than if she had been sitting down there alone.

After some more small talk about the weather, she said, "I sure do hate to see you move out. You've been one of the best renters I've ever had. You don't know how much trouble it is to rent to good people."

"I've certainly enjoyed living here," I told her, "but I'm going to be traveling so much and we've got to get a new factory set up in Cullman, I just don't have any other choice."

"I understand," she said. "I just hate to see you go. I hope you didn't mind me sending my nigger up to clean up for you a couple of times. I like to give her a full day's work when she comes and when she finished with me early, I would send her up to clean and dust a little for you."

"No, I certainly didn't mind. I just hope she didn't."

I couldn't help but think back to that first time I came home and found everything straightened up and dusted. I was terrified and didn't make a sound until I had checked out the whole apartment, under the bed, the closets, the lamps, the telephone, and everything else I could think of, looking for an electronic bug. My paranoia subsided somewhat when I went down and asked Mrs. Armstrong if someone had been in my apartment. But a hint of it returned on all future occasions when I came home to find my apartment cleaned. I had purposely left a lot of Klan literature lying around the apartment just in case a visitor came calling when I was at home or even when I was not. I also had my certificate of Klan membership framed and proudly hanging on the wall right next to my bogus Army discharge. I couldn't help but wonder how her "nigger" felt each time she saw such a flagrant display of racism. I'll bet she wanted to pee in my orange juice.

"The way things are now," she continued, "you've got to rent to just anybody that comes along or they will sue you. I've been awful lucky. But I was fooled one time. It was about four years ago and the apartment was for rent. I had an ad in the paper. This fellow called up, and I could usually tell by their voice if they were niggers. But this man didn't sound like a nigger. He fooled me. If I had thought it was a nigger, I'd just tell them that the apartment had already been rented. It was late in the afternoon when the man called and I told him he could come on over and look at the apartment if he wanted to. I saw as soon as he got out of the car that he was a nice-looking nigger man, but I didn't know what to do. I met him at the door and the only thing I could say, and I said it over and over, was 'You're not going to like my apartment, you're not going to like my apartment.' That man just smiled and looked at me right in the eye and said, 'Mrs. Armstrong, you're probably right.' Then he walked back to his car and drove off. I was shaking all over. I worried for weeks that some lawyer would call me up with a lawsuit, but they never did. He was probably a nice man, but niggers just don't live around here."

I got a little more insight into the kinds of feelings that can stoke the fires of a Klan. And the tornado never happened.

I called Tucker in Cullman the following day and told him that I had been referred by Torbert. He was expecting my call, he said, and he would put my name before the next meeting. "We'll vote on it a week from tomorrow night," he said, "and I'll get back with you, J.W."

"Well, I'm going to be living on South Second Street in Cullman, but they won't have my phone in until the first of next week. I'll call you as soon as I get it and give you my number."

"You say you live on South Second."

"Yea, right on the corner of Second and Hickory."

"Well, I'll be dad blamed," Tucker said. "I don't live but about a block from there. It'll be good to have you as a neighbor as well as a member, J.W. I'll be back in touch."

I knew that Klan activity in Birmingham would be slow until after I was accepted into the Invisible Empire, because

Black didn't have anything planned. I would let Tucker and
Torbert and anyone else in the Invisible Empire think that I
had completely severed my association with the Knights, but
at the same time, I also planned to keep participating with
them if I could do so without being discovered by someone in
either group. I thought the worst that could happen would
be that I would be kicked out of both, but I planned, if I
were found out, to make a big, noisy split with the Knights,
telling them how disappointed I was that Duke tried to sell
me out and I didn't even know about it. Fortunately, it never came to that.

I first heard from Ben Walker of Black's plans to picket
and heckle President Carter. "We're going to march against
the President," he told me on the phone a few days before
Carter's scheduled visit, which was to kick off his reelection
campaign. "Get yourself ready. Don is already up in north
Alabama demanding a parade permit from the Tuscumbia
officials."

I asked about the chances that he'd get it.

"They don't want to give us the permit," he said. "But if
they don't, I'm willing to march anyway and let them arrest
us."

Seigenthaler and I had, on numerous occasions in the past,
talked about the prospect that a demonstration could result
in my arrest. Publicity could damage my new relationship
with Bill Wilkinson's Klan faction, especially if my picture
were published with Don Black's.

I asked Walker how strongly Black felt about marching if
the officials denied him a permit.

"I know him pretty well," Walker said. "I fear that he
might back down on it without permission from the officials
for us to march."

That bore out my long-standing belief that Black was less
an activist than he was rhetorician. It was also somewhat
surprising to me to hear Walker, one of Black's key support-
ers, tell me that he thought our leader might "back down."

And it served to validate my belief that Black's support was paper-thin, even among his cadre of security guards.

Black, as he planned the protest against President Carter, clearly feared that Wilkinson and his group might try to upstage him and cut in on his action, since the bitter confrontation between Wilkinson and Duke in July had left the rivalry between the two groups more intense than ever. But, much to Black's relief, this never happened.

When Black returned to Birmingham from his initial trip to Tuscumbia, he told me about his discussion with the officials (who were obviously also discussing the President's visit with the White House and the Secret Service).

"They won't give us a permit, but they can't stop us from being there and demonstrating," Black told me. He did not seem to be backing down. "What I plan," he said, "is a rally the night before Carter gets to Tuscumbia. We'll meet at the new National Headquarters in Tuscumbia and we'll have a cross lighting. Next day we'll hit the streets and stage a protest against Carter. After he gets through talking, we'll march through the streets again in a group."

Black's security guards usually go armed, but he laid down the law for the presidential activities: "No guns."

During the year I spent around Don Black's operation, I had participated in many activities. But, in terms of status, Black obviously hadn't yet planned anything to match the scope of his march against the President.

We gathered in Tuscumbia the night before Labor Day at the modest concrete block building that serves as the NATIONAL HEADQUARTERS OF THE KNIGHTS OF THE KU KLUX KLAN, its hand-lettered sign more imposing than the structure itself.

Only about sixty of us were Klan members, but a huge crowd showed up for our rally and cross-lighting ceremony, as the protest had been announced nationally. Many were curiosity seekers and others were reporters from distant places. But the largest proportion of the more than one thousand people who showed up that night were unmistakably

sympathetic to the Klan. This turnout on the eve of Carter's
visit to the area was another example of the covert support
the Klan has among "respectable" people who would never
carry a membership card or be publicly associated with the
Klan.

Black's speech in Tuscumbia was his usual. "Ladies and
gentlemen," he shouted, "just look around you. Just notice
all these brave people in white robes. These people have
made the most important decision in their lives. They have
dedicated their lives to making this a better country, returning it to the greatness it was when our forefathers shed their
blood to make it free. As I've said, many of us have made our
decision. Won't you make yours to join us so we can work
together for such a worthy purpose?"

There was almost no applause from the somber crowd.
However, the applause came when he launched into an
attack on President Carter, the federal government, blacks,
and Jews. He lambasted Carter for his support of affirmative
action programs, which, he said, were eliminating jobs that
could, and should, be held by white Americans.

"Jobs are going to all the many thousands of Cuban refugees that Carter has welcomed with open arms," he said.
"He has opened the border between the United States and
Mexico by placing the son of an illegal Mexican immigrant
in charge of the Border Patrol."

Afterward, about sixty Klan members gathered in the
small headquarters as Black outlined the plans for the next
day. "We don't have a permit, but we are going to do it
anyway," he said. "We've got as much right to be on the
sidewalk as anybody else who is here."

The authorities had already conceded that they could not
stop the Klan from bringing a group to the President's
speech, but they did intend to prevent a formal march without a permit.

"We will remain on the sidewalks and march two by two,
four feet apart," he said.

Our march was to begin about three hours before Carter

arrived. We would walk, on the sidewalks, through the downtown area and later attend the President's speech in a group.

Black didn't try to disguise his elation at the huge turnout for the rally and cross burning. I was surprised at the turnout myself. Often Black had told me to expect large, enthusiastic crowds and I was usually disappointed to find a showing of only a few Klan members and, on occasion, even fewer spectators. I'm sure Jimmy Carter would regret it, but I'm convinced it was his scheduled visit, and not the magnetism of the Klan, that was responsible for Black's audience.

"Tomorrow," Black told the group huddled in the small headquarters building that night, "there is going to be the closest scrutiny we have ever been under. We will be dealing with the Secret Service as well as the police. They will be checking us for weapons, and I want it clear that there won't be any guns. I am urging you not to bring any weapons."

His plan was that he, Gene Russell, and Stanley McCullom, the Tuscumbia Titan, would walk at the front of the parade. "If anybody is to be arrested it will be the three of us. You all just do as you are told," Black said.

On the way to my motel that night, I heard on the radio that the details Black had outlined to us had been tentatively approved by the authorities. It was apparent that his defiance was somewhat less than genuine. I felt better about the coming day.

On Labor Day, right on time, about fifty of us showed up at the headquarters for the short trip to town. I rode from the headquarters building in the back of Ben Walker's pickup. He was unarmed as far as I could determine. Also in the back of the truck were some placards we would carry during our picketing.

We assembled in the courthouse parking lot downtown, donned our robes, and joined about eighty Klan sympathizers in civilian clothes who would march through town with us. Black was right about the scrutiny: There were almost as many police officers as demonstrators.

My own hood was still being made, so I wore a white cowboy hat. When Black first noticed me at the headquarters that morning he threw me off guard. Noting my cowboy hat and sunglasses, he said without smiling, "Traveling incognito today, J.W.?"

I had no idea if he meant anything by the remark. And I worried about it all day.

The sun was already hot that Labor Day morning—the temperature would rise into the nineties before the President finished his speech—but that wasn't the reason I began sweating profusely again. I was nervous once more. Did Black suspect me? If he did, would my nervousness, or my actions, confirm his suspicions?

I trekked the six city blocks of the march, winding up back at the courthouse parking lot, where we disrobed and returned to the headquarters. No one paid much attention to me, or to any of us for that matter, except for the prisoners who heckled us when we passed by the city jail. "Hey, you crazy mothers," one shouted, "what the hell do you think you're doing?"

As always, when I marched in Klan regalia, I felt silly. But wearing a Klan robe with a cowboy hat made me feel even sillier than usual.

There were a lot of people in town that day, many of them supporting Jimmy Carter and many others taking advantage of a once-in-a-lifetime opportunity to see the President in person. Their response to our presence was hardly noticeable.

The picket signs we carried protested everything negative you could think of about the Carter administration: busing, the admission of Cubans and Asians to the country, "Jew control" of his government, the failure to free the hostages in Iran, the downturn of the national economy. The one I carried said END WELARE [*sic*] GIVEAWAYS! (I was sure that some of my fellow reporters back at *The Tennessean* would accuse me of writing that sign myself.)

I had been told months earlier that if we were ever attacked during a march our picket sticks could be used as clubs. It wouldn't be necessary this day because most people just ignored us. And, besides, the picket sticks were pretty flimsy.

After the march, our numbers began dwindling rather rapidly. It was obvious that many of the Klan members had no intention of returning for the President's speech.

"I wouldn't listen to Jimmy Carter for fifteen seconds," one of them said as he was leaving. But about a dozen of us went, still wearing our robes as a further form of protest.

When we arrived at the park where the annual Quad Cities Labor Day Picnic was being held, the crowd was already gathering to hear Carter. We drew stares and glares as we made our way through the crowd to a little mound in front of the President, to his left and about a hundred yards from his bank of microphones.

While our morning march, under the watchful eyes of the cadre of police officers who kept their distance, had been less than eventful, my Klan associates were feeling that the crowd they had drawn the night before provided them with the "exposure" they were seeking—the exposure that Black felt would rejuvenate his disintegrating organization.

And so, there we were, a band of a dozen KKK members in a throng of thirty thousand who had come to hear the President. And, except for us, the majority of the huge audience was overwhelmingly supportive of the President. He had begun his speech and was only a few minutes into it when three members of our group unfurled the Confederate flag. As the Stars and Bars suddenly billowed, it caught the President's eye. He looked straight at us, as if seeing our white robes for the first time.

"I say these people who wear white sheets do not understand what our country stands for," said the President. "The

Klan," he continued, "represents cowardice, fear, and hatred."

As I listened to Carter dish out those Klan labels, I had to agree silently with his every word. But, at the same time, I couldn't help but feel a bizarre sense of recognition; after all, this was the first time I had ever had a President personally call me a coward.

When Carter went back to his prepared remarks, a slight scuffling began. A group of black youths stood talking with a white teenaged boy and girl. One of my group of Klan members said he feared the white teenagers were in trouble and being "surrounded" by the blacks. We rushed over. They obviously had engaged in some hot words. The girl was wiping tears from her eyes.

"Get back," one of the Klansmen ordered the black youths.

"I don't have to back up for you," the black youngster retorted.

The Klansman—who was a stranger to me and whom I have never seen again—responded, "Boy, you haven't been smacked until you get smacked by a Klansman."

I could see the situation was fast getting out of hand, since neither side showed any inclination to retreat. As more Klansmen gathered around, so did more black youths. Where in the hell were all those police officers who had watched us this morning?

Finally, several sheriff's deputies rushed in, ordered us back to our place on the hill, told the group of youths to disperse, and the tense moment passed.

The President finished his talk and wandered off. It had been an eventful day for Don Black, and when I next talked to him on the phone he was elated. He had elicited a blistering attack from the President's bully pulpit. "We got his attention," Black told me.

Black gloried over the headlines that kept his ego soaring for several days when Carter and Ronald Reagan kept the

Klan alive as a campaign issue. Never in all the time that I knew Don Black did he seem so elated about the future of the Klan.

But, as events of the next few weeks would demonstrate, the presidential campaign controversy was not enough to bolster the Klan leader's organization. Increasingly, it became apparent to me that Black and his group would soon dwindle into near obscurity.

As a reporter, I was fortunate to have already begun my move on to the more successful—and more violence-prone— Bill Wilkinson Klan group.

Although our official Klan business was finished for that day, I still had one matter I needed to take care of before leaving town—I had once again been discovered by another newsman. It was ironic. A television crew from a Nashville station had photographed our march with none of the crew recognizing me or getting me in any of its news film. Yet, Joe Holloway, a photographer for The Associated Press in Atlanta, did recognize me. I felt the same sudden pang of terror I had felt when I looked up that afternoon in Florida and saw Jon Smith and his camera. Holloway had actually recognized me before I noticed him. He was looking right at me when our eyes met, but the change in his expression was barely perceivable. For just an instant, there was a look of puzzled bewilderment on his face. Then, just as suddenly, it was gone.

I knew immediately that he had sized up what I was doing because he knew me too well—well enough to know that I would never become a Klansman unless it was to get a story, and well enough to know that if he made any attempt to communicate with me, he would place me in great jeopardy. I also knew immediately that my secret was safe with Joe Holloway. He was more than a good photographer. He was also a good friend. I had had dinner at his home in Atlanta when I was there for the furniture show. In the past, we had fished together, drunk together, worked together, and traveled on assignments together. I felt he deserved an explanation of my strange behavior.

After my Klan associates—and the President—had left town, I called his office in Atlanta to find out where he was transmitting his pictures from. I then drove to the Holiday Inn in Florence and knocked on his door.

"Just a minute, I'm in the dark," he responded. He seemed to be expecting me. "Damned if it isn't the great dragon," he said, as he opened the door.

We talked about fishing, the day's activities, and our families, as he developed, printed, and transmitted several pictures. Finally, he had satisfied his editors and had a moment to relax.

"Well, Thompson, unfortunately none of the pictures you were in were good enough to put on the wire," he said. "But that's not your fault."

I thanked him profusely for not giving me away when he first saw me and explained how important it was that my clandestine activities remain so, and he handed me an envelope containing the negatives of every picture I was in. "If you ever have the occasion to use these," he said, "just give AP a credit line."

My luck was holding.

Furthermore, in the matter of my fear about Black's suspicions that day, it turned out to be just my paranoia about being discovered working overtime. Within a week, a hood was delivered to me in Cullman, with Gene Russell's card: "You are white today because you're ancestors practiced segregation."

THE NEXT FEW DAYS I stayed in Birmingham helping out around the cabinet shop. At night I would either sleep on David's sofa or in Chris's spare bedroom, alternating between the two so as not to wear out my welcome at either.

Late Thursday afternoon I decided to call Linda. I had intended to call her at the store but subconsciously dialed our home number. Just as I realized my mistake, she answered the phone.

"I meant to call the store," I explained. "What are you doing home this time of the day?"

"I'm not feeling well," she said. "I've been in bed most of the day."

The main purpose for the call was to tell her that I wouldn't be able to come home before Sunday because, just the night before, Black had invited me to a rally in Brookside the following Saturday night and I had assured him I would be there.

"I hope it's nothing serious," I continued. "Why don't you stay in bed and maybe you'll feel better tomorrow?"

"Jerry, I'm afraid it is something serious. I've felt rotten all over for the past week and I'm spitting up blood, lots of blood, especially in the mornings."

I was beginning to panic now. "Have you seen the doctor?"

"No, I haven't felt like moving, much less going to a doctor."

What was I to do? I said, "I called to tell you that there's a thing I just have to go to Saturday night, but . . ."

"Go ahead," she interrupted, "there's nothing you could do if you were here."

"The only way I'll go is for you to make sure to get to a doctor tomorrow. Otherwise, I'm coming home right now." What a mess. "I really do need to go to this thing, though, because Black personally invited me."

"Okay," she said. "I'll try to get to the doctor tomorrow. You be careful."

"I'm going to be careful and I'm also going to call back tomorrow to make sure you've seen a doctor."

For the rest of that day and night and throughout the next day, she was on my mind. I felt guilty as hell not racing home the night before. She was right that there was nothing I could do, but dammit, I could have been there. She could be dying, or something could happen to me down here. I could be wiped out in a wreck or something—and I thought of several somethings. But, I rationalized, by staying here and going to that rally I could be shortening this assignment, which would allow me to go home for good: if I missed the rally I might miss something that would take me months to find out otherwise. I finally made myself believe that I was doing best for the both of us by staying—gambling that nothing was seriously wrong with her, and gambling that I would learn something at the rally that would make the stay worthwhile.

The next day seemed to drag on forever. I called home twice before getting an answer. Finally I reached her. She sounded a little better than she had the night before, but still her voice had a note of serious concern. The doctor had told her she was suffering from a bleeding ulcer and directed her to watch her diet closely.

"You don't know how relieved I am," I told her. "I'll leave here as soon as the rally is over and see you sometime early Sunday morning. I love you."

"I love you too," she said. "Please don't go to sleep on the way home."

Driving south from Cullman on Interstate 65, headed for the Brookside rally, on Saturday night, I took the Warrior-Robbins exit and traveled down a long, dark, twisting road that took me through Robbins, which resembled nothing so much as a ghost town. There were no visible signs of activity and it was just barely past dark when I went through town. The road on the other side of town was even more desolate. There were few houses and even fewer cars on that lonely stretch of road between Robbins and Highway 78.

At the bottom of a winding hill, just past a crossroads and a small store, I met a black-and-maroon-colored Chevrolet. Just as I approached the car, which didn't dim its lights, I saw the unmistakable flash of fire that comes from a gun barrel at night. I instinctively ducked down in the seat just as an earsplitting blast rattled my truck. There was only the one shot as the car sped past and turned up the crossroads I had just passed. I never looked back, but if I ever had the guts to drive again the way I did that night, I could probably qualify for the pole position in the Indianapolis 500.

Maybe someone in the Klan had found out who I really was. Possibly some black assumed I was heading to the rally, which had been well publicized. Or maybe some good ole boy had had just a little too much to drink. After carefully considering all the possibilities over the next several days, I came to the conclusion that it was just a random act of terror, probably inspired by alcohol. I never mentioned the incident to anyone in the Klan, and no one acted surprised when I turned up at the rally. (I also didn't tell Linda until after I had been home for several months and she noticed the rip in the pickup—a scant six inches above my head. She said it made her weak in the knees when she found out. But if you haven't seen the streak of fire from a gun barrel, heard the blast, and felt the shuddering concussion of a bullet ripping through the vehicle you're riding in, you don't truly know the real sensation of weak knees.)

I had calmed down considerably by the time I arrived in "downtown" Brookside. The rally was held in a vacant lot behind a tire company under a railroad viaduct. It was already under way when I finally found the location, and Black was speaking. I didn't really miss anything: I had heard the same speech on numerous occasions. However, when I peered over the edge of the viaduct, I was surprised to see Black speaking from the bed of a trailer with his back to the elevated street.

My first thought was for his security. He presented an almost inviting target for an assassin. What if the same person who, just minutes before, had taken a potshot at me happened along that street? The invitation would be too much to resist. I couldn't do anything to prevent it, but I could possibly shout a frantic warning if I saw the same car coming, so I stayed on the viaduct until he finished speaking and left the platform. My God, I thought, I was even thinking like a Klansman. Although I didn't agree with what Black was preaching, I was willing to help him defend his right to preach, and I certainly didn't want anyone, especially through physical violence, to attempt to deprive him of that right.

After he had finished, he immediately went into a closed meeting with the local Klan officers and I went down to the vacant lot and mingled with the Klan members I knew. Black had told me earlier that many of the members of the new Brookside den had been former members of Wilkinson's Invisible Empire who had become disenchanted when he didn't stand behind them when they were among the two hundred Klan members arrested a year earlier in Montgomery when Wilkinson attempted to retrace the route of Dr. Martin Luther King, Jr.'s, Selma-to-Montgomery march. I could see evidence of this crossover in the number of weapons visible at the rally. I had never seen as many weapons at a rally of the Knights of the Ku Klux Klan. But this time, an old Dodge van parked at the edge of the lot had more than a dozen rifles and shotguns propped up against the front seat. The fellow driving the van, a former Wilkinson member, was offering several of the guns for sale during the lull between the end of the speeches and the time the crowd dispersed. I didn't see any buyers.

Ricky Fitts, the north Alabama Klansman I had met at the first meeting I attended in Muscle Shoals, Don Oliver, and several other Klan members I had met at other meetings gathered, at Fitts's invitation, at the trunk of his car, where he had a large chest full of cold beer iced down. Several of us were sipping beer when Black sauntered up after the closed meeting.

Fitts offered Black a beer, but he refused. "I don't think I should right now," he said. "There's still too many people around."

"Well, boss, I was sure uneasy the whole time you were speaking," Fitts said to Black. "There's no way in hell we could provide security for you when anyone who came down the street had a clear shot at your back. Of course, we had security people at both ends of the bridge and they wouldn't have gotten away, but you would have still been shot."

"There's really no way you can keep from getting shot if someone wants to shoot you bad enough," Black responded. "The main thing is keeping them from getting away."

"We would have done that," Fitts assured him.

"And, if I've got to get shot, I'd just as soon get shot in the back," Black said, smiling.

I couldn't help but wonder if any of the others standing around knew what I knew—that Black had once been shot in the back. If anyone did, he didn't indicate it.

Black was relaxed and in a good mood. There was a good turnout for the rally, the people were apparently accepting him as Grand Wizard, and the support from north Alabama was better than usual, since most of the north Alabama Klan members were jockeying for position, hoping for an official title in the reorganization of the Knights and the shifting of the National Headquarters from Louisiana to Tuscumbia.

Black was joking and laughing. It was one of his rare displays of humor. He finally took a sip of beer from a Styrofoam cup and suggested that we all go to a truck stop down on Highway 78 for coffee.

I declined, explaining that I had to drive to southern Mississippi the next morning for a meeting with some furniture dealers. Deep down, I really wanted to go because it was so unusual for Klan members to laugh and joke about anything, but with ten or twelve people going I didn't want to push my luck. After all, I had been shot at already and slipped by. I didn't want someone to ask me about my Army days—something that would surely give me away.

I walked back up to the viaduct where I had parked my truck and, on the way, I decided that I would go back to Birmingham and take I-65 to Cullman. One thing was for sure: I wasn't going back up that same lonely road. The only problem was I didn't know exactly how to get back to Birmingham. I knew the general direction, I just didn't know which road to take.

As I left Brookside, a fellow sort of swung out from a signpost and thrust out his thumb to hitch a ride. I picked him up, reasoning that he could at least direct me to a main road, or better, he might be going to Birmingham too. I had had only one beer, but it was immediately obvious to me that he had enjoyed several more than that. He was going to a club on Bessemer Cutoff, and if he could get me there, I could get to Birmingham.

I found out that he too had witnessed the Klan rally from the viaduct and that he was duly impressed with Black's speech. He must have introduced himself at least a dozen times, each time insisting that I shake his hand. Each time I shook it, and each time I told him I was J. W. Thompson.

"You know, that feller really knew what he was talking about back there," he said of Black.

"Yeah, he tells it like it is," I said. "He's a smart man."

"You know the niggers are just taking over," he said. "We've got to do something about it. It may get to the point that we just have to get our shotguns and go out 'n' mow 'em down."

"Well, some people are saying that a race war is coming and if they know what they're talking about, you might be right."

We continued this type of small talk, with him repeating himself several times, until we reached the Bessemer Cutoff. For the first time in several miles, I knew where I was and how to get where I wanted to go.

"Here's the place," he said, pointing to a club up ahead with a large neon sign out front proclaiming it THE BUNK-HOUSE.

"This is a fine place," he said. "You ever been here?"

"No, I'm afraid this is one of the places I've missed."

"Well, I'll tell you what, J.W., you come on in and I'll buy you a drink."

On the outside there was a huge padlock on the front door, but loud music was coming from the inside and there were several cars in the parking lot.

"How in the hell are we going to get in?" I asked. "The door is locked."

"Aw, that door is always locked. We'll go around and go in the back door."

"No, I think I had better get back up to Cullman."

"J.W., they've got some real purty girls in here, and if you tip 'em about five dollars, they'll take everything off. You better come on in."

"That sounds mighty fine," I said, very honestly, "but I've

got a long drive ahead of me tomorrow. Maybe some other time."

"Well, we don't have to go here," he said persistently. "You wanna go get some nigger pussy?"

By this time I was convinced that he didn't have a gun, and, in his condition, he couldn't have fought his way out of a paper bag, so my response was my best macho manner: "Dammit! Get your ass out of my truck right this minute. We have both just left a Klan rally and we both know how the niggers are taking over the world. If you think I'm gonna screw one, you're crazy. Get out."

"Wait a minute, J.W.," he said, almost pleading. "I didn't mean to piss you off. I know some white whores too. You wanna white whore?"

"Get out, dammit, before I kick your ass out."

He got out of the truck and gently closed the door. The last words I heard from him were, "I'm much obliged for the ride. J.W. I'll be glad to pay you. I'm sorry I pissed you off. Have a nice day."

Before I had driven a mile, I was sorry that I had left the ole fellow on such a sour note. He was only trying to be accommodating, and I was trying to be a super bad-ass. I would have really liked to go into The Bunkhouse, but it reminded me too much of the Pine Grove Country Club on Whites Creek Pike near Nashville. I had been there twice and twice I had to fight my way out. After all, I had experienced enough excitement for one day.

I drove back to Cullman.

It was raining through a low-lying haze the next morning, which made the two hundred miles between me and home seem much farther. I decided to sleep in, but sleep did not come easily.

I had already called Seigenthaler, only to be told by his son that he was out of town. Finally, I decided to venture into the rain and drive down to the service station on the corner and get a Sunday paper. I had enjoyed all the television preachers I could stand.

After leisurely reading the paper—all the paper—I decided to go down to Jack's Truck Stop for lunch. I really hadn't thought much about the gunshot from the night before until I started out the door for the second time that morning. It was then that I noticed the jagged tear above the cab of my truck. If I had ever had any doubt about being shot at, all doubt disappeared when I noticed that ugly gash. My knees got weak again.

I went back inside and called Wayne Whitt. "Whitt, somebody took a shot at me last night," I began.

"Did they hit you?" he asked.

"No, but they came too damn close. The slug ripped through the metal, just above my head."

"Did you report it to the police?"

"No, I didn't. I didn't find the bullet hole until just a few minutes ago."

"What are you going to do about it?"

"I don't really know what to do. What would you suggest?"

"If you think it could have been someone in the Klan, I'd say get the hell out of there and come home today. But it was probably some drunk coal miner from Jasper trying out a new pistol and you just happened along. If you think somebody is shooting at you because they know who you are, come on home now. I'm going to leave that decision up to you. Hell, you've been shot at before; are you sure it wasn't just another jealous husband?"

"Well, I don't guess anyone can ever really be sure, can they?"

"You do whatever you feel best. I'm certainly not going to tell anyone to stay in a situation that might get them shot."

"Well, I feel a lot better after telling you about it. I don't think the Klan had anything to do with it. But if they take another shot—and if they miss—I'll be in Nashville quicker than a hiccup."

I was trying to sound much braver than I actually was. If I had experienced even one fleeting hint that I might be shot at again, I would have already been back in Nashville.

Meanwhile, I spent that rainy afternoon doing not one constructive thing. I watched television, took several naps, read, and finally began to feel guilty. So I called Roland Torbert to further express my disgust about Duke's attempt at selling me out and to subtly solicit an assurance that Wilkinson wouldn't attempt a similar deal with someone else.

"Mr. Torbert," I began, "I've been thinking a lot about being a member of the Invisible Empire, and I'm really looking forward to it. . . ."

"We're sure glad to have you coming over," he interrupted. "I'm sure you will see a big difference with us."

"I'm sure I will, but I've been thinking about that too. I would never have believed it, even if someone had told me, that David Duke would try to sell me out like he did. I would really like to talk to Mr. Wilkinson to make sure he doesn't plan to do the same thing sometime in the future, at least without first bringing it before his members. Is he going to be in Alabama any time soon?"

"Mr. Thompson, I can assure you that Bill Wilkinson will never sell you out or even attempt to. You've got my word on that. He won't be back up here for at least two months—or at least he's not planning to be—but I'll be glad to give you his phone number and you can call him up and talk to him."

"I'd like that," I said. "I don't really expect it to happen again, but I never thought Duke would do it either. You know how it is—if you get burned once, you don't get too close to the stove the next time. I'd just like to talk to Mr. Wilkinson to let him know how I feel."

He gave me the number and told me it would be best to try to contact Wilkinson during the day. He also told me he had been in contact with Tucker, who told him that I had been unanimously accepted by the membership of the Cullman Klavern.

"If there's any way I can," Torbert said, "I'll try to make it up there for your naturalization."

"I'll be looking forward to seeing you there, and I'll call Mr. Wilkinson the first thing in the morning."

I did try to reach Wilkinson the next morning. The number Torbert gave me was the Empire's National Headquarters in Denham Springs, Louisiana. However, I was told that the Imperial Wizard would not be in until the following day. I told the woman who answered the phone that I would call back then. I had no way of knowing whether or not she was being truthful with me, but I wondered.

I had been talking frequently and freely with Black and members of his Klan and with Torbert and Tucker of Wilkinson's Klan. I fantasized that somehow they had gotten together and discussed J. W. Thompson. I discovered that my worries and fears were directly proportionate to the amount of free time I had just to sit around and think about them. So I drove to Birmingham and puttered around the shop with David and Chris for the rest of the day.

I called the headquarters the next morning only to be greeted by the same woman's voice and the same message: Wilkinson would be in the following morning. I called again at about ten the following morning, fully expecting a repeat of the two previous mornings' conversations. I was surprised when she asked, "May I tell him who's calling?"

"Sure. I'm J. W. Thompson from Cullman, Alabama."

"Jerry?" I froze momentarily, but managed to answer rather quickly, "J. W. Thompson, from Cullman, Alabama," I said once more, very slowly and clearly. Had it just been my imagination?

"Just a moment, Mr. Thompson."

"You don't know me," I told Wilkinson when he got on the line, "but I'm J. W. Thompson and I've been a member of David Duke and Don Black's Klan. Now I'm getting ready to come over to your group. Roland Torbert suggested that I call you." I kept talking before he could say anything. "I'm doing this because I'm so upset that Duke tried to sell my membership. I've got to ask you, Mr. Wilkinson: If and when you decide to sell my membership to someone, will you notify me first?"

His response was immediate: "I don't sell anyone out," he said. "And I don't buy anyone either. My record will show that."

"That's all I wanted to hear, Mr. Wilkinson. I just wish I had asked Duke that question before I joined up with him, but who would have ever thought he would do what he did? I'm looking forward to seeing you when you get back up here."

"Well," he said, "I'll be up there in a couple of months. I've got some good people in Alabama, so I don't have to come up there very often. But I'll see you when I do."

I was still shaking after I hung up the phone—not from my conversation with Wilkinson, but because I was sure that woman who answered the phone had called me Jerry.

I had taped the conversation, as I always did when I talked to Klan members from home. I played the tape back, again, and again, and again. Each time I listened to it, I became more convinced that the woman called me Jerry. I called Seigenthaler.

"Are you sure?" he asked me.

"Hell, yes, I'm sure. I've listened to that tape a dozen times and each time I hear it, I'm more sure."

"I need to get that tape up here where I can hear it. How can we get it here the fastest? Could you put it on a plane?"

"I could, but I'd have to drive back to Birmingham. Why don't I just bring it? I could drive it up there in four hours or less."

"That's fine. Do that. When you get near the office, call

me and I'll meet you somewhere and get the tape. If they were expecting you to call and the secretary slipped up and tipped you off, it's probably time to come home anyway."

During that drive toward Nashville, I was plagued by a variety of emotions. Subconsciously, I hoped that Seigenthaler would also be convinced that the woman had called me Jerry, that she was expecting my call, and that they probably knew who I was and what I was trying to do. If so, I could go home and immediately start writing the series of stories on what I had learned up to this point and beat the Klan to the punch. I would disclose my participation before the Klan figured out some way to make it sound beneficial to the Klan. I would also be home to see some of Todd's football games, I'd have time to put in a late fall garden, and get some work done on the house, especially the heating system. All that would be nice, I thought.

At the same time, however, I knew I hadn't gone as far in the Klan as I wanted to. After all, Black's Klan hadn't really done enough to make my stay worthwhile. It seemed the Wilkinson people were the only ones doing anything in the Klan, and I wanted to find out what they were doing, how they were doing it, and why they continued to attract new members while Black's organization was withering on the vine.

I knew Seigenthaler would listen to the tape as carefully as I had. He would probably even ask some other people to listen to it to see if they heard the word "Jerry" too. But I knew the ultimate decision on whether or not to continue the assignment would be left to me. Even if he had some doubts, we would talk about it and subsequently persuade ourselves that it was an honest slip of the tongue on the woman's part. Then I would consciously decide to go back and be especially alert for any other tip-off that I had been found out, and if I didn't see any other indications, no matter how subtle, I would continue.

That's it, I thought, that's the way it will work. And that's exactly the way it did work.

When I called the office, Seigenthaler told me he had some people with him and that he would send Whitt to meet me and pick up the tape. When Whitt and I met, he got into the truck with me and together we listened to the tape several times, Whitt was noncommittal.

"It sounds like she is saying 'Jerry,' but maybe she didn't understand you when you said J.W. After all, J.W., if you don't say it real plain, could sound like Jerry. John and I will listen to it some more tonight and you call him the first thing in the morning."

I was somewhat less than honest with Linda about why I had suddenly come home. I told her that Seigenthaler was eager to wind up the story and wanted all the tapes and notes I had in order to get them transcribed. I certainly didn't tell her what I suspected one particular tape contained.

Now that I was home, even if it was only for one night, I found that she had not told me everything the doctor had told her. When I asked how she was feeling, she said, "The doctor said he could give me some medication for the ulcer, but after running some tests he discovered a complication that rules out the use of medication right now. But he assured me he could clear it up for me about next May."

"Why then?" I asked, truly puzzled.

"That's when the baby is due."

"You're pregnant?"

"That's right. You know, as much as I like to have you home, I kinda wish you had spent one more weekend in Alabama in August."

"I think that's wonderful," I said, giving her a big hug. "Joe needs a little brother."

"If that's the case, he'll have to be awfully tough. The girls and I have already decided she'll be named Julie. Unfortunately, I just haven't decided how I'll be able to handle another baby."

'That's simple, I'll be here to help."

"Somehow I knew you were going to be tickled to death

when you found out, that's why I didn't tell you on the phone."

"Weren't you tickled when you found out?"

"No, I cried. I still don't know how I'm going to be able to handle things. I've always heard that the good Lord won't give you more burdens than you can carry, but with another baby He's coming awfully close to my load limit."

I spoke with Seigenthaler the next morning. He succeeded in persuading me that Wilkinson's secretary had just simply misunderstood my name. He said he and Wayne were convinced of it after listening to the tape dozens of times. Within an hour of our conversation, I was on the way back to Cullman.

I WOULD STILL have more than a week to look for any other indications that the woman's slip was more than an accident. If there weren't any, I would be naturalized into the Wilkinson group as scheduled. Meanwhile, I would attempt to talk with Torbert and Tucker as often as possible without appearing too eager.

I also kept in touch with Don Black. He scheduled another rally in Athens the following Saturday night, hoping for a better turnout than our previous rally there. I assured him I would attend, but as I had learned long ago in my dealings with Black, his plans were subject to change on short notice. So I wasn't really too surprised when I called him late Saturday afternoon to find that the rally had been postponed for a week because "some of our people in north Alabama had a conflict and wouldn't be able to be there."

I wished I had called earlier so I could have already been home for the weekend. But I still had time for an abbreviated trip.

I didn't talk to Seigenthaler or Whitt over the weekend and left at 5:00 A.M. on Monday to return to Alabama. I was shocked when I stopped just south of Nashville and bought a copy of *The Tennessean* from a rack at a convenience store. Splashed across the front page was a copyrighted story, with fantastic pictures, of the Klan's paramilitary training camp in my new hometown—Cullman. There was a picture of Tucker, of a man known only as "Tony," and a woman holding a semiautomatic rifle—all members of the Cullman Klavern of the Invisible Empire. The story said the members had been "handpicked" by Wilkinson.

I didn't leave the parking lot until I had finished the story. It was frightening. Within days, I would be a member of this group. This story said members with prior Army experience were given preference for membership in the elite fighting squad. Would they ask me to join, since I had a discharge from twenty years in the Army? What should I do if they did?

The story said that in the camp near Cullman, the group was training to kill blacks in the coming race war. In addition to killing blacks, according to a quote from Tucker, the group would also kill policemen who opposed their actions. "We're preparing for survival and war," Tucker said, "revolution." The camp was named "My Lai," he said, "in honor of Lieutenant William Calley and the good deed he done in Vietnam." The story went on to say that state and federal agents were "alarmed" by the goings on at the camp and by what they termed a "new kind of terrorism."

The word "alarmed" was certainly inadequate to describe my own feelings at that particular moment. Before I got to Cullman, the story was already on the national news on the radio. That night, news of the camp and the people who trained in it were major news on network television. The next day, it was in the Birmingham papers, replete with quotes from local officials who acknowledged that as long as the Klan members confined their training to private property, with the obvious consent of the landowner, there was nothing they could do.

When I called Tucker on Tuesday night, I could tell right off that the national publicity had elated him.

"J.W., the news media has been calling from all over the country. *The New York Times* called, the *Los Angeles Times*, a whole bunch of newspapers, radio stations, and television stations," he said proudly. "We have sure stirred up a mess of publicity. That's for sure. Everybody wants to know where the camp is, but everybody we took in there was blindfolded. Hell, other members of the Klavern don't even know where it is. We done a good job of keeping it secret, even among the other members. I'll bet there's some uneasy niggers out there. If they knew how much firepower we had, they would shore nuff be uneasy."

"I'll have to agree," I told him, "you sure have stirred up the publicity. I can't wait to get with you folks because everybody in the country knows you're doing something. Is the meeting still on Saturday night?"

"Yeah, and I think we're going to meet at the Klavern where we've been meeting, but I'm not real sure yet. Could you call me back tomorrow night? I'll know for sure then and I'll tell you exactly how to get there. It ain't too hard to find."

"Sure, I'll call you back tomorrow night. Just hang in there and don't let those news people get to you."

"They are kinda getting to be a pain in the ass, but we're gonna let the niggers and the nigger-loving liberals—we call them white niggers—we're gonna let everybody know that we've got the people and the equipment to stand up and fight for the white people. Everybody's gonna know we mean business. I'll talk to you tomorrow night."

When I called again the next night, Tucker was still high on the publicity that the story continued to generate. "Boy, I ain't never seen anything like it, J.W. People are still calling from all over the country," he told me. "We got a call today from a Klavern over in Mississippi that wants to bring the Special Forces over there Saturday to provide security for a march they're having. I've talked to several members ot our group and I believe we're going over there."

"Does that mean that the meeting will be postponed?"

"Naw. It's still on and we found out today that we could still use the old meeting place. I may not be there for the first part of the meeting, but I'm leaving Gerald Briscoe in charge. He's a good man. He will be doing the naturalization. I believe we've got four or five more members we'll be naturalizing Saturday night. You just see Gerald when you get there and he'll take care of everything. If you could, try to be there about six-thirty so you all can get the naturalization over with before the regular meeting. It would be better because the other members won't be held up by the ceremony that way."

"That will be no problem. I'll be there early," I assured him.

And he told me how to get there: "It's about seven miles out of town toward Hanceville. You turn to your left right beside Willingham's Cabinet Shop. There's an old farmhouse out in the middle of the pasture there. You can see the lights strung up where we've had some rallies, and there will be several burnt crosses out there in the field. You can't miss it, but if you do have any trouble, just call Gerald and he'll meet you somewhere. I'll probably be back before you all get through."

Tucker was right—I couldn't miss it. I drove down the mext morning following his instructions, and went right to the old house with the burnt crosses in the pasture. The place looked spooky enough in the daylight; I could imagine how it would look after dark. It was situated about a hundred yards off the road, down a long narrow drive right beside Willingham's Cabinet Shop. I was sure that the main highway would seem a lot farther away when viewed from that pasture. I would find out for sure Saturday.

As I left the old farmhouse, I carefully noted the mileage, the landmarks, the road signs, and anything else that would make the house easy to find, and slowly and clearly dictated everything into a tape recorder as I drove north toward Nashville.

I had never trusted anyone connected with the Klan, and I recalled the double cross perpetrated on David Duke in that same farmhouse. I wondered if the cameras and recorders were still in place. Would this be where the Klan exposed me as an infiltrator, a newspaper reporter? Would I be the guest of honor at yet another "low-down media stunt," all for the benefit of Bill Wilkinson? That would be the perfect way to destroy everything I had gathered for my story and the perfect way for Wilkinson to grab national headlines once again and to prove further to his members that he was "a smart man." Would they even go through the naturalization, or would they put me off and slow-walk me as Black had done?

The more I thought of all these possibilities, the more possibilities I thought of. Many of them were even worse. The remoteness of the vacant farmhouse would be a perfect place to lure someone for the grisliest of physical retribution imaginable. I tried not to think of those kinds of possibilities, yet they kept popping up.

Before I reached Nashville, I had even simulated another scenario, as unlikely as it seemed at that time: No one suspected a thing, I would be naturalized as scheduled, and then welcomed warmly as a member of the Invisible Empire, with Bill Wilkinson as my new Imperial Wizard.

Hell, I didn't really know what to think or what to expect, and I wouldn't know until Saturday night. I did know that the various possibilities of physical danger kept surfacing and I'd never been so preoccupied with them while I was a member of Black's Knights. Was I losing my nerve? Would I get scared and do something stupid that would give me away?

I did know that the members of Wilkinson's group were more violent and better armed than Black's group. But, at the same time, I couldn't help recalling a conversation I had with Roger Patmon back in July when he directed a Klan

roadblock that I participated in and the cold, matter-of-fact
way he described shooting "a nigger right in the face" with a
shotgun. And Patmon was an officer in the less militant, less
violent, of the two Klan groups.

"We was over in Carbon Hill working a roadblock like
this," Patmon told me, "and this nigger drove by and stuck
an ole pistol out the window. It was pointed right at me. He
had a wild look in his eye and just threatened outright to kill
me. I felt naked. I didn't have a damn thing to get behind
and I didn't have a sign of a gun with me. I'll never know
why he didn't shoot me then and there, but he just drove off.
I went and got a shotgun out of the truck when I noticed
that he had backed in a parking lot right down the street. I
was walking down toward where he was parked when I saw
him level his gun at two Klan ladies walking down the
street. I knew he was going to shoot them and I couldn't let
that happen, so I shot him. The first shot went through the
windshield and hit him right in the face. I was loaded with
buckshot, but he was a tough bastard. You know, he raised
up and fired a shot back at me even after I had hit him good.
When he shot back, I put two more blasts in him and he
didn't shoot back no more."

"Did you kill him?" I asked.

"Hell, no, I told you he was a tough bastard. Naw, it just
messed up his face and got an eye, I think, but he's still
alive."

"What did the law do? Did they rule it self-defense?"

"They didn't even charge me. They took it to the grand
jury and I just told the grand jury the truth. I told them I
was sure the nigger would have shot those two ladies if I
hadn't shot him first and that I felt I was only doing my duty
to prevent it. I told them that any one of them would have
done the same thing in that situation, and when they
stopped to think about it, they would have. They didn't even
indict me. The police gave me back my shotgun—in fact,
that's the gun right there in the cab of the truck. I've been

expecting to hear from the FBI, though. I figured the nigger would run to the FBI and claim I violated his civil rights and they would jump right on it. You know white folks ain't got no civil rights according to the FBI—just niggers. But I ain't heard nothing yet and maybe I won't."

If Patmon could be considered nonviolent and less militant than members of Wilkinson's group and if he could coldly, and without even a tinge of remorse, recollect shooting "a nigger in the face" with a shotgun, what could I expect from members of the group I was about to become a part of? I didn't want to think about it anymore.

I stopped in Nashville and called Robert Sherborne at the paper. Since he knew what I was doing, I thought he'd be the one I could talk to about my apprehensions regarding my naturalization on Saturday night. He served often as a sounding board when I needed someone I could honestly talk with. I could openly admit to Sherborne that I was afraid and he would understand. I didn't feel comfortable admitting fear to Seigenthaler, although I'm sure he knew I was fearful on several occasions. In fact, after the assignment was over and the stories had run, we discussed the various fears we'd had while I was associating with the Klan, and neither of us was surprised that many times we shared the same fears about the same things; we just didn't admit it at the time.

And I would never even let on to Linda that I was afraid; she was already worrying enough for both of us. So that left Sherborne. I asked him to come out for a drink after work Friday.

I grilled some steaks and we had a late dinner. Linda and the baby went to bed early, since Linda had to open the store early the next morning. The rest of the kids soon followed.

Although it really wasn't cool enough to warrant it, Sherborne and I decided to build a fire in the fireplace. Then we talked. I caught up on what was happening at the paper and then unburdened myself of some of the thoughts and apprehensions I had about my upcoming naturalization. He didn't really try to alleviate any of them but did offer suggestions on how to handle some.

We both knew that such feelings would persist, but somehow they didn't sound as serious when we talked about them out loud. It was the silent workings of the mind that made them appear so real.

I had talked to my friend and lawyer, Phil Turner, earlier in the evening. We had planned to get together and watch a football game on Saturday, a commitment I had made before my naturalization was scheduled. I explained that we'd have to make it at a later date since I would be out of town on Saturday. I had never mentioned to Phil that I was working on the Klan, just that I was on an assignment I couldn't discuss. He subdued the innate curiosity that characterizes all good lawyers and didn't pry.

As Sherborne and I sat in front of the roaring fire and planned a fall fishing trip, we were interrupted by the telephone.

"Are you still up?" Phil asked when I picked up.

"Sure. Sherborne and I are sitting here in front of a beautiful fire telling fish tales and planning another trip."

"That's good," he said, "Ginger and I aren't sleepy either. We thought we'd drive out and join you if that would be all right."

"Fine. Linda and the kids are already in bed, but Sherborne and I will probably still be reeling in speckled trout."

I told Sherborne they were on the way, and we both thought it a little strange that normal people would go visiting at midnight. If they had worked for a morning newspaper, it wouldn't have seemed the least bit strange.

After they arrived and we had talked about the family, fishing, the fire, and other things of equal significance, Phil announced, "Thompson, you folks must think we're a little crazy for driving out here at this hour, but I need to talk to you about something."

"Well, we did wonder," I said. "But we're night people too, you know. I'll say this, if someone has named me in a paternity suit, it's a damn lie."

"No," he laughed, "that would be simple. I'd just call Linda as a witness and we'd beat that. I may be just nosy, but I would like to ask you just a couple of questions, and if you feel it's none of my business just tell me and I'll understand. Fair enough?"

"Sounds fair enough to me. You're my lawyer and I'm confident you wouldn't let me say anything that would incriminate me," I said with a glibness inspired solely by the flicker of firelight and Budweiser.

"First, let me ask you if Sherborne knows what you're doing. I know he knows you're working on a story, but does he know exactly what you're working on?"

"Matter of fact, he does, Counselor."

Sherborne chuckled and Ginger giggled at my response, but Phil remained serious.

"That's good," he said, "because I didn't want to put you on the spot when I asked you to confirm or deny what I believe you're doing. And I can assure you that neither Ginger nor I will ever mention anything that's said in this room tonight. Are you working on a story about the Ku Klux Klan, maybe even as a member of the Klan?"

Sherborne's expression didn't change, Ginger was silent, and suddenly I was serious. But I made a feeble attempt to maintain the façade. "Could I plead the fifth, or better, could I plead for a fifth? Do I have to answer that question?"

"No. You can just tell me to butt out."

"Well, I'm not going to do that. Yes, I am working on a Klan story. Yes, I am a member of the Klan. And, although you didn't ask, yes, I am going to join even another Klan group tomorrow night and then I'll be a member of two Klans. Damn, wouldn't that performance have made a fit-

ting climax for a Perry Mason show—the witness breaking
under the intense interrogation of the tough lawyer?"

"Well, I really hoped I was wrong, but I was afraid I was
right. And I was."

"Now it's my turn to do the questioning. What did I do or
what have I said before tonight that tipped you off? I really
need to know that."

"Nothing. Absolutely nothing. I knew you were working
in Birmingham and that you had recently moved to Cullman. I really had no idea what you might be doing until I
picked up the paper last week and saw the story about the
training camp in Cullman and saw the cold, hard look in the
eyes of those people holding those guns. I'll tell you, those
people are mean. You can see it in their eyes. Then it hit me
that you were involved with these people, and it's bothered
me ever since. I hope not many people know where you live
or where you work."

"I hope so too."

"Now, if I may, I'd like to offer a little advice. Not as
lawyer to a client, but friend to friend. Don't go back down
there."

"I appreciate your advice, but that's a possibility I haven't
even considered. I've got to go back. I have to be there
tomorrow night."

"Why?"

"I've worked too long and too hard and been through too
much to quit now. The information I have won't justify the
time and effort I've already put in. I've got to finish the job I
went to do."

"What more can you possibly learn?"

"I don't know. I just know that I learn more every day,
and I believe that would hold true if I stayed another ten
years."

"What do you think, Bob? Don't you think he shouldn't
go back?"

"No," Sherborne answered, "I think he's right. I think he

does have to go back. Getting into this new group opens up a whole new area, and I think he has to take advantage of the opportunity. As long as he feels comfortable with it, I believe he has to continue."

"Wait," I interrupted, "I didn't say I was comfortable with it. Hell, I haven't been comfortable in over a year. I'm just saying that I believe the benefits will outweigh the potential risks."

"Boy," Phil said, "I wish you fellows would let me get a good laboratory to take a blood sample from you both. I'd like to have it analyzed to see what's in it that makes you think the way you do. I'll bet they would find some combination of ice water and insanity."

"No, it's just that newspaper reporters don't make the money that a lawyer does, so they have to work harder," I offered.

"No, it's not that, not that at all. You guys enjoy it too much. I've got another suggestion: Since you're going back anyway, Ginger and I will go to Cullman too. We'll drive down in the morning and get a motel room. We need to get away for a weekend anyway and we'll just be there if you need us."

"I haven't said anything to Jerry, but I was going to before I left here tonight," Sherborne said before I could speak. "I'm going to be down there. I'll be staying at the Day's Inn right at the interstate."

"Talk about insanity, you guys are crazy," I said. "Although these folks view the naturalization ceremony as a once-in-a-lifetime event with even greater significance than a wedding or a college graduation, or whatever, I don't think they would appreciate my bringing guests. So what the hell could you do if you were there?"

"Nothing probably," Sherborne said. "I really believe if they do suspect you, they'll just put you off and won't naturalize you. But if anything should go wrong, you'd have some help three hours closer than Nashville."

"Look, fellows," I said, "if I thought I would need any help, even the slightest suspicion that I would need help, I wouldn't go at all."

"We know that," Phil said. "But Ginger and I have been wanting to go to Cullman, Alabama, for some time now, and tomorrow just seems like a good day to go."

"I feel the same way," Sherborne said. "I've wanted to go to Cullman for a long time too."

Cullman, the popular new resort! Still, I knew it would be futile to try to dissuade either of them, and deep down inside I didn't really want to.

"I think you're both silly—and I'm not including Ginger because I think she's a victim of coercion—but I'm really touched by what you're doing. None of you know how reassuring it is to see such a caring, warmhearted silliness and how it contrasts with the silliness I'm accustomed to—a silliness inspired by hatred. Thanks."

Since we were all going to be in Cullman the next day, we discussed some of the basic logistics of our journey. We decided that we wouldn't travel together. I was to call Phil and Ginger about thirty minutes before I left home and they would leave then. Sherborne would leave about an hour later. Sherborne said he wanted to be there early enough to drive by the farmhouse—"So if you don't come out, I can tell the cops where to start looking for your remains."

After Phil and Ginger went home, Bob and I talked some more and watched the fire go out. Then he left.

I felt good that night as I slipped in bed and snuggled up to Linda. I had told her the night before, for the first time, that I was planning to become a member of Wilkinson's group. I had put it off as long as I could because I had expected another "Why don't you come home now? Don't you think we've been through enough? We can't take it anymore. We need you. Everything is falling apart" response. But she surprised me.

"When I read about the paramilitary training camp where the Klan is teaching its members to kill, I knew you'd have to get involved with those idiots too," she said when I told her. "You've got one son who lives in constant anxiety that something will happen to his father. I hear him crying many nights. You've got another son that barely knows you. He thinks his daddy is a ring of the telephone. And you've got another child you'll probably never meet. But you can rest assured that when that child is old enough to understand, whether it be a he or she, I will tell it that when its father was killed by the Ku Klux Klan, he was doing exactly what he wanted to do. I love you, we love you. Good night."

That was it. No lecture. Not really much of anything, as I thought back on it.

"Linda, darling, we've always been able to talk to each other. We've enjoyed excellent communication, but suddenly all that's gone to hell."

"It hasn't been all that sudden," she interrupted. "I realized several months ago that you communicated with me like you communicate with the television set—if I say something you don't want to hear, you turn me off. When we enjoyed communicating with each other, I was your first love. Right now, you're in love with your job and the Klan. Maybe someday I'll win your love back, but right now I don't have the energy to compete. Good night, again."

"Good night, my darling. You'll always be my first love."

She was just tired, I reasoned, as she walked toward the stairs that night and I walked toward the refrigerator for another beer.

We changed our plans slightly before Sherborne left in the wee hours of the morning. I would call him first and he would then notify Phil and Ginger.

By 10:00 A.M. the next day, I had made the call to Sherborne and was pulling out of the drive for the trip back to Cullman. Sherborne was to have checked in to the Day's Inn under the name of Bob Alan (Alan is his middle name). He was to pay cash upon arrival in the event he had to leave on

short notice. This would avoid the usual delay of the formal
check-out procedure.

When I arrived in Cullman, I called the Day's Inn from a
phone booth near my apartment, only to find they had no
guests by the name of Alan or Turner. This was no great
surprise; I had anticipated that this would be one of those
"nothing could possibly go right" kind of days. I drove down
to the old farmhouse once again to double-check my mileage
figures and again spoke my findings into the recorder.

When I returned to my apartment, the message light was
flashing on the answering machine.

"J.W.," the machine squawked, "this is your old buddy,
Bob Alan. I was just passing through Cullman and thought
maybe we could get together for a beer."

I always assumed that all my phone conversations and
messages were being monitored. As it turned out, this was
an unnecessary caution, but it served to keep me constantly
aware that I was living a precarious charade in which one
inadvertent slip of the tongue could have dangerous consequences.

However, after listening to Sherborne's message, I kind of
hoped someone had heard it. They would have known
immediately that he was not too familiar with Cullman
because he obviously was not aware that the nearest "beer"
was forty miles away.

I returned his call and we agreed to meet at a shopping-
center parking lot. When we met, I got into the car with him
and we drove to the farmhouse so he would know exactly
where it was. He also told me that he and Phil had decided
that it would be best for Phil and Ginger to stay in Nashville
but that they would be readily available if they were needed.
(It wasn't until later that night after my naturalization that
I learned there was a colossal misunderstanding and that
Phil and Ginger had never been called. Instead, they had
been waiting all day at home fearing something had happened but reluctant to call my home or anyone else for fear
of causing undue alarm.)

Since my induction was scheduled for six-thirty and was to be followed by the regular business meeting, Sherborne was to drive by the farmhouse at ten-thirty if he hadn't heard from me before then. If he saw any cars or signs of activity, he was to check back every thirty minutes. Although I didn't really feel it was necessary, I did feel reassured just knowing I had a friend nearby regularly checking on the progress of my second-most-important day with the Klan.

I also felt more comfortable than I had when Black lowered the lights and administered my first oath. These folks knew I was a convert from Black's rival group, and this knowledge gave me a certain amount of credibility that I didn't have when I joined Black's Knights. By this point I could talk their language. I was able to use the word "nigger" frequently in casual conversation, I laughed at their "nigger" jokes, and I freely cussed—and discussed—the "niggers" and the "white nigger liberals" that were preventing the country, as the Klan envisioned it should be, from getting back on course.

I kept telling myself these things over and over, but I knew the real test was still to come. I actually had to do it. This felt like my first solo landing. My instructor was on the ground watching, but he really couldn't help. I had to do it and I had to do it right. Tonight wouldn't really be any different. Sherborne would be no farther away than that flight instructor. And he would be just as helpless.

Finally, it was time. When I arrived at the farmhouse, there was a pickup truck backing up to the front porch. Two men were getting out when I parked and started walking toward the house. One was well-muscled and square-shouldered and dressed like a television cowboy, from his well-shined Western boots to his cowboy hat with a peacock feather in the band. He also, I quickly noticed, had a shooting iron—a large-caliber revolver in a holster that he carried in his hand. In his other hand he carried a briefcase, which seemed a little out of character for a cowboy or a

Klansman. The other fellow was slight of build. Both of
them had red hair, both were friendly, both had briefcases,
and both had guns.

I introduced myself. Both had strong, firm handshakes.
The cowboy was Gerald Briscoe and the other fellow was
Red Willingham, an independent trucker.

"Glad you could make it, J.W.," Briscoe said as he shook
my hand. "We've got three or four more that are coming in
tonight. They oughta be here in a minute or two. You know,
I've set through this ceremony several times, but I've never
conducted it before, so you all will have to bear with
me."

"I'm sure that won't be a problem," I said. "Terry told me
you were an all-around man, could do anything that needed
to be done."

"I'm glad he's got that much confidence. I can't even get
the door open," he said, fumbling with a large padlock on
the front door of the old house, which was made from wood
that had never felt the closeness of a coat of paint.

As Briscoe fumbled with the lock, I talked with Willingham. Then Briscoe asked us to try our luck. It was immediately obvious that the key he was using would never fit the
lock.

"Terry just left me the wrong key," Briscoe said. "I'll bet
he has the right key with him over in Mississippi. We may
have to call the whole thing off if we can't get in."

Oh, hell, I thought, they're going to put me off. I could
feel all my earlier anxieties creeping back with all the
subtlety of a stampede of wild horses. By this time, several
other members had arrived, and with them came more
guns—more guns than I had ever seen at any function of
Black's Knights.

"Doesn't anyone else have a key?" I asked.

"Mr. Logan sold this place to his daughter," Willingham
said. "She might have a key. I'll walk down there and
see."

The daughter apparently lived beside the cabinet shop

down on the highway. Within minutes, Willingham, accompanied by the daughter, her husband, and Jim Logan, her father, were coming across the pasture in the direction of the house. Logan had a key that fit. I hoped the great sense of relief I felt inwardly wasn't obvious on the surface.

Inside, the spooky appearance of the outside was amplified. The windows had been boarded up, chairs were placed in rows, along with several recycled church pews, and a single naked light bulb swayed at the end of an electrical cord in the center of the room. In the front room, before what was once the front window, now securely boarded up, sat a bare table and the fiery cross adorned with thirteen red candle glasses. Behind the table and cross, hanging on the wall, were the Klan flag and the American flag.

Many of the regular members elected to stay outside and talk during the naturalization ceremony. Briscoe and Willingham placed their briefcases on the table, opened them up, and took out their robes. Logan, who served as Chaplain, had already donned his. Briscoe, the elected Nighthawk (security guard) of the Klavern, assumed the role of the Exalted Cyclops for the ceremony and Willingham read the part of the Klaliff (vice-president). Harliss Self, wearing a pistol in a shoulder holster, served as the Nighthawk.

Only one other recruit, a fireman, showed up for the ceremony. The other two recruits, I learned at the next meeting, had been unable to find the farmhouse. They apparently lost interest, however, since they never appeared at subsequent meetings either.

Both Briscoe and Willingham seemed as nervous as I did as they read their respective parts from the official Klan handbook.

NIGHTHAWK: "Your Excellency, your faithful Nighthawk has important documents and information from the alien world."

EXALTED CYCLOPS: "Faithful Nighthawk, you may now speak and impart to us the important information in your possession."

NIGHTHAWK: "Your Excellency, pursuant to my duty in seeking laudable adventure in the alien world, I found these men [saying our names], having read the honest introduction to our Klan, and prompted by unselfish motives, desire a nobler life. In consequence, they have made the honorable decision to forsake the world of selfishness and racial alienation and emigrate to the racial community known as the Invisible Empire, and become loyal citizens of the same."

EXALTED CYCLOPS: "Klansmen, you have heard the publication of the petition for citizenship in the Invisible Empire. Does any Klansman, on his oath of allegiance, know of any just reason why these aliens should be denied citizenship in the Invisible Empire?"

The wait for someone to speak up seemed like an eternity. I was thoroughly terrified at the thought that someone might speak up with something like, "Yep, one of 'em is a damn newspaperman." I was just as thoroughly relieved when Willingham continued with the Nighthawk's response in the absence of an objection to our joining.

"I am officially instructed to inform you that you are about to take a vow of blood and honor."

Just as before, the part about my blood made me feel uneasy and there was certainly nothing about the ceremony that made me feel honorable.

Except for the sixth section of the oath, it was almost identical, word for word, to the oath I had taken five months earlier in the eerie flicker of the single candle in Don Black's apartment. In this oath, the Invisible Empire had substituted the section headed "Honor" in Black's oath with a section headed "Power."

It read:

> I swear that I will work diligently in the campaign of any candidate for public office who has been officially endorsed by the Invisible Empire Knights of the Ku Klux Klan, and that I will cast my vote for that candidate.

I swear that if I am called upon to do exceptional and difficult work during a campaign, that I will answer that call with energy and faith, and that I will make the utmost effort to fulfill my mission.

I have always suspected that David Duke, knowing his political aspirations, had this section in his original oath and changed it to the section of "Honor" only after Wilkinson absconded with the papers and documents when the two split in 1975.

Nevertheless, the lengthy ceremony that for the second time I considered ridiculous—the same ceremony the Klan considers sacred—was finally over. Twice I had been rescued from the "alien" world of "selfishness and racial alienation" and now held dual "citizenship" in two rival Klan organizations.

Hence, another charade was added to the one I was already living. I couldn't help but wonder how long I could keep my membership in the "other" Klan a secret from whichever group I happened to be participating with at the time.

At the conclusion of the ceremony, Jim Logan instructed us on the ways of the Klavern, mainly the meeting dates, and we were greeted by the other members with the secret handshake of the Klan.

Briscoe then instructed Self to summon the members who had stayed outside. The regular meeting was called to order and Logan, reading from the handbook, offered this prayer:

"Our God, we as Klansmen acknowledge our dependence on you and your loving kindness toward us. May our gratitude be full and constant and inspire us to walk in thy ways. Let us never forget that each Klansman, by his conduct and spirit, determines his own destiny, good or bad. May he forsake the bad and strive for the good.

"Keep us in the powerful bonds of fraternal union, of

clannish fidelity toward one another and of a devout loyalty
to this, our great Klan movement. Let us always remember
that the crowning glory of a Klansman is to serve his race,
his community, his nation, and his own high principles. God
save our race, help us to be free people, master of our own
destiny. Amen."

The only "business" of the regular meeting was Briscoe's
admonishing us all not to talk with anyone, even among
ourselves, about the Special Forces training camp.

"This camp thing is a real hot potato," he said. "Terry
asked me to tell you not to say a word about it to anybody. If
you don't know anything about it, that's good. If you do,
don't talk about it with anyone. If the law starts asking questions, we're all better off the less we know."

The regular meeting took far less time than the naturalization ceremony, which suited me fine. Reading again from
the handbook, Briscoe began the closing ceremony:

EXALTED CYCLOPS: "Fellow Klansmen, the sacred purpose
of this gathering of the Klavern at this time has been fulfilled; the deliberations of this klonclave have been ended.
Klaliff, what is the fourfold duty of a Klansman?"

KLALIFF: "To worship God, be patriotic toward our race
and nation, be devoted to our Klan and its leaders, and to
practice Klannishness toward our fellow Klansmen."

EXALTED CYCLOPS: "Faithful Nighthawk, what does a
Klansman value more than life?"

NIGHTHAWK: "Honor to a Klansman is more than life."

ALL MEMBERS: "The truth has been spoken."

Logan then gave the benediction and Briscoe signaled the
official end of the meeting with two raps of the gavel.

Despite the overwhelming urge to make a dash for my
truck and speed away from these people and back to sanity, I
mingled with the other members around the front door after
filing out of the old house.

One of the older members got everyone's attention when
he announced: "Oh, by the way. I meant to bring this up
during the meeting, but I forgot about it. There was an old,

yellow Camaro, with the back end raised up and four niggers in it, seen in town two or three nights last week. Y'all be on the lookout for it."

"Got a license number?" one member asked.

"Naw, but it's Alabama tags and the driver is supposed to have a big, fuzzy Afro hairdo."

"We'll be looking for it," another member answered.

"Yeah," said another.

No one bothered to suggest what to do if the car and its occupants were located. I lived constantly with the threat of discovery. I wondered if those four black people in a yellow Camaro knew they should have the same fear. I have often wondered if the car was ever located and, if so, what happened to the people in it. Just thinking of the possible consequences still sends chills up my spine.

I called Sherborne and Phil and Ginger to report that the naturalization was over and I was fine. Of the four of us, I don't know who experienced the most relief. Collectively, our relief couldn't match Linda's. I had called her first.

"Thank God," she said when I told her that everything went off without a hitch. "I can actually feel the knot in my stomach starting to loosen up a little. It started to tighten up this afternoon when Todd asked me to remind you when you called that you had lost a dollar on the Alabama-Kentucky game. Then it got rock hard when I thought of the possibility of having to tell him you had lost a lot more than that. I won't have to go through that now—at least not today. Oh, Jerry, we all love you, we miss you, and we need you. Please be careful coming home."

"I will, darling. I will."

FOR THE NEXT two weeks, I spent my days in Birmingham at the cabinet shop (we were still waiting for tools for the new factory) and my nights in Cullman contacting my Klan associates. For the first time in more than a year, I really felt I was making progress on the assignment.

The only real way I had of measuring progress was by the number of legitimate contacts I had with Klansmen and Klan leaders. By "legitimate," I mean contacts that didn't make it appear I was being too eager to participate in Klan functions. I could also gauge progress by personal participation in the various activities, and now that I was a member of two different groups, it seemed one or the other was planning or doing something almost every week.

I was still in almost daily contact with Black, but his most pressing plans concerned the organization of a national leadership conference he planned for late November in Birmingham.

I was also checking regularly with Terry Tucker, and each conversation served to further highlight the stark con-

trast between the two groups. Tucker was always making
plans to demonstrate and to hold money-raising events; during this particular period, his most pressing concern was to
secure a place for the next meeting to avoid even the slightest interruption in the regular meeting schedule.

Our next meeting would be held in the basement of Mel's
Fashions, a clothing store on Cullman's main street. "You
can park in the City Parking Lot and just walk across the
alley," Tucker told me.

Although I had talked to him frequently on the telephone,
I had never met Tucker. I learned later that he and the
group of Special Forces troops he had taken to Mississippi on
the night I was naturalized had decided to spend the night
there. That was why they didn't make it back for the meeting.

Tucker was removing some sacks from his truck when I
walked down the alley that night and introduced myself. He
was younger than I thought he would be. He was not a big
man, but it was obvious he was in good physical condition
and full of energy—always seeming to be in a hurry. He
accompanied me to the basement door of the clothing store
and led me back through a narrow aisle between rows and
rows of clothes hanging on rolling racks. An area had been
cleared at the back of the room and several members were
already seated in the small area where we would meet.

I took a seat in the front row next to Red Willingham and
for the first time noticed the walls of the basement, constructed from huge, limestone rocks stuck together with
cement. I imagined that a dungeon in a medieval castle
would have been similarly constructed.

Tucker sat behind the table at the front of the room. The
flags hung on the wall behind the table. A woman, Peggy
Parsons, sat at the other end of the table behind a box of file
cards. Dudley Ham, a young man with a boyish face but a
very manly-looking .45-caliber automatic pistol snuggled in
a shoulder holster, sat in the middle.

Mrs. Parsons was a young, attractive woman in her thir-

ties and the only female member of the Special Forces. She
was the Klavern secretary. Her husband, Tommy, was also a
member of the Special Forces. Ham was the Klaliff of the
Klavern. Gerald Briscoe had resumed his normal duties as
the Klavern Nighthawk and was carefully watching the
door—with a large revolver strapped to his hip. Several other members had entered with a variety of weapons either in
their pockets or brazenly strapped on their sides. A military
type of semiautomatic rifle was leaning against the rock
wall near Tucker's seat, and a large revolver in a holster lay
on the table in front of him. The muzzle of the gun was
pointed right at my ear; the barrel looked as big as a stove-
pipe. Willingham, apparently noticing me eyeing the gun on
the table, got up and turned it in another direction.

Tucker, after calling the meeting to order, thanked the
store owner, "Jim," for allowing us to use the building.
Apparently Jim was well known to the others there, but I
never learned his last name.

"I'm glad to do it," Jim said. "I just want to warn you
about one thing: The cops come down the alley regularly
and shine their lights in here, so if you see a light just stay
cool and I'll take care of everything."

This statement might have calmed most of the others, but
it did nothing but make me more nervous. I could imagine
seeing some rookie policeman mistaking our presence for a
burglary in progress and maybe in his excitement ringing off
a shot. I could just see me scrambling under the racks of
clothes as a gun battle raged with bullets ricocheting off the
rock walls. What made this vision even more frightening
was that I knew which side had the most firepower.

Tucker reported on the trip the Special Forces had made
to Mississippi. "Boy, we sure got the attention," he said.
"This thing is still hot. News people are still calling me from
all over the country wanting to come to the camp. We might
invite some more out when it dies down a little, but we still
don't need to talk about it. We ain't never done anything
that got us this much national publicity, and good publicity.

I'll bet there's niggers all over the country still shaking just knowing we've got such a camp."

He then asked for a vote on an application for a new member. He read the name and asked if anyone knew the man. No one did.

"It's just really a transfer," Tucker said. "He's been a member of the Jasper Klavern and has moved up here. I think I know him. I believe he was EC down at Jasper. What do you think? Should we vote on him?"

"Since none of us know him," said one man in the rear of the room, "I think some of us oughta go talk to him and make sure he'd be a good member."

"Okay," Tucker said, "why don't you go see him before our next meeting and we'll take a vote then."

I knew my application, probably on the recommendation of Torbert, had been voted on the first time it was brought up. I couldn't help but think of the many ways I could have screwed it up had they sent a delegation to see me before voting.

Before I left that meeting, I paid my monthly dues, $3.00, bought an official handbook, $1.50, and purchased a new, sparkling clean robe that still had the laundry tags stapled to it, $20.00.

I commented on the laundry tags. Tucker explained, "Yeah, we like to start everybody in our Klan off with a clean robe. The lady that makes 'em sends them to the laundry the first time, but you have to keep it clean from now on."

Thinking back on the trouble I had just getting a copy of Black's handbook and the months I spent trying to purchase a robe, then the hood to go with it, I felt this group really had it together.

We agreed to meet again two weeks later, again at Mel's.

The next two weeks went by fast. I puttered around the shop some and spent a few days at home organizing some of the notes and information I had gathered over the months and even took time for a few leisurely walks over the farm, wrapped in the aroma of woodsmoke from nearby tobacco barns and engulfed in a virtual sea of vibrant fall colors. The many months of boredom and repetitious routine were finally giving way to a mounting rush of adrenaline. I felt as though I had already crashed through the secondary and caught sight of the goal line, although it was still in the distance.

I arrived early for my second Klan meeting in the basement of Mel's Fashions. Several other members, including Tucker, Ham, and Briscoe, were milling around the City Parking Lot as I pulled in.

"J.W., we're not going to be able to have a meeting tonight," Tucker told me as I walked toward the group gathered around Tucker's pickup truck.

"Why?" I asked.

"We got information that the cops were going to raid us if we had a meeting here tonight."

"What the hell for?" I asked. "We weren't planning on doing anything against the law, were we?"

"Naw, they couldn't get us for anything against the law," Tucker said, "but they could bring a bunch of news people with them and try to embarrass us, and that wouldn't do anything but hurt this man's business and we don't want that to happen."

"What the hell is this country coming to?" I asked in feigned disgust, "when people can't get together for a perfectly legal meeting without being harassed by the cops. I wonder if they're gonna raid the Church of Christ in the morning."

"You can bet your ass that will never happen," Tucker said, laughing. "We've just got to get us a place to meet outside of town. I think we've just got some young cops trying to get their pictures in the paper. We'll get a meeting place somewhere this week and definitely have a meeting next Saturday night. Hell, we'll meet at my house if we have to. We're gonna have a march down in Birmingham in about two weeks and we need to get everybody together on that. We hear the nigger mayor down there is giving some of the white policemen a bunch of shit and we're going down there and march to show our support for the police. Looks like if we're gonna support any police anywhere, it'll have to be somewhere besides Cullman."

We all agreed with Tucker, then he polled us individually to see if any of us knew of a building the Klan could use for a permanent meeting place. I obviously had no knowledge of a suitable place, but some of the others had suggestions of vacant houses and stores that might be available. One fellow offered the use of his garage, another his basement. Tucker said he would consider them and we would discuss it at our next meeting.

"Listen," Tucker announced to the group, "I'll be in touch with you all sometime this week and let you know where we're going to meet next Saturday. If you see any other members be sure and tell 'em. We need to get everybody together before that march. I'll be in touch."

Several of us stood around and talked for a few minutes in the parking lot before breaking up and going our separate ways. Dudley Ham told me he was a truck driver and offered to accompany me on any trip I might have to make to deliver furniture. He gave me his Klan calling card and asked me to be sure to contact him. He wrote his phone number on the card, and then the unlisted phone number of his parents, explaining that "me and the old lady is having a bunch of trouble, so if I'm not at home, I'll probably be at my folks'."

I never called him.

Tucker called me at home on Wednesday night to inform me that our next meeting would be at the home of Tommy and Peggy Parsons in Hanceville, a small town seven miles south of Cullman on Highway 31.

"Just go to the red light and turn left," Tucker instructed.
"You can't miss it. There's a big vacant lot right beside their
house; you can park there. We want to start at seven."

No small talk, no wasted words of idle chatter, Tucker
was concise, serious and to the point. The conversation was
brief and unlike any of our past conversations. Did he suspect me? Was he inadvertently tipping me off to this suspicion?

I arrived at the Parsons home, a neat, white frame residence, about 6:45 P.M. Several people were already there.

Bill Riccio, the man I had first met when I accompanied a
group of Klansmen to the public meeting in the Birmingham
City Council Chambers months before—the meeting we
purposely interrupted—was holding forth on the front
porch.

Decked out in a green beret, camouflage fatigues, and jungle boots, Riccio fingered his .45-caliber automatic as he
talked—or possibly a better term would be "preached"—to
the group gathered around him.

"When we come to power," he told the Klansmen, "we
will be the most powerful force in this nation." Anger distorted his face, and his chin quivered as he warmed to his
subject: "I can't tolerate—and none of us should tolerate—
anyone who would infiltrate any group and gain the confidence and the friendship of the people in it, then publicly
turn against us."

I was standing just a few feet from Riccio. I had no doubt
he meant what he said.

He warned that anyone who would pose as a sympathizer
to gain entrance into the KKK and then "betray" the Klan
should be dealt with in the harshest way.

I felt Riccio was talking directly to me. I tried hard not to
show how uneasy I felt. I never said a word, but I had a very
serious, attentive look on my face and nodded in agreement
several times.

As Riccio kept spewing forth his bitter hatred and his

death threats, I realized that he was worried about federal
agents, not journalists. Still, I was afraid his threats would
just as easily apply to me. I even wondered if Tucker had
expressed some concern about my sincerity to Riccio; I had
certainly been uneasy since talking with Tucker the Wednesday before.

I listened intently to Riccio and tried to look and act nonchalant. But the sweat trickled between my shoulder blades.
It occurred to me later that I did a lot of sweating in Alabama and very little of it was caused by the weather.

Riccio, Alabama Chaplain for Wilkinson's Invisible Empire, talked to us that night about the conviction a few days
earlier of two former top FBI officials, W. Mark Felt and
Edward S. Miller. The two agents were found guilty of conspiracy to approve illegal break-ins in the search for fugitive
radicals in the early 1970s. Riccio was quick to note that he
despised the radicals whose civil rights were violated by the
FBI but just as quick to point out that his contempt was
more intense for "the feds" who would infiltrate any
group.

"When we come to power," he said, as several of us stood
around nodding our assent, "we must never let ourselves
slide into complacency and let a fed go. If he is a fed, he is
our enemy." Then he said, "We must be prepared to kill the
enemy."

I shuddered in disbelief, first at hearing him say this and
again upon the realization of his seriousness. Of all the
people with whom I came in contact as a Klansman, Bill
Riccio disturbed me the most, even though our encounters
were brief. During those times I was around him, I tried to
stay within earshot because he seemed to be the ultimate
example of a totally committed Klan member: not only men-
acing but also downright frightening.

I never will forget that the words in the manual of the
Invisible Empire give the penalty for violating the secret
oath of the Klan: "Disgrace, dishonor and death."

Riccio never once struck me as even coming close to what a Chaplain should be. At a street rally in Birmingham later on, Riccio offered the prayer and thanked God for creating the white race and asked for heavenly guidance to preserve it. Minutes afterward, he took the same pulpit to tell those gathered how they could help the Klan achieve "racial purity." It was like watching one of those old movies in which a perfectly normal-looking person is transformed into a grisly werewolf. Riccio's face took on a red flush, his voice got louder and higher pitched, his eyes narrowed, and his overall appearance and personality seemed to undergo a drastic change. He repeatedly referred to blacks as "ape niggers."

As Riccio continued his sermon of hatred and intimidation that night in Hanceville, he was interrupted by the arrival of one of the strangest-looking vehicles I had ever seen: a square, boxlike affair resembling an Army tank, constructed from what appeared to be aluminum siding and sounding like a huge lawn mower.

"I'll be damned. It's ole Charlie Schwiegert," said one of the Klansmen, as a tall, lanky man in a huge cowboy hat emerged from his "homemade car."

Schwiegert, grinning broadly, approached our group with a confident, bouncy gait. He shook hands with everyone there, cracked a few jokes, and, within seconds it seemed, shattered the mood of gloom and doom that Riccio had set with his sermon. He was the only Klansman I had met who had an open sense of humor. He didn't seem the least bit fearful that the world was about to crumble down on top of him, nor did he appear to be a dyed-in-the-wool, true Klan believer. He seemed too secure to need the Klan in the way most of the others did.

Riccio attempted to regain his audience. "I'll tell you, men," he said, "we're hot as a firecracker right now. The feds are watching our every move, and it's probably the ATF [Alcohol, Tobacco, and Firearms agents of the U.S. Treasury Department] and not the FBI. Those bastards can come in your house without a warrant and check out every gun you own. And if they find something wrong, you'll be in federal court before you know it."

"Yeah, somebody's been following me," said one of the Klansmen. "Ever time I looked around for the last two weeks, they was always right there."

"Aw hell," Schwiegert said, "y'all ain't gotta worry about them fellers you see. If somebody is spying on you, you won't never see 'em. It's them fellers up in the woods with the bi-noculars that you've got to worry about. When you drive a car like mine, there's always somebody following you. I bet the cops have stopped me two hundred and fifty times just to check out my car. If somebody is really watching you, you'll never know it till some feller walks up on your porch with the papers in his hand."

While Schwiegert was quashing the atmosphere of tension Riccio had established, Terry Tucker arrived. Dressed in his jungle fatigues and carrying a semiautomatic rifle in one hand and his briefcase in the other, Tucker seemed worried and was obviously in a hurry.

"I'm sorry I'm late, men," Tucker said. "Come on in and let's get this thing under way 'cause I've still got to meet a man when we get through."

We all crowded into the Parsons' living room. I took a seat toward the far end of the room. Tucker and Peggy Parsons were seated on the couch, Riccio sat on the floor at the end of the couch and to my right. Others, most of whom I had never seen, sat to my left and behind me.

"Since we're running late," Tucker began, "I'd like to consider this an informal meeting and dispense with the regular rituals. Is that all right, Jerry?"

I froze. He was looking right at me and calling me "Jerry." There were too many people between me and the door to make a run for it. I hadn't moved or said a word. Fortunately, while I was trying desperately to think of something to say or do, a big fellow seated in the corner behind me said, "Sure, that's fine with me, Terry. Any way you want to handle it."

"Oh, by the way, in case some of you don't know him," Tucker said, "this is Jerry Jones, the Giant for this region. We're glad to have you with us, Jerry."

That was the first time in my life I ever had the urge to hug a giant.

As I bathed in a warm glow of relief, Tucker seemed suddenly to be overtaken with nervous tension. His hands shook as he told us, "Some of you already know that some nigger-loving lawyers got together with the niggers up in Decatur and sued us this week for a million dollars apiece. We was up there all day yesterday looking at pictures and it looks like they're gonna be able to identify forty-one of us besides me and Bill. They served the papers on me and Joe [Willingham] this week and there will be others served. It's very important that you contact me or Roger [Handley] the minute you get your papers. Call us at work or any time during the day or night."

I had heard Klan members talk of being arrested, of past Klan violence, and even of shooting people, and it never seemed to bother them. But this lawsuit had their undivided attention—they were visibly shaken. All the Klan members in that room whom I knew had never before shown fear even in circumstances that would make most people quake in their boots. But it was suddenly obvious that they feared a court confrontation. Despite the macho image most of them try to project publicly, they made no attempt to disguise their concern over the lawsuit. Suddenly, they were reacting as humans and not as Klansmen.

I learned later that the Southern Poverty Law Center had filed a $43-million damage suit against Wilkinson, Tucker, and forty-one others on November 4, 1980. The suit stemmed from the shoot-out at Decatur, Alabama, on May 26, 1979. Members of the Invisible Empire, mostly from the Cullman Klavern, and a group of blacks protesting the imprisonment of Tommy Lee Hines—a mentally retarded black man charged with raping three white women—had clashed on the street, with two blacks and two whites suffering gunshot wounds.

"I believe we can win this thing," Tucker told the gathering. "God, I hope we can win it. But we've got to have money and we're going to have to get out and raise it ourselves. It's gonna take time and money to win this thing, and we're gonna try to get just one lawyer to represent us all."

Jones interrupted Tucker's comments with a request from Wilkinson: "Bill wants every Klavern to take up an extra donation each month to establish a national legal defense fund for things like this."

"Well, I'll tell you this," Tucker retorted quickly, "we're just about donated out. We've got to get some money for a defense fund in Cullman before we go worrying about the rest of the country."

We then discussed scheduling a series of turkey shoots to raise money.

"Now, we don't need a bunch of Klansmen down there shootin'," Tucker said. "But we do need you to work. In fact, we don't even have to let anyone know that the Klan is sponsoring the shoot. Meanwhile, you all can start going to the merchants and business people around here and let them know we're in trouble and need some help. Just point out that we've always been there to help them. I'm sure a lot of them will give us a donation. They always have in the past."

Then Tucker asked if there was any other business that should be discussed.

"Yes, they is, Terry," said an older man whom I'd never seen before and haven't seen since. "I don't get to a lot of these meetin's anymore, but I need some help. They's a man—a married man—that keeps calling one of my neighbors, a widder woman. Her husband passed away last spring and this feller's been callin' ever since. I want some of you younger fellers to go see him and see to it he quits calling this lady. He just keeps deviling her and deviling her with them calls."

"Has she called the phone company?" Tucker asked. "They've got the stuff to stop that kind of thing or they will put his butt in jail."

"I'll tell you all something," said Riccio from his seat in the corner. It was the first time he had spoken during the whole meeting. "We had all better keep our noses clean right now. We can't afford to get in any kind of trouble right now. We're being watched too close."

Compared to Riccio's, my own frequent waves of paranoia didn't seem severe at all.

The old man was persistent in his efforts to have the Klan contact the man about the calls until, finally, Peggy Parsons offered a suggestion that seemed to satisfy him. "You just tell the woman to tell him the next time he calls that the Klan knows what he's doing," Mrs. Parsons suggested, "and that if he calls her again a Klan lady will be calling his wife. When I get through telling her what he's been doing, I'll bet he won't think I'm a lady, but I bet he won't call any other woman either."

Several of us had a good laugh at that.

"Now that we've got that settled," Tucker said, "we need everyone we can get to come to our march in Birmingham next Saturday. We're gonna leave Cullman at ten o'clock. We'll meet in the parking lot of Food World. If any of you miss us there, we're gonna assemble in the Woolco Shopping Center in Center Point at noon and you can meet us there. We've got to make a good showing with a lot of people."

Tucker went on to explain that the purpose of the march would be to protest the "nigger" mayor's restrictions on when police could use their weapons. I felt his unstated purpose in going to Birmingham was really to embarrass Don Black, who managed to muster only a few dozen members for some of his biggest marches. However, Tucker put it another way: "I'll tell you this, if we go down there with just a handful, we're going to get our butts kicked."

At this point I was not overly concerned with the Klan getting any butts kicked, but there was one particular butt that did concern me—mine. If I went to Birmingham with the Cullman Klavern of the Invisible Empire, I would almost certainly be recognized by someone in Black's group. That would put an end to my affiliation with Black and his Klan and could even possibly jeopardize my standing with the Invisible Empire, since Tucker, Torbert, and all the others just assumed that I had severed all ties with Black's group when I became a member of theirs. I discussed all this with Seigenthaler, hoping he would decide that it would be too risky for me to go. But, despite my hopes, his decision was exactly what I expected it to be: Go ahead, and if you're recognized make a big break with Black's group, preferably with some of Wilkinson's people witnessing it.

Tucker didn't elaborate on his butt-kicking statement at the time, so I asked him about it in a telephone conversation a few days later. He told me he had "information" that we might be confronted "by those damn Communists down there. I don't think those damn Commies will have more than fifty or sixty members down there," he continued, "so we'll need to have three or four times that many just to let 'em know that we have come to town to march and we're gonna march." I vividly recalled the confrontation between members of the Communist Workers party and members of the Klan and Nazi party in Greensboro.

I called Seigenthaler and alerted him to what Tucker told me. I also told him I would be in Nashville the following day, and he suggested we meet at our lawyer's office and discuss this matter further.

As we talked about the possibilities of a confrontation, Al Knight stressed and restressed that under no circumstances was I to go armed.

"They never have," I told him, "but what can I do if the Klan decides to issue us weapons before we get to Birmingham?"

"You've got to refuse," Knight said. "I don't know how you can do that without raising suspicions, but you've got to do it. Just being there will put you in a certain amount of jeopardy, but being there armed could put you in jail. If you're there with those folks and something happens and you have a gun, you could be charged with conspiracy to murder."

"Okay," I said, "I know I have to refuse to go armed, but how, if they shove a gun at me?"

"Just run like hell," Bill Willis said. "Just saunter off when no one's looking and race like hell to the state line. We'd rather fight extradition than a murder charge."

I have always liked the way Willis has of coming up with a quick, simple solution to complex legal problems. I didn't tell him that day how many times I had carefully planned that mad dash to the state line. I had already computed that my truck would make it from Cullman to Birmingham and back to exit 6—six miles inside Tennessee—on one tank of fuel.

I didn't relish the prospect of a personal involvement in a confrontation such as the one in Greensboro. Nor, for that matter, in any confrontation that might result in violence. I made that clear to Seigenthaler after we left the lawyer's office—clear that I felt uneasy participating in this particular march. I could tell he wasn't too comfortable about my going either.

When I got back to Cullman, I spoke to Seigenthaler again. He told me he too was apprehensive about my safety, as well as the safety of others. Therefore, he had already alerted the Justice Department in Washington in an effort to head off any violence that might occur at the march. He didn't tell me so, but I suspected that he also told them he would keep in close touch with me to provide them with a running update of any additional information I might come across. He also told me that, as part of the deal he made with Channel 5 in Nashville in return for their protecting my identity, the station would be sending a news crew to film my participation in the march. Our photographer, Jimmy Ellis, would also be there.

I ended that conversation with a promise—which I kept—to call him before leaving to meet my Klan buddies for the trip to Birmingham and again as soon as I could after the march was over.

I was at the Food World parking lot by nine-thirty the next morning, with the first call to Seigenthaler behind me.

"Be careful," he told me. "I think you'll find adequate security protection when you get to Birmingham."

Terry Tucker, a young man named "Jack," and a red-haired fellow named "Roger" from Huntsville (I believe he told me) were there when I arrived. Dudley Ham and several others arrived a few minutes later. After waiting until we were sure no others were coming, we left Cullman in a convoy of six pickup trucks heading for Birmingham.

Ham took the lead because he had a police radar detector mounted on the dash of his truck, the others fell in, and I brought up the rear. We all had CB radios and Ham suggested we all tune to Channel 14 to avoid interfering with the truckers on Interstate 65.

I had filled my tank right up to the top just before leaving Cullman, just in case I had to take Willis's advice and "run like hell" toward Tennessee.

We were zipping along much in excess of the speed limit and nearing the northern edge of Birmingham when I noticed a large cloud of steam billowing up from under the hood of my truck. The temperature gauge indicated the engine was far past the boiling point. I picked up my CB microphone and called Tucker, telling him that I had apparently ruptured a hose and would be forced to stop and have it repaired. I said I'd meet them later at the Woolco Shopping Center where the march would begin.

"We'll pull over at this package store just ahead and help you get it fixed," Ham replied.

I couldn't really refuse.

"I know this fellow there," he said, after we had all pulled in to the package store parking lot and I had raised the hood—to be greeted by a wall of steam. "It's too hot to work on now. Why don't you leave it here and we'll fix it this afternoon on the way back."

"It's just the heater hose split out at the end," I said after the steam had cleared enough for me to see the problem. "I'll just wait for it to cool down a little and cut it off just past the split and put it back on. I'll be right on over."

"Naw, we can't leave you here with your truck broke down," Ham said. "I'll go in and ask this fellow to watch it for you and you can ride on over with me. We'll get you back right after the march and help you fix it."

I really had no other choice. I got in the truck with Ham and the Jack fellow I had met earlier. I kept thinking to myself, If I couldn't refuse a ride, how in the hell will I refuse a weapon if they offer me one? Once inside the truck, I had no right of refusal. I was literally surrounded by deadly weapons. A large revolver, in a holster, was on the right side of the dash, a .45-caliber Army-type automatic pistol rested on the other side of the dash, and a semiautomatic military rifle with bayonet attached, hung in a gun rack in the back window. After all the admonitions from Willis and Knight just a few days ago against going armed . . . If they could only see me now, I thought.

When we arrived at the shopping center in Center Point, several dozen other Klan members were already milling around. We were greeted also by police who had assembled enough security for several heads of state. Dozens of tactical squad officers rode motorcycles through the area, while plainclothes officers, riding in unmarked cars, roamed the neighborhood. Helicopters whirled overhead and four horse-mounted officers trotted through the parking lot. I felt much better.

A plainclothes sergeant in the tactical squad approached us and told Tucker and Riccio, who were waiting when we arrived, that certain ground rules had to be complied with on this particular day. "Look," he said, "we are going to let you fellows have your protest march and we'll protect you. But we're not going to allow you to go armed. Just tell your people, if they have weapons, to lock them up in your trucks and we'll watch after them for you. We don't want to have to conduct body searches. We'll take your word for it. You still have thirty minutes before the march begins to get them all locked up."

Three large locked toolboxes in the backs of three pickup trucks were filled with a variety of weapons during the next half hour. As additional Klan members arrived, they were directed to one of the trucks to disarm.

The Channel 5 news crew and Jimmy Ellis had arrived and were filming and taking still shots of us getting ready for the march. As I pulled on my robe, I noticed Roger donning a bulletproof vest that he would wear under his fatigue jacket. The weather was unseasonably warm and I knew that vest would be hot, but I secretly wished I had one too—especially if Roger felt it might be needed.

"Here comes the bunch from Nashville," someone shouted as an old green-and-silver bus pulled into the parking lot. There must have been fifty people on that old bus. As they filed off, I stood behind a truck, wondering frantically what I would do if anyone recognized me. After all, my truck was broken down fifteen miles away. I could almost see my heart banging against the underside of my white robe as I carefully studied the face of everyone who got off the bus. Fortunately, I didn't see a familiar one, but I still kept my distance from that group as much as I could. One of the first to get off the bus was a stocky, gray-haired man wearing a small microphone clipped to his necktie and carrying a small camera. He seemed to know many of our group and several seemed to know him.

I noticed that the robe he pulled on was decorated with bright red markings. He was obviously a high officer. Indeed, he was later introduced to me as Stanley King, Grand Titan, in Tennessee—Nashville, Tennessee.

I tried to dodge King's camera but I did not succeed totally. One of the members he had brought with him to Birmingham—a matronly-looking, gray-haired grandmother—was
arrested in Nashville on Memorial Day 1981 in a bizarre
bomb plot. The woman, Gladys Girgenti, had left the Invisible Empire only a few weeks before she was arrested in the
bomb plot and formed her own Klan group. King acted
quickly after her arrest to make it clear that they were no
longer associated. In this regard, he offered *The Tennessean*
the use of a photograph he had taken in Birmingham that
day: It showed me marching alongside Gladys Girgenti.
King offered us the picture in an effort to be helpful to the
newspaper. In return, he hoped the paper would clearly
point out that Mrs. Girgenti and the others were no longer
connected in any way with the Invisible Empire—his Klan.
He wanted no part of this kind of publicity and wanted
everyone to know it.

Once all the guns and knives and billy clubs were locked
securely in the pickup trucks, the wife of one Klansman was
told by her husband to drive one of the trucks to the halfway
point on our parade route and stay in radio contact so that,
in the event of trouble, she could deliver the guns to the
marchers in minutes.

The march proceeded without incident, however. We
were told that it would cover three and a half miles, but it
felt much closer to twice that. As the Klansman marching
beside me—a man from Arab, Alabama—put it when he
leaned over toward me near the end of the march, "Whoever
said this was a three-and-a-half-mile march? I sure would
like to buy land from that feller."

The march terminated in East Lake Park with a public
rally and several speeches. Riccio, in his capacity as State
Chaplain, opened the rally with a prayer. Then Alabama
Grand Dragon Roger Handley led off the speaking by shouting warnings that "a race war is coming. The niggers are
itching for a confrontation and when it comes they are going
to wish that it hadn't."

These people certainly didn't share the restraint of Wilkinson, Duke, and Black, who were always careful not to use the word "nigger" in public.

Riccio, decked out in his fatigues and green beret, the standard uniform of the Special Forces, echoed the racist rhetoric of Handley, only louder and in more alarming tones. "I'm telling you white people, we have got to be prepared when the ape niggers think they have enough power to challenge us on the streets of Birmingham. We're going to meet that challenge, and we're going to turn it back, and we're going to take our country back from the ape niggers. The government has given them everything they want, and we're going to take it back. Get yourself in shape, go to the library and get books on guerrilla warfare and study them and learn how to survive. Get at least two thousand rounds of ammunition for every gun you own and make sure everyone in your family knows how to use them. Lay in some food. We'll be ready, and the white niggers who support the ape niggers won't be. They will just have to go down with them."

I had never heard this kind of talk sounded in Black's organization. These rantings scared me, and Wilkinson's people hoped it would have that effect on anyone else within earshot—they hoped it would scare people into their ranks for promised security and survival.

While several of the marchers began to drift off from the rally—they had obviously heard this kind of ranting and raving before—the police officers stayed. The rally crowd was constantly surrounded by the security officers. A line of communication seemed always open between the Klan and the police. Whenever we had a march, demonstration, rally, or some other event, someone had always discussed it with police and learned the ground rules. This was the only event that I participated in, however, in which the police demanded that all the Klan members go unarmed. I never discovered who initiated the communication between the Klan and the police, but at the functions I attended, I always found the police cooperative and friendly to us.

During the march, as we passed a small tavern on Birmingham's east side, I noticed Don Black's security officer, Ben Walker, standing outside on the sidewalk watching us file by. Since there were approximately 150 of us, not the hoped-for turnout, but more than Black had ever been able to assemble, dressed in white robes, I'm sure we all looked alike to him. I was confident he didn't recognize me.

However, as I left the rally and walked across the park to a lot where several trucks had been waiting to return us to the shopping center, I noticed Dennis Thomas, another member of Black's security force, mingling with the members of our group who had participated in the march. He seemed to know many of those among our group and was going from truck to truck talking with them. Every time he would start in one direction, I would go in another. He would recognize me for certain if we ever came face-to-face. I thought he noticed me several times, but I would always quickly look away or busy myself with the literature that was distributed at the rally. Still, I wasn't sure he hadn't seen me. And I worried that he had until my next conversation with Black, who made no mention of it.

The following week, I was one of seven Klan members who accompanied Black to picket a Birmingham television station that was showing a Klan documentary. Thomas was also in that group. The march and rally by the Wilkinson organization were not mentioned.

Black was openly disappointed with the turnout for the television-station protest but decided to go on with it anyway. As we gathered in the street outside the station, someone apparently notified the police. A few minutes later an unmarked car pulled up and a uniformed tactical sergeant got out.

"How are you doing, Don?" the sergeant asked Black.

"I'm fine, Jim," Black responded. "How are you?"

"What are you folks planning to do here tonight? If

you've got a lot more people coming, I need to get some more officers over here, maybe a couple of motor scouts too."

"We're just planning to picket during the broadcast," Black said, "and this is probably all the people we'll have."

"In that case, I'll just stick around until you all finish."

What a contrast with my last Klan function in Birmingham, just the weekend before. When I marched with the Invisible Empire, we were surrounded by dozens of police officers. Tonight, in my role as a member of the Knights of the KKK, our security would be provided by a lone police sergeant in an unmarked car.

Within minutes after the police sergeant arrived, the station's news director, Wendell Harris, walked down to the street where we had gathered. He and Black greeted each other by first names. I was already decked out in my robe, holding a placard: JEWSMEDIA TELLING ONE SIDED STORY.

"What's the problem, Don?" Harris asked.

"We think this documentary you're showing is distorted and incorrect," Black said. "It depicts the Klan as a bunch of lawless hoods, and that is far from the truth. I would think your station would want to present an accurate account to your viewers."

"Well, this series we're running was not done locally," Harris said. "It's a package deal we purchased."

"That may be true," Black said, "but you, as a news director, have a responsibility to make sure it's accurate, and if it's not you could certainly refuse to show it. You know I've been here six years and our group has never been arrested or accused of violating the law."

"I know that, Don, and I will certainly see that you have a chance to voice your objections. I'll send a camera crew right down here. Incidentally, the piece we're showing tonight is sort of a historical piece on the origin of your robes and some of your symbols and markings."

"I hope you all didn't really find out what those black

stripes on our sleeves mean," Black said smiling. "There's really one for every nigger we've killed."

Black seemed pleased that a camera crew would be coming down and Harris seemed pleased that Black was pleased.

A photographer from the *Birmingham News* also showed up and began snapping pictures. I purposely avoided his camera, knowing that if my picture appeared in the Birmingham paper, I would surely be recognized by some member of the Wilkinson group and my charade would be over. As soon as the cameras were gone, we left too. Black, I'm sure, rushed home to watch himself on television.

I called David and we had a beer.

I HAD TOLD Tucker I would help with the turkey shoot scheduled for the following Saturday morning. It was raining when I got up and I greeted the rain with mixed feelings. On the one hand, I didn't want to work at the turkey shoot to begin with and I certainly didn't want to work at a turkey shoot in a cold, steady rain. On the other hand, Tucker might call it off altogether because of the rain and I would miss out on a useful occasion.

I called Tucker at home. "What's this weather going to do to our turkey shoot?" I asked.

"We just can't have it," he said.

Music to my ears, despite what I might be missing. I wanted to shout out in gleeful relief.

"It's just too dang messy and muddy. It looks like it's gonna rain all day too. We'll just try again next Saturday. Boy, we've got to do something to raise some money. It's gettin' serious."

"Well, I'll be ready again next Saturday," I told him. "Right now, I think I'm gonna go get some beer and lay back and watch the football game this afternoon. Too messy to do anything else."

"That sounds like a good idea to me, J.W. I'll see you next Saturday."

I failed to tell him that I planned to do my laying back on my couch in Tennessee to watch the game. I had already checked with Black and he had nothing scheduled. I headed home. What a beautiful rainy day. I welcomed that rain more than the cotton farmers in the Tennessee Valley in north Alabama.

I talked with Seigenthaler on Sunday and we decided that I should go to the lawyers' office on Monday morning and begin writing the first story. He had already made arrangements to set me up in a vacant office. We had tentatively decided to start the series on the Sunday after Thanksgiving, but since I still planned to participate with the Klan right up until the first story ran, we thought it best for me to continue to stay away from the office. We felt it was necessary to maintain the secrecy that had become commonplace in both our lives for more than a year.

This decision made me happy because I could spend my nights at home. And it made Linda happy because it signaled an eventual end to this assignment. It wouldn't last the rest of our lives, as she had begun to think.

After about three days of struggling behind the typewriter, I discovered, much to my dismay, that I felt more confident building cabinets. I told Seigenthaler that I might have to consider trying to get my old job back in the cabinet shop. He said he would come to the lawyers' office every day to look over what I'd written and offer suggestions. And he always left me with words of encouragement, usually something like, "Keep putting it on paper, pal. It might start making sense."

But only the recollections persisted. Vignettes kept flooding back at me.

There was that day in Birmingham, a bright sunny afternoon, when suddenly, in the midst of dozens of robed and hooded Klan members, I spotted a petite girl, about ten, I thought. Her beautiful young face, framed in the white hood, reminded me of our Tanya. Her left arm was in a cast, bent at the elbow. Her eyes looked straight ahead, expressionless. There was no way I could read her thoughts. The other Klan members kept saying how cute she was. I wanted to cry.

I had felt the same way at other times when I saw young boys and girls, their faces illuminated by the flickering flames of burning crosses, laughing and playing in vacant lots while their parents turned their attention to serious hatred.

At a rally in Collinwood, Tennessee, I saw a young mother with her toddler, who was dressed in a tiny tee shirt proclaiming WHITE POWER and a small Klan hood. For a while the baby attracted more attention than the featured speakers, as Klansladies and Klansmen alike posed for photographs holding the baby.

The Klan always plans marches for maximum visibility, and there would invariably be black people watching as we walked by bellowing, "White power!" and, "Wake up, white people, wake up!" Once I happened to glance to my right and locked eyes with a wrinkled old black woman seated on a bench. I knew that she hated me. Worse, her look of contempt made it clear that she pitied me. I wanted, just for a fleeting instant, to rush over, smile at her, and say, "I'm not really part of all this."

Sequestered in that small, windowless office, I found myself more than once reliving some of these experiences: wondering if the cute little girl's arm healed, if the old wrinkled black woman still pities me. Those memories still linger.

Fortunately, after about a week of reliving all this—the two naturalization ceremonies, the marches, the rallies, the rhetoric, the venomous hatred being taught Klan children, and various other aspects of the past year—suddenly the whole assignment began to make more sense than before.

Meanwhile, the Nashville Klan organization was thrust into the limelight in a flap with the state and local officials over the Klan's plans to hold a national convention in Nashville.

Sherborne was on top of the local activities and was writing stories almost daily on the ongoing controversy. He learned that the Klan had rented the National Guard Armory for the convention and the state's adjutant general had already accepted fifty dollars as a deposit on the facility. Once this was made public, a howl of protest rose from the Nashville community, both black and white. Governor Lamar Alexander issued a strong statement which, in effect, took up the Klan's welcome mat to Tennessee. The adjutant general reviewed the rental agreement for the use of the armory and revoked the lease and returned the deposit. He did this on the grounds that the woman who had initially applied for the use of the building had misrepresented its intended use. She told state officials that the building would be used for a large family reunion. What she failed to tell them was that the only family ties commonly shared by those attending was the Ku Klux Klan.

Tex Moore, the Invisible Empire's Grand Dragon for Tennessee, announced that the Klan would bring a civil suit against the state because it was deprived of the use of the public building, and he vowed that the Klan would continue with plans for a KKK national convention in Nashville on the weekend of December 6 and 7. And, he said, since the Klan was expecting people from all over the United States that weekend, they planned to march in Nashville's Christmas parade on the seventh.

The Nashville Gas Company, sponsor of the parade, said the Klan had not been invited to participate in the parade and would not be welcome. Nashville Mayor Richard Fulton issued a strong statement against the Klan's planned visit to his city and pledged that he would mobilize the entire police force, if necessary, to prevent its participation in the Christmas parade.

All this did not dampen the Klan's determination. Moore said the Klan would defy local officials, the parade sponsor, and the police, if necessary, to march in the parade. The battle lines were drawn and the controversy continued.

Meanwhile, I would go to my little room in the lawyers' office each morning and try to make sense out of what I was writing. Each night I would phone my Klan contacts in Alabama.

While opposition to the Klan was mounting in Nashville, I learned that support for the Nashville Klan was growing within the ranks of the Klan in Alabama. Terry Tucker told me, "Looks like we might be going up to Nashville on the seventh to march in the Christmas parade."

"That's great," I said. "When did they invite us to come up there?"

"Well, they didn't exactly invite us," Tucker said. "In fact, the mayor and the police say they ain't gonna let us march, but Tex Moore, the Grand Dragon up in Tennessee, says it's a public parade and the local Klavern is going to march in it. We're just going up to help them out. They are in a big fuss over it up there now, but Bill says that if it is a public parade we've got just as much right as anybody to be there. I think he's even gonna be there himself."

"You mean Mr. Wilkinson is going to march with us?"

"I think he is. He's gonna be in Cullman for our meeting on the sixth and he'll probably go up to Nashville with us the next morning. By the way, our meeting on the sixth is the one where we elect officers for next year. Try to be there if you can and tell everyone else you see."

"I'll try to be there," I told him.

"You say you're over in Georgia?" I had told him I was calling on some furniture dealers in Georgia when I called long-distance.

"Yeah."

"Can you get a hundred and one proof Wild Turkey over there, or do you know? We can't get nothing but eighty-six proof down here."

"I'm sure I can. I'll be going to Atlanta before I come home and I'm sure I can get it there." I could get it down the street, here in Nashville.

"Boy, if you can I would sure appreciate it if you would pick me up a bottle of that hundred and one and I'll pay you for it."

"I'll be glad to," I assured him.

I told Seigenthaler about my conversation with Tucker.

"How do you feel about going back for that December sixth meeting?" he asked me.

"Like I have felt about going to all meetings. I've never looked forward to going to any Klan meeting."

"What I was thinking," he said with a slight hint of a smile, "is that it would give you a chance to meet Wilkinson and we could have the first stories in the can. We could start the series on the seventh. I think it would be a great way for us to 'welcome' the Klan to Nashville."

I had to admit that the "welcome" part of that suggestion appealed to me. It was the thought of going back to another meeting that didn't. For one thing, there was certain to be another confrontation with Linda. I had thought, and had led her to believe, that I wouldn't be going back, that the newspaper series would start on the Sunday before the seventh, which would preclude my attending that December meeting. But one more trip, this particular trip, would surely provide me with additional insights into the Klan. It would, I hoped, allow me a face-to-face meeting with the man I considered the most effective Klan leader in the nation—Bill Wilkinson. It would give me some insight into the democracy of the Klan election process; it would let me know who the new officers were. It would also allow me another week to work on the stories that I was having such a hard time with. At the same time, it felt very much like risking one more roll of the dice before dragging your money off the table.

"Sure," I said, "I think that will be a terrific way to wind this thing up."

"Well, don't forget to take the whiskey," Seigenthaler said. "That could really get you in trouble."

On Wednesday before the Friday I was to leave, I was having a particularly hard time with a lead. I had written it and rewritten it a number of times and it still didn't convey what I wanted it to. I called Seigenthaler to solicit his help.

"I'm a little tied up right now," he said. "I've got some people coming in and I can't leave. How would you feel about coming to the office?"

"I've been waiting for almost a year and a half to come back to the office," I said. "I'd love to."

"That's fine, then. Come on down. I wouldn't say anything about what you're working on, however, since you still have a trip to make. I'm sure there're a lot of people who would like to see you. Also, I'd like to send Sherborne and a photographer on down to Alabama today to talk with your landlady and your friends at the cabinet shop and to get some pictures of that doctor's house and Black's apartment. Do you feel comfortable about Sherborne's knowing what you've been doing?"

"Sure. No problem at all." I didn't tell him how long, how many months, I had felt comfortable about Sherborne's knowing what I was doing.

"Okay, call me when you get to the front door and I'll come out and walk in with you. I want to see the reactions too."

I quickly gathered up my papers and cardboard boxes filled with notes and headed to the office. I'll never forget that day. It was good to be home.

I felt like a new baby at his first family reunion. I have never been hugged and kissed as much in one day as I was on that first day back. I got reacquainted with old friends, met some new ones, and got absolutely nothing done on the story.

Almost everyone knew by this time that I had been working on a Klan story, but not once was the Klan mentioned

that day. Some told me they had worried about me, some
said they had prayed for me. One fellow, though, apparently
still believed the cover story. He came up to me in private
and said he had undergone a similar experience while he was
a patient at a mental institution. He assured me that there
was no longer a stigma attached to a hospitalization or treatment of this type. He shook my hand firmly and assured me
he would be available to help if I had any further problems.

The next day I worked on the story again, and on Friday
morning I went to the office to discuss a rough outline for
still another installment before returning home to prepare
for my final trip to Alabama as a member of the Ku Klux
Klan.

I had told Linda that I was going back one more time. She
was visibly upset—so upset that she didn't even want to discuss it. I had tried to explain to her that the final trip was
necessary because of what I hoped to gain, a meeting with
Wilkinson, the election . . . She just gritted her teeth,
obviously trying to stop the quiver in her chin, and walked
off with tears welling up in her eyes. She didn't say a word.
She didn't have to.

But now that I was ready to leave, already later than I
had planned to, it was Linda who said, "I need to talk to you
about what you are doing."

I knew I had to hear her out.

"Jerry, this thing has pushed me to the breaking point
emotionally. I couldn't talk the other night when you told
me you were going back one more time because I couldn't
control myself. I was irrational. I may still be. But we have
been through so much here and you have come back alive so
many times, this is a real crisis point for me. Do you realize
that you are going to be in Alabama when the first story goes
to print? People in the computer room will know what
you're doing, the people in the composing room will know,
the pressroom people will know. The danger has never been
greater than it will be at this point because of all the addi-

tional exposure. You don't have to risk life and limb just to get a final few drops of information that probably won't make any difference anyway."

There was nothing I could say, so I said nothing.

"Why do you have to do this one last thing, since your original objective was to try to become a member of the Klan? You accomplished that not once but twice. It seems to me you have it all. You have the Klan's oath of secrecy, you've seen the danger, you've participated in Klan activities, rituals, and ceremonies. Literally all the things you set out to learn you have achieved many times over. It seems like one last bit of insanity to push your luck to go back down there for one more night. Why?"

"Maybe," I stumbled, trying also to be rational. "But, Linda, you don't understand the crazy bastards that make up the Klan. I haven't accomplished a lot in this life and I may never, but I've got to do all in my power to put an end to the spread of this vicious cancer that is eating away at the world—our world. You don't understand the real hatred, the violence, they are teaching. And, most important, I don't want that little fellow"—directing her attention to Joe, who was sleeping peacefully on the living-room couch—"or that baby you are carrying in your belly, or Todd, Niki, or Tanya, to grow up in a world where that kind of hatred is not only taught but openly encouraged. That's why I have to go back. Do you know what I'm saying?"

By this time, tears were flowing unchecked down our faces.

"I know I love you," she said. Then we held each other tightly in a lingering embrace for several minutes, silently letting our feelings and emotions trickle down our cheeks.

Then I left.

Walking out the door on that cold December night was the hardest thing I did during the whole assignment. On that long, lonely drive, my thoughts were consumed by Linda, the kids, the unborn child, the farm, and just being back home for good, although I was still heavily courting another lady—Lady Luck. She had to remain at my side for at least another twenty-four hours, I thought.

We had been careful to take additional security measures, but I was still uneasy. During the past few days, the building security at the paper had been alerted to be on the lookout for any "visitors" who might show up asking for me. Seigenthaler and I had met with the local sheriff and discussed the upcoming story and our expected response to it. He assured us he would have his patrol cars check more regularly around my house. The sheriff also lent us a small walkie-talkie radio for Linda to keep near her; she could call directly to any car in earshot and it would respond directly.

A full-time armed guard had been hired and had established himself and his dog in a travel trailer near the front of my drive. Large floodlights had been installed around our house, which was now illuminated like a football stadium. The day the lights were installed, I had a sudden start while driving home. I was still more than a mile from home when I noticed the glare of the large lights on the horizon and momentarily thought the house was on fire. Our home telephone had been changed to an unlisted number—a move that no doubt spared us some crank calls and possibly some threatening calls but offered no deterrence at all to young country boys calling our little daughters. In fact, it seemed as if the calls from the young boys suddenly increased. Maybe it was because the line was no longer cluttered up with calls from relatives, news sources, or friends.

While all these things were instituted for the security of me and my family, the initial effect was more discomforting than reassuring.

Linda's tolerance to all the hustle-bustle around the house soon wore thin—a decline that was accelerated, I'm sure, by the anxiety she felt about my going back for "just one more time."

"Do you realize we've lost all control of our lives?" she asked me the day before I left. "We moved to the country for peace and tranquillity, and both have suddenly vanished. I

can't get the baby to sleep because he thinks it's still daylight
outside. Strange people have been running around everywhere putting up lights, putting in a trailer, checking
around the house, and your mother couldn't even call on the
phone because she didn't have our number. I came home and
a strange, snarling dog wanted to keep me out of my own
house. I'm sure all the neighbors are wondering what's
going on too. Will we ever be able to get our lives back to
normal?"

I couldn't answer that. I still can't.

All this raced through my mind as I drove down that lonely stretch of road that had become so familiar to me over the
last sixteen months. It was kind of like the last day of school.
I had become accustomed to this old road and I wanted to
put it behind me quickly—had wanted to for months—but I
would still miss it.

Sherborne and Jimmy Ellis were already in Birmingham
waiting for me. They had reserved a room for me at the
Rodeway near the cabinet shop. Our plans were for me to
instruct them on how to find the doctor's house, Black's
apartment, my landlady, Mrs. Armstrong, and David and
Chris the next morning. While they were getting the pictures and interviews, I would drive back up to Cullman and
pack the remainder of my belongings, so that when I left my
apartment to go to my last meeting, I'd be leaving for the
last time.

It would be a busy day.

But first there was one thing I wanted to do. I arranged to
see David and Chris: I had to be the one to tell them what I
had been up to. I had long felt they both suspected that I was
really doing something other than working at a cabinet
shop—and goodness knows David had reason to wonder—
but neither of them had ever asked me about it.

"Fellas," I just blurted out, "I've really grown very fond
of you both during the past months, and because of that it's
been harder and harder to keep bullshitting you." And I told
them.

They both looked stunned and were silent for a
moment.

"I was closer than you were, David," Chris said finally. "I
said you were writing a book." He laughed.

"Yeah," David said. "I thought you were working for the
government. I've thought that ever since you took me to that
Klan rally in Florida."

Their curiosity, curtailed for so long, produced an endless
stream of questions. I tried to answer them all and then
stressed how important it was for them to keep my secret for
just a few more hours, since I still had this last meeting to
attend.

We were all up early on the morning of December 6. I
called David and he met us for breakfast. Ellis was to get his
pictures and catch a 3:00 P.M. plane back to Nashville with
his film. Sherborne, once he finished with his interviews,
was to drive on to Cullman, meet me, and remain nearby
until I was safely out of the meeting.

Seigenthaler had arranged a plan with Metro sheriff, Fate
Thomas, to get me back to the paper after the meeting and
to get my truck home. Thomas, a personal friend of both of
us, had agreed to come to Cullman with two deputies, at his
own expense, to see me home. One of the deputies was to
drive my truck, the other the sheriff's car in which I would
be riding, and Sherborne was to bring up the rear. We all
thought it would be safer if I didn't drive my truck after this
last meeting, since many of those I would be meeting with
would also be traveling up the same highway at the same
time to assemble in Nashville with the Klan for the protest
and defiance of police to march in the Christmas parade.

Thomas and his deputies, Jerry Burns and Mel Harders,
were waiting in a room at the Holiday Inn in Cullman when
I got up there that afternoon. I made contact with them by
phone and agreed to come by once it got dark to show Harders the location of the Klan meeting place. Sherborne was
waiting in the motel room when I got there. Harders and I

drove in Sherborne's car to Willingham's Salvage Co., better known in Klan circles as Joe's Junkyard. I had never been to a Klan meeting there before and was not familiar with the layout. However, it appeared to Harders and me that the office would be the only suitable place to hold a meeting, and the office was several hundred yards off the main road— Highway 278.

We returned to the motel and made the final plans for getting home. I would return to the motel immediately after the meeting and would call Seigenthaler at the newspaper to tell him that I was safely out and on the way home. He had told me the presses wouldn't start until he received that call, even if it meant holding up publication of the paper. We expected that call to be near the first-edition deadline, since we anticipated a long meeting, believing that a Klan election would take a considerable amount of time.

As the meeting time grew near, there were several last-minute details to attend to. I made one final call to Don Black at his home. His wife, Darlene, answered the telephone and was warm and friendly, as always. She had talked to me earlier about the small turnout for Black's national leadership conference of the Klan held in Birmingham the week before. She told me, "We'll have to concentrate on quality members, not quantity." I don't know whether she considered me quality or quantity, but in just a few hours she could consider me gone, a former member, or whatever.

Black was also cordial and, unlike Darlene, boasted about the results of his national conference, especially the wide variety of people from as far away as "Canada, Texas, and Arkansas." He told me he was still searching for a building in Birmingham to set up a national Klan media relations office. I mentioned a building I knew was vacant and suggested he contact the owner, whose name I furnished. Black said he was definitely interested and asked if I would contact the owner "because he'll probably be more willing to talk with you than with me."

Then there was one more call—to the new preacher of
the small country church that sits at the edge of our farm.
Peter van Eys had recently come to the church and I had
never met him, but I personally knew every member of the
congregation and I knew they must be full of questions and
he could answer many of them at services the next morning.
Seigenthaler had told me right before I left Nashville that he
had been in contact with Tom Brokaw of NBC's *Today*
show in New York, adding, "I think he's going to want you
on the show Monday morning. I would plan on leaving here
Sunday."

It was obvious that the fast pace of the last few weeks
wouldn't slow for at least a few more days.

Knowing that all the neighbors had noticed the floodlights around the house, the armed guard, the trailer, the
police dog, all very much out of character for the small,
quiet community, I asked Peter to tell the church members
that I was all right, and would be home soon. I also asked
him to ask them to be available to help Linda and the family,
should they need it. None of us really knew what to expect
once the story broke. I also didn't really know what to
expect from the neighbors, even though I had known most of
them since childhood.

Since my childhood, the community had always been all
white, with third and fourth generations of families still
farming the same land cleared from wilderness by their
ancestors. The only black people I ever saw inside the small
church were our guests when Linda and I were married
there.

The people in the community are all strong-willed and
staunchly independent. I couldn't help but wonder how they
would react to my being an undercover member of the Ku
Klux Klan, then writing about it. Did any of them have
underlying sympathies for the Klan? I didn't think so, but I
had met members of the Klan who many times reminded me
of some of our neighbors back home—people who just didn't

fit my image of Klansmen. Would the neighbors view me as a maverick or, as they always had in the past, a friend and neighbor? I thought I also knew the answer to that question, yet a slight tinge of doubt remained.

After the call to the preacher, I still had about thirty minutes before I would leave for that last meeting. It was a long half hour and I was becoming more jittery by the minute. I felt the way I used to just before going onstage in a school play. But in that case, the jitters always disappeared as soon as I got onstage. Maybe that would happen tonight, too. I certainly hoped so: after all, I was probably playing the most important role of my life. My acting during the last sixteen months had certainly been acceptable—I was still around for the last act. At least, I wanted this last meeting to be my swan song with the Klan. I would know very soon.

I was more nervous about this particular Klan meeting than any of the others, of course. Within the next three hours, it could be that my fear of being discovered would be ended and I would be safely on my way out of there.

I gave myself about ten minutes for a cushion and left the motel to go to the junkyard. On the walk across the parking lot I took a deep breath. I noticed the stars above: They seemed brighter than usual. And I felt the warmth of an uncommonly warm December night. For that brief moment, all seemed right with the world. Then I remembered where I was going. When I arrived, several Klansmen were milling around in front of the office. Many of them were openly wearing guns. My only concern, aside from the outside chance that a gun would accidentally go off, was whether my luck would hold out for just a little while longer.

I spoke first to Joe Reynolds, a quiet, strictly-business type of Klansman and a member of the Special Forces team, who had frequently been mentioned as a possible candidate for Exalted Cyclops of the Cullman Klavern. I offered my support.

"I will take it," he said of the Klavern's top post, "but I

really don't want it. There's really a lot of people who could
do a better job."

"Like who, for instance?" I asked.

"Like you," he said—what?!—"or Terry again. You all
can talk to people, you're level-headed, and you can get
things done."

For a fleeting instant I thought, What a perfect way to
wind up this assignment. I could resign the post publicly in
the story the next morning. Fortunately, I quickly regained
my rationality. If I had fooled these people so well that they
would even suggest entrusting me with the Klavern's top
position, how much more embarrassed and furious they
would be when the first story appeared. I didn't want to rub
their noses in it and risk the chance of intensifying their fury
to the point of violence.

I said thanks, but argued that I was out of town selling
furniture too often to be an officer.

As it turned out, Reynolds' name was not put in nomina-
tion for the top job. Tucker and William Parker were the
only two nominated. I voted for Tucker, but Parker won.
No count was ever announced, only the winner. Tucker told
Parker, as he congratulated him on his victory, that he had a
big year ahead of him.

Later that night, at the paramilitary camp where Wilkinson was giving a tour for invited newsmen, Tucker and Wilkinson laughed about the election results. Reporter Bob
Dunnavant, one of the newsmen visiting the camp, said
Tucker told Wilkinson his loss was "arranged." Perhaps he
had the vote count arranged as well.

Although Reynolds was not nominated for Exalted
Cyclops, he was nominated for Klaliff, to run against Peggy
Parsons. I voted for Reynolds, but Mrs. Parsons won.

Reynolds was finally elected secretary.

I thought it somewhat strange that in each race Tucker
was not announcing the vote totals, only the winners. Not
once were there more than two candidates in each race, but
I was curious to know how many people voted for each. I

counted forty-two people in the room, but I never heard any number associated with the votes.

As they handed out small pieces of paper on which we were to cast our secret ballots, I accidentally took an extra piece, but I put it to good use. Each time I would write down my vote, I would also write the winner of the previous race on the extra piece of paper and any comments made from the floor. My Klan affiliation was quickly coming to an end. I could feel it, and it felt good. I could also feel myself becoming more confident and courageous—I was actually taking notes.

Inside the meeting room, I had felt comfortable, until a tall, loud fellow I had never seen at a meeting before, and who was obviously drunk, kept acting as if he heard noises outside and repeatedly reached for his pearl-handled automatic pistol, holding it behind his back as he stood directly in front of my chair. Since I was sitting and he was standing, the gun was right at my eye level. I soon decided to shift to another spot in the crowded junkyard office and moved to a table near the door, pushing aside a semiautomatic rifle so I could sit on the tabletop.

The rest of the meeting moved along briskly. Tucker was apparently in a hurry to get back to Wilkinson and the camp. As in the past few meetings, location of a meeting place was a worrisome topic. One Klansman volunteered the use of a former restaurant building, but it needed repairs and electricity. We decided to meet again at the junkyard until the necessary repairs were made to the restaurant building. We also decided to hold future midmonth meetings on Tuesday nights instead of Wednesdays, to allow Klan members the opportunity to attend Wednesday-night church services.

Finally the meeting was over. It had lasted a few minutes over an hour, but to me it seemed much longer.

Tucker rushed to the door, asking me to follow him to the parking lot so he could pick up the bottle of 101-proof Wild Turkey I had brought him. He seemed to be in a hurry. But, then, so was I.

"You'd better let me pay you for this, J.W.," Tucker said.

I vehemently refused his offer, promising, "The next time we get together with a fifth of Wild Turkey, we'll enjoy it together."

"Okay," he said. "I sure do appreciate this."

I have since hoped that he finished the bottle that night. After he learned of the story the next morning, whatever was left of the whiskey would have to taste bitter.

I calmly walked to my truck, suppressing the near overwhelming urge to break into a dead run and speed away.

The sheriff, the deputies, and Sherborne seemed surprised that I returned to the motel so soon after I had left. At the same time, they were relieved . . . but nowhere near as relieved as I was.

I was trembling with relief as I phoned Seigenthaler. "I'm out," I told him. "By God, it's finally over and I'm headed home."

"That's fantastic!" he shouted. "We did it. No, you did it. Be careful on the way home. We'll all be here waiting. This calls for a celebration."

"Since I'm not driving home," I said, "I'm starting now. When I bought Tucker's whiskey yesterday, I also picked up a bottle for ole J.W."

"Go ahead. You probably need a drink. We'll wait thirty minutes to give you time to get out of Cullman and then we're going to release the story to the wire services."

Burns drove my truck and I climbed into the back seat of the sheriff's new Continental with a pint of Old Charter. Harders drove, the sheriff and I talked, and I just kept sipping the whiskey as we closed the distance between Cullman and Nashville.

I hoisted the bottle and took a sip in salute as we crossed the Tennessee state line and I saw the huge WELCOME billboard. This was my homecoming.

Somewhere between the state line and the office, I slept.

It could have been the events of the long, eventful day, the
overwhelming sense of relief, or the sheer physical exhaustion that precipitated my nap, but more likely it was the Old
Charter.

I was wide awake, however, when we pulled up in front
of the office shortly before midnight.

An atmosphere of festive jubilation prevailed in the city
room. Seigenthaler started in our direction holding the
paper up in front of him. Finally, I thought, I can be Jerry
Thompson again. That particular edition was the most
beautiful newspaper I had ever seen. The headline, the big
color picture of me holding a burning torch, and the space
devoted to that story made me feel almost as proud as when I
saw my very first by-line in *The Tennessean* twenty years
before, on a story about a woman wrestler who was arrested
for arson. There had been hundreds of other stories in
between, but at that moment, only those two came to
mind.

I took the paper, looked it over, then turned to Seigenthaler and said, "Haven't seen that fellow's by-line in a long
time. Is he back?"

"He's back, pal," Seigenthaler said, chuckling, "and I
don't know who's more relieved, me or you." He gave me a
hefty slap on the back.

On any normal Saturday night, the city room is almost
deserted at that hour. This was not a normal Saturday night.
It seemed the whole staff was waiting for me. I called Linda
who answered on the first ring. "Darling, I'm home. I've
quit the Klan and I won't—repeat won't—be going
back."

"Oh, Jerry, do you realize I've been waiting for more than
a year for this call?"

"I know you have, because I've been waiting just as long
to make it. I love you and I'll be home soon."

"I love you too and I'll be waiting, so take your time and
be careful. I felt reasonably sure that everything went all

right when I began hearing your story on television and radio more than an hour ago, but it sure is good to hear it from you."

Seigenthaler was holding forth for the deputies, the sheriff, and several staff members in his office.

"Thompson, let me tell you," he said as I walked in, "this may be a better story than we thought. As soon as it went out on the wires, we started getting calls from all over the country and even a couple from Canada. We learned several months ago that the Klan was more than just a Southern phenomenon, but the immediate widespread interest is more than even I expected. I'll tell you, within minutes after the story went out, our switchboard was flooded with calls." Even the *Birmingham News* had called. They wanted my landlady's name.

"Tell me about your last meeting as a Kluxer," Seigenthaler said. "How did it go?"

"A lot better than I expected," I answered. "I got a hint that it would be all right when Joe Reynolds suggested that I might be nominated for Exalted Cyclops. Then I got braver and more confident as the meeting went on. Hell, I even took notes."

"Hey, pal," he said, laughing, "you also took drunk. Hell, I don't blame you a bit. I might be drunk too before this night is over. You did a hell of a job and tonight we're going to celebrate. I've already ordered steaks and drinks for everyone."

And the celebration began.

I had seen the immediate interest in the story within hours of my return from Alabama. But I was not really prepared for the interest to continue and even intensify. The wire services, AP and UPI, which have bureaus in the newspaper's building, both reported that newspapers all over the country were requesting more information. Although the story occupied much of the front page of our paper and sizable column space inside, the wire services necessarily condensed the first and subsequent stories. But their subscribers wanted more.

Seigenthaler called me at home the next morning and asked me to be at the airport early because an ABC-TV crew would be waiting there for an interview before I left for New York to do the *Today* show. At the same time, he told me that a good-sized contingent of Klan members had already arrived in Nashville to prepare to march, as uninvited participants, in the city's Christmas parade. This made me nervous, as did the upcoming television appearances— but in different ways, of course.

That's the way my first day as a former Klansman started. For the next several weeks the pace seemed to accelerate rather than settle down.

The office called me in New York to inform me that Don Black had called a press conference in Tuscumbia that afternoon to denounce my series of articles as a "farce." He also told *Tennessean* reporter Saundra Keyes, who covered the press conference, that the Klan would initiate immediate proceedings to banish me. Those proceedings, he said, would involve convening a Klan jury to try me on banishment charges. I would be invited to appear on my own behalf.

"Under the circumstances, there is not much doubt what they [the jury] will decide," Black told the press conference.

Alternating between calling me a "spy" and claiming that my stories revealed nothing of significance, Black said:

"He found out that I was anti-Semitic, but he didn't have to infiltrate the Klan to find that. He found out our members have guns. Big deal. With spiraling crime rates, riots, and the possibility of armed insurrection, certain citizens being armed is nothing sinister or ominous. The real threat is not from the Klan—it's from black militants and Communist groups."

Black went on to say that he and some Klan members were "a little suspicious" of me because they were unable to check my background fully. This made all that boring preparation seem a lot less boring and a lot more important.

"Aside from that [the background check], if you'd asked me two days ago if he was a spy, I would have said no. I would never even have suspected him of being a reporter, and I congratulate him on that," Black said, adding that my appearance on *Today* that morning was "the first time I ever saw him in a suit."

He also accused my newspaper of trying to "get us," and said the Klan was "making some attempt to limit that kind of thing."

I didn't realize it at the time, but during my stay in the Klan I developed some good confidential news sources who have since provided me with various bits of information. It was through one of these sources that I learned that Wilkinson's group also took immediate, though not public, action to banish me from his Klan.

During the long-drawn-out periods of frustration I experienced trying to get in the Klan, I was relieved to find how quickly I was able to get out.

Although the last story in my series ran on December 15, 1980, the Klan story did not die—Klan members throughout the country kept it alive.

January 9, 1981: The U.S. Immigration and Naturalization Service moved to prevent a group of Canadian Klansmen from entering the country for the purpose of demonstrating at a Nazi-sponsored rally in Buffalo, New York, on January 15, the birthday of Dr. Martin Luther King, Jr. It marked the first time the INS had acted to prevent aliens from demonstrating in the United States.

February 13, 1981: William H. Seward of Memphis was kidnapped from his home and tortured by two men he identified as Klansmen. His hair was cut to the scalp in several places and he was splattered with yellow paint and feathers. An anonymous caller to a Memphis newspaper said Seward was punished because he was a suspected infiltrator and government agent. The caller also told the paper "that Thompson fellow up in Nashville won't always have police protection. He'll pay too." Four days later, Seward was placed under police protection after informers told police a murder contract had been let for his life.

March 21, 1981: Twenty-one people were injured in Meriden, Connecticut, when a Klan rally turned into a bloody confrontation after anti-Klan protesters hurled rocks and bottles into the midst of the robed Klansmen.

April 26, 1981: Imperial Wizard Bill Wilkinson and twenty-one other Klansmen were arrested in Manchester, Tennessee, for parading without a permit. Wilkinson refused to post bond and remained in jail to bring attention to what he termed the denial of his constitutional rights. *The Tennessean* learned in September that Wilkinson had quietly dropped his appeal of the illegal parading conviction, and an additional charge of illegal soliciting (a roadblock attempt, of course), after striking a deal with city officials under which the guilty verdicts would stand. He paid $174.00 in fines and court costs for his conviction and $137.50 in fines and court costs for his followers.

April 27, 1981—the day after Wilkinson's arrest: Don Black, Grand Wizard of the Knights of the Ku Klux Klan—the man who recruited and swore me into the KKK—was arrested with nine companions in Slidell, Louisiana, on the shore of Lake Pontchartrain. The group was preparing to board a boat when federal agents surprised them and confiscated a variety of explosives and automatic weapons. They were charged with trying to overthrow the government of the Commonwealth of Dominica, a tiny island in the Caribbean. Seven of those arrested pleaded guilty to reduced charges in exchange for their testimony against Black, Joe Daniel Hawkins of Jackson, Mississippi, and former Klansman Michael Norris, of Tuscaloosa, Alabama. Those three were tried in June. Black and Hawkins were found guilty and Norris was acquitted. Black immediately appealed his conviction and federal prison sentence. The appeal is pending. During the trial, a Memphis attorney,

J. W. Kirkpatrick, whose name surfaced during testimony as a ten-thousand-dollar contributor to the bizarre scheme, died from a .410-gauge shotgun blast in the mouth. His body was found in his car along with a suicide note. An associate said he apparently chose "death over dishonor."

May 3, 1981: Todd Thompson celebrated his fifteenth birthday by attending the birth of his youngest brother, John Matthew Thompson, whom I delivered. The birth brought our whole family together for one of the few times since the story broke in December. The Klan was the furthest thing from our thoughts that day.

May 4, 1981: *The Tennessean* learned through confidential sources that a splintering disagreement among members of the Invisible Empire's Cullman Klavern, long considered Wilkinson's flagship Klan unit, had led to the virtual dissolution of the group's Special Forces commando group. As many as twenty-five members of the Klavern left the Invisible Empire and formed an independent Klan group with no national affiliation. After the dissolution of the paramilitary group, which was originally set up to protect Wilkinson and to provide security for Klan activities, we found out that the hoopla surrounding the special forces training camp late in 1980 was mostly Klan malarkey. The camp was set up mainly as a promotional gimmick, the sources said, and virtually no training took place there.

May 13, 1981: The U.S. Attorney's office filed a petition in Birmingham to revoke the probation of Bill Riccio, Wilkinson's Alabama Chaplain, who was considered by many law-enforcement officials to be one of the most dangerous members of the Klan. In 1979 he had been found guilty of carrying a sawed-off shotgun and had been given three years probation with the stipulation that he obey all state and federal laws. He was, as a convicted felon, also prohibited from carrying a firearm. However, federal prosecutors obtained photographs of a masked man—believed to be Riccio—holding a rifle at the Special Forces training camp. Also, he allegedly killed a small dog with a bow and arrow the week before, violating Alabama's animal cruelty statute.

May 21, 1981: Riccio was found guilty of violating the provisions of his federal probation and sentenced to ten years in prison. He began his sentence at the federal holding facility in Talladega, Alabama—the same one he arranged to protest in summer 1980 for holding Cuban refugees. At the hearing in this matter, it emerged that Riccio had called the Cullman Klan members together prior to the hearing to warn them they would be assassinated if they testified against him at the hearing. Two members of the Special Forces team identified Riccio as the man behind the ski mask.

May 25, 1981: Two men and a fifty-year-old grandmother were arrested in Nashville by federal agents who thwarted the trio's plans to bomb a synagogue, a Nashville television station's transmission tower, and every Jewish-owned pawnshop in the city. All three were tried in federal court in November 1981 and found guilty of multiple charges. In January 1982, Gladys Girgenti was sentenced to fifteen years in prison.

June 17, 1981: *The Tennessean*, in a copyrighted story, revealed that Wilkinson had issued secret orders to his followers to stop displaying weapons in public. "It shall be our policy from this moment, until further notice, that there shall be no open display of firearms at any public Klan function," he wrote. In the same *Klan Action Bulletin*, Wilkinson disclosed that his Klan was encountering serious financial difficulties that could force him to spend all his time fund-raising. In addition, he said Klan members had been forbidden from challenging local authorities who deny them parade or solicitation permits. "We must raise money fast or we are in trouble," he wrote. "In the past we have marched and passed out literature in open defiance of local officials, knowing that our chances of being arrested were extremely high. In a number of cases, as you know, we have had arrests and as a result it has cost us thousands of dollars in legal

fees. It has been agreed upon by myself and all grand dra-
gons that we must avoid any future confrontations which
might be likely to result in arrests, even if we feel we are
right. Only when we are free of these debts and have a sub-
stantial defense fund in the bank shall we knowingly place
ourselves in jeopardy of going to jail."

August 31, 1981: Wilkinson suffered probably the most
damaging blow to his image as a national Klan leader. We
broke the story on the front page of *The Tennessean* that
Wilkinson became a secret FBI informant in 1974 after
agents assured him his identity would remain confidential. A
Klan source had provided me with confidential federal documents, some marked URGENT, that Wilkinson acted as a
federal informant, both when he was a member of David
Duke's Knights of the Ku Klux Klan and also after he established his own rival Klan faction in 1975. Wilkinson
acknowledged to the newspaper that he had provided information to the FBI on a confidential basis for the past several
years but said he never divulged any information he
wouldn't tell the news media. Nevertheless, the repercus-
sions were quick in coming. It was reported the next day
that some of Wilkinson's top people—Alabama Grand Dragon Roger Handley, one of his most trusted lieutenants, and
Tennessee Grand Dragon Tex Moore—had met with Don
Black to discuss reorganization and unification of the Klan
under one national leader—someone other than Wilkinson.
Black, in acknowledging the unity with rival Klan leaders,
said, "It was understood with Handley and Moore that I
would not be a part of the Klan under Bill Wilkinson's leadership."

The Klan source who volunteered the documents had
never been too friendly toward me before, so I couldn't help
but wonder if his offer of this juicy information was just a
ploy to lure me away from the office. But if he was telling
me the truth, I certainly wanted the information—though I
didn't want to meet him alone. I asked Sherborne to go with
me.

We went to the appointed restaurant, ordered coffee, and within five minutes the man came in, carrying a briefcase. While explaining each document, he spoke in a friendly manner, laughing often, as if he were getting a certain amount of delight out of putting his Imperial Wizard on the spot—or at least providing me with the materials to do it for him.

After he had given me all the documents, he brought out a small plastic device about the size of a pack of cigarettes. "Know what this is?" he asked.

Both Sherborne and I professed our ignorance.

"You fellows drove up in that white pickup outside, didn't you?"

I acknowledged that we had indeed driven to the restaurant in my truck.

"And you were driving a two-tone brown Thunderbird yesterday, weren't you?"

I still don't know how he knew that, but I was driving a friend's car, the one he described, the day before.

"Well, Mr. Thompson," he said with a note of delightful sarcasm, "this little device will detonate the bomb that is attached to your truck just near the gas tank. I can detonate it from more than three blocks away with this thing."

Without missing a beat, I hauled out my practiced don't-show-what-you're-really-thinking ability and said, "Why don't you go on and push the button, then, and just blow up that son of a bitch while you're this close to me?"

Sherborne sat in silent disbelief.

"No," the man said, "it's not armed. I'll go out and get it. You all can watch me take it off."

He walked out to my truck, as Sherborne and I watched from inside, and removed a small white plastic box from the side of the truck near the gas tank. He brought it back to the table and opened it up, revealing several tiny transistors and a maze of colored wires.

"This is a little radio receiver," he explained, pointing to the inside of the box, "and it attaches to metal through this magnet. If you ever see anything like this on any of your cars, don't try to take it off because it'll probably be triggered to blow up if anyone tries to remove it. They usually are."

"Why are you telling me all this?" I asked.

He smiled at me. "I just want you to be careful. I'm not going to do anything to you, and I hope no one else does. But there are people who will if they get the chance. The U.S. Secret Service couldn't keep Kennedy and Reagan from getting shot, so if the Klan wants you, the Klan will get you. Just keep your eyes open."

I assured him I planned to keep them open for many years to come.

I'll have to admit, however, that both Sherborne and I were mighty uneasy as I started to turn the ignition key for the drive back to the paper.

September 4, 1981: We reported that Wilkinson, strapped for funds, as his earlier secret memo had said, had relinquished his private airplane to a Montgomery, Alabama, attorney in lieu of legal fees. Ironically, the aircraft has been used on at least one occasion since then by an attorney and an investigator for the anti-Klan arm of the Southern Poverty Law Center to fly to Muscle Shoals to take a deposition from a top Klan official to be used in a Texas lawsuit against the Klan.

This is only a sampling of the incidents that *The Tennessean* has reported since I left the Klan on that balmy December night in 1980. There have been many more. After my experience, I feel confident that there will be even more examples of the virulent racism espoused by the Klan that gives comfort to the respectable racism of many others. There are decent people who would never wear the sheets and hoods of the Klan but whose attitude toward persons of other colors or creeds is no less hateful. They believe they are respectable because they don't wear the robe and the hood. The lead on my first article after leaving the Klan read: "The Ku Klux Klan today holds a strange, disturbing attraction for frustrated, fearful middle-income men and women—and a dangerous potential for violence and terror." Unfortunately, I've not learned anything about the Klan since then that would compel me to write that lead differently today.

Once that initial story broke, the names of several people I had met during the past year cropped up again.

Several newsmen in Birmingham contacted Mrs. Armstrong, my landlady. She was not too cooperative, saying she wanted to avoid the publicity. She did tell Bob Sherborne that she had "no idea" that I was anything other than a retired Army sergeant and a cabinetmaker. "If I had known he was notorious, I would have had him down for coffee," she said.

And then there were the doctors, Dr. Sanders and Dr. Abernathy. Sanders, contacted in December 1980 by *The Tennessean*, said the meeting at Abernathy's home was supposed to be a community gathering of citizens concerned about lawlessness and Communism—not a Klan meeting. He added that he attends many meetings like the one at Abernathy's, to discuss the "creeping Socialism" which he feels is destroying this country.

Several attempts were made to contact Dr. Abernathy for his comments on the meeting. He was always unavailable when anyone from the newspaper called, but he did grant United Press International an interview in which he contended the meeting was not a Klan meeting "per se."

"I don't even know who is a Klan member," Abernathy told UPI, but added, "I did know Don Black was a Klansman."

Abernathy, who says he is not a member of the Klan, said the meeting I attended was one of about six "informative meetings" he held in his home on a variety of subjects.

"I have held a number of meetings in my home," he said, "including meetings of just about every group you can speak of. There was never a Klan meeting per se. There were meetings in my home that anyone interested in speaking out

about a subject could. They were open and advertised to the
public."

The physician said speakers at his home meetings
included Republican and Democratic congressional candidates and a member of the John Birch Society.

"We once had a Jewish toastmaster speak out on patriotism," Abernathy said. "I believe in individual rights. If
someone wants to join the Klan, let them. I don't know anyone who's planning on joining the Klan."

Abernathy, on the other hand, said he never had any personal interest in joining.

"I don't know of any reason for me to join the Klan, but I
think I ought to know what's going on," he said. "I don't
intend to join the Communist party, but I feel I need to
know what it's about. This country is looking at things in
black and white, instead of right and wrong," he added.
"Whether you are black or white, if you commit a vicious
crime you should be punished. Blacks shouldn't be promoted
to jobs just because of their color. And I don't think this has
anything to do with the Klan."

That twinge of doubt I had earlier about how our neighbors would react to the story was removed once and for all
when I called home from the airport before leaving for New
York on the day the story broke. I wanted to see if Linda had
detected any reaction, one way or another.

"Well, I'm not too confident about the effectiveness of the
armed guard," she began.

"Why?" I asked, sort of bewildered.

"Right after church," she said, "there was a stream of cars
coming down the drive and none of them paid any attention
to the guard. They just waved as they drove by. One after
another, they told me how proud they were of what you did
and how they had prayed for you, even though they didn't
know what you were doing. All of them told me not to worry
and if I needed anything to just call. Forrest Pratt sent word
that we were not to worry about the cow being out, that he
would keep her up with his cows until you get a chance to

fix the fence. They were wonderful, and they all told me to tell you that you don't have to worry because you're home now and they will take care of you. You know, I realized as they left, some with tears in their eyes, that although this is a long way from Iowa, this is really home. You be careful in New York but have a good time. I feel much better."

I felt much better too that Tommy Reasonover, a long-time friend and a hulk of a man who lifts weights regularly, had volunteered to serve as my personal bodyguard whenever I traveled. He was right beside me as we boarded the jet for the Big Apple.

During my assignment, I became aware of the world I shared with millions of others—the world I shared with the Klan. Along with this new awareness came a sadness that I had never experienced before. I recall the sadness I felt each time I saw Klan children at a KKK function. In the flickering firelight of the huge crosses in vacant fields there were always the beautiful, shining faces of small children—boys and girls not yet in their teens: Klan children, being indoctrinated with that racist polemic of white supremacy. I never felt this sadness more profoundly than when I read reports of the testimony of Robert Girgenti, age sixteen, before a grand jury investigating his mother, Gladys Girgenti, the grandmother arrested in the bombing plot in Nashville. After his appearance, he said that he was fully aware of the KKK plot and his only regret was that it was unsuccessful. As for his mother, he said, "She will probably get some time, but she told me not to worry about it. We've had other members in the same situation, but it's a little different, I guess, when it's your own mother."

Each time I marched in robe and hood, the symbolic uniform of deep-seated hatred, I felt a special sadness—and guilt—when my eyes met the gaze of a black person standing along our parade route.

During the last four months of my Klan affiliation I was actually living a triple role—reporter and member of each of two competing Klan groups—which compounded my fears.

When I was with the more violence-prone and more heavily armed Invisible Empire, I was constantly afraid of carelessness that could lead to disaster—a weapon accidentally discharging, an automatic rifle inadvertently knocked off a table and spraying the room with bullets.

And, of course, there was the ever-present fear of being discovered by either Klan members or some news reporter who knew me.

I remember worrying that night I sat in on my first den meeting with members of the Invisible Empire in Cullman, Alabama. Many of the members there routinely flashed and fondled their pistols and automatics. That's when it suddenly dawned on me: These people *are* ready for the race war Wilkinson keeps predicting.

And I worried that day in April when I sat in the Birmingham City Council Chamber with a group of Klan members who sneered, jeered, and applauded as a black Army veteran told how Klan members had shot a rifle through his home at night. Not one of those Klansmen would have wanted his own wife and children to go through such an ordeal, still they clapped their hands in joy as the retired sergeant told the group conducting a hearing on Klan violence that police had ignored his pleas for help because they were investigating the theft of a television set. Although I was posing as a Klan member and fearful of being discovered, I couldn't bring myself to applaud.

Those were some of my feelings while I was in the Klan. When it was all over and I was back home, I had a whole new set of fears and concerns.

I was concerned about the safety of Linda and the kids (and they had never stopped being concerned about mine). Our quiet log home down in the woods had suddenly become an illuminated fortress with armed guards, a police dog, two-way radios, and confusion in general. I was asked repeatedly for radio interviews, television appearances, and speaking engagements, which was not easy on them, especially Linda. I returned home one Saturday in January from

an out-of-town engagement, followed by a lengthy meeting
with Seigenthaler, to find nothing but a note on the kitchen
table.

> Jerry, the girls are at Ronnie's and Todd is with
> his grandparents and I have the baby with me.
> Things are just happening too fast for me to adjust.
> It seems we no longer have any control over our
> lives. I need some quiet time away from it all to try
> and sort things out. I'll be home tomorrow. I love
> you.

I didn't sleep much that night, but I did do a lot of thinking. While I was away, sometimes I thought Linda was
whining and nagging too much. Sometimes I felt she was not
giving me the support I needed. I was lonely many nights
when I called and she was surrounded by people she loved.
Sometimes I felt she was being unfair.

But that night, I got just a taste of what she had lived
with for sixteen months while I was gone, and the reality
smacked me with the subtlety of a sledge hammer blow that
she was far more considerate, understanding, supportive,
and concerned than I could have ever been had our roles
been reversed. We shared a very warm greeting the next
morning.

I realized that at some point during my time undercover—early on, indeed—I went through a transformation: I
moved from being a reporter on an assignment to being a
citizen with a deep personal commitment to unearthing the
truth about an insidious force in our midst. So what started
as an engrossing undertaking became an all-consuming passion.

Perhaps that passion distracted me from noticing another
transformation taking place at about the same time. My son
Todd was still noticeably jealous and a little resentful of
Linda when I first left for Alabama. And those emotions
were heightened, if anything, when that incident occurred
about halfway into my assignment when he threatened to

run away from a home where I was temporarily—and, he feared, maybe permanently—absent. But by the time I came home to stay, all of that had somehow changed, somehow been truly transformed. What exists between them now is a loving relationship that couldn't be more sincere between a natural mother and child. Todd's hostility toward Linda has been replaced by adoration. He's quick to give her a hug when he comes home from school and rarely goes to bed without a good-night kiss. Seeing these two people whom I love openly express love for each other makes the hardships we all endured more than worth it for me.

I'm also proud of the community-wide support of our neighbors—good people who don't hesitate to speak up in one voice that says, "We live in a neighborhood where the Ku Klux Klan will never be welcome—or tolerated."

I'm proud of my own awareness now. Before this story I never really considered the Klan a threat to me—after all, I'm not black, I'm not Jewish. But I'm aware now, and firmly believe, that as long as the Klan presents a threat to anybody, we're all threatened—as long as a single human lives under the influence of fear and intimidation, we all live under that influence.

When I look back more than thirty years and recall that warm spring day when our neighbor came in and saw Willie Biggs, the black farmhand, eating at our dinner table, I know now why they looked the way they did.

Afterword

My undercover investigation into the activities of the Ku Klux Klan came about because the publisher at *The Tennessean,* John Seigenthaler, was concerned that the Klan was using our newspaper to spread its message. Seigenthaler is not a man who takes well to being used or to having his newspaper used. So it was my assignment to find out the truth about Klan activities, especially those in our circulation area.

The Klan had been promoting itself as a non-violent group committed to protecting the rights of white people. Seigenthaler obviously didn't believe this, and neither did I. But as a journalist, I was accustomed to dealing fairly and factually with the subjects of my stories. That is how I would approach the Klan story, too. Seigenthaler agreed that if I should find that the Klan was indeed a non-violent group that promoted white rights and, as it claimed, did not promote hate, I would report that as enthusiastically as I would any other findings.

My investigation, however, proved that the Klan was the same as it had been for more than one hundred years: a group motivated by hate and violence with a mission to obstruct the rights of a number of minorities, most notably Jews and blacks. My investigation also proved that at least one member of the Klan was determined to circumvent the First Amendment and obstruct my rights.

I had been ready for the Klan story to be over several months before it was. I kept telling myself that I would have time to become reacquainted with my family, time to catch up on the things I had missed, time to rest and rejuvenate. Throughout the eighteen months undercover, I kept my sanity and suppressed my homesickness by promising myself that once the assignment was over I would have more time than ever before to spend with my family. I dreamed of quiet privacy and candlelit dinners. But it wasn't to be.

It has been nine years now since I packed up and left my home to temporarily assume a new life and lifestyle, and I still haven't been able to find the time I kept promising myself and my family.

The story took longer than we had anticipated. I had sacrificed more than just eighteen months of life with my family. When I left to go undercover, we were a close, loving family. When I returned, I was more like a guest in my own home.

As the assignment lingered on and on, Linda and the children began to experience feelings of abandonment. We had planned on the assignment taking three to six months. But when my absence stretched past the first six months, I could feel the patience and support at home stretching, too. Before the eighteen months were over, there was almost nothing left to return to at home. Everyone there had become accustomed to my being gone, and suddenly it wasn't such a big deal anymore. I wasn't prepared for that.

None of us were prepared for the immediate media reaction to the Klan story. The day the story broke, I was called to New York to appear on the "Today" show. This time I left my family to fend for themselves under care of an armed guard. Just twenty-five miles away in Nashville, a large contingent of robed klansmen had showed up uninvited to march in the Christmas parade. There they confronted local police and made speeches in front of the newspaper condemning Seigenthaler and me.

I looked at my appearance on the "Today" show as an opportunity to tell the truth about the Klan to a larger audience, to tell millions of people that the Klan was still fueled by hatred and violence. I also realized I was accepting the invitation to appear again at the expense of my family. I was no longer undercover; yet I was again separated from them, and they would have to face the unknown without my presence and support.

It has been almost a decade now since that story broke, and we are still trying to resolve some of the issues which were raised during that turbulent period of our lives.

From a journalist's standpoint, there is the issue of where my commitment to my job—to a story—begins and where it ends. From the standpoint of being a husband and a father, there is the question of when my responsibilities to my family outweigh my responsibilities to search out and expose the truth. Perhaps even more important, though, is the question of where my responsibility as a human being who shares this fragile planet with other humans begins and ends.

If I meet my family's needs for support and love while neglecting other issues which carry the potential for making our world a more violent, hate-filled place where racial and religious groups are pitted against one another, am I living up to my goal of being the most responsible person I can be?

I neither want to overdramatize nor minimize the effects of any of these issues. Yet I still catch myself at times wondering if I've made the right decisions, for my family, for society, or for myself.

When we moved to the country, we built our log house deep in the middle of the largest stand of timber on the farm. Both Linda and I cherished our privacy and adored the natural setting. Linda still has not put up curtains, contending they would restrict her from enjoying an unobstructed view of the deer and squirrels playing and the birds flitting from tree to tree. Our dogs keep us informed of unexpected visitors long before they arrive.

That we had enjoyed this kind of privacy made it very difficult to adjust to an armed guard protecting our house day and night.

Instead of quiet solitude in the woods, the singing of birds was frequently interrupted by the squawk of a police radio kept handy in case of an emergency.

It was awkward getting used to the police dog and the armed guard, but it was outright frightening trying to deal with the wave of threats that begin pouring in when the first story hit the streets. The threats were delivered in the mail or called in to *The Tennessean;* occasionally I was confronted on the street or in a restaurant by a member of the Klan who always had some choice words to accuse me of betraying "the white race."

After the initial wave of threats came the harassment. Sometimes it was as simple as a heckler disrupting a speech. At other times it was as serious as someone shooting out the windows of Linda's country grocery store with a deer rifle. The most damaging harassment, however, came in a lawsuit brought by a Klan member mentioned in this book—Roland Torbert.

Torbert was the man who personally recommended me for membership in Bill Wilkinson's Invisible Empire of the Ku Klux Klan. When the story broke, Torbert, according to his court testimony, also began getting threats from his fellow klansmen. In an effort to save face and to get his buddies off his back, he sued me for $1 million. He also named G. P. Putnam's Sons, the original publisher of *My Life in the Klan,* and *The Tennessean* as co-defendants in the lawsuit.

To say I was unconcerned by the lawsuit would be untruthful. I was concerned. I didn't have a million dollars, and I had covered many court trials and knew that juries are unpredictable. I was never concerned about the accuracy of the quote I attributed to Torbert. He said what I said he said, and he knew I had quoted him accurately. More importantly, I knew I had quoted him accurately.

It had been more than a year since the series of stories had appeared in *The Tennessean* when Torbert brought his suit. Since his name was never mentioned in the newspaper series, the paper was quickly removed as a defendant in the lawsuit. But the commitment of John Seigenthaler and the newspaper in helping me prove my innocence remained steadfast to the end.

My Life in the Klan had been out four months when I received notice of the lawsuit. It was gaining sales momentum in several areas of the country, and I already had toured the East Coast promoting it on talk shows and radio and television programs. Sales were brisk.

I was preparing for a two-week swing through South Florida when the legal papers arrived. They arrived simultaneously at Putnam's offices in New York. On the advice of counsel, Putnam decided not to ship additional copies of the book. They apparently feared it might possibly compound the company's potential liability in the event I was unsuccessful in defending myself against Torbert's charges.

I made the South Florida tour, speaking to several civic groups and being interviewed by newspapers in Hollywood, Fort Lauderdale, Orlando, and Miami. I appeared on several television shows, and the *Miami Herald* carried three stories about the Klan and the book in one week. Yet there was not a copy of the book to be found.

While I disagreed with the decision by Putnam, I also understood it. At the same time, I also realized that Roland Torbert had accomplished what he had set out to do. He had, in effect, killed any future sales of my book. Once Putnam had decided to take the book off the market, Torbert was in no hurry to have his lawsuit tried. He knew that the longer it took to get a court decision, the less interest there would be in the book. He was right, too.

It took almost two and one-half years to get my day in court. As it turned out, it was three days in federal court in Birmingham, Alabama. After the third day of testimony, the case went to a seven-member jury to decide whether or not I had libeled Roland Torbert, a former Exalted Cyclops of the Mount Olive, Alabama, chapter of the Ku Klux Klan.

The jury took twenty-six minutes from the time it left the courtroom to return with its verdict. As I nervously waited, I felt the brief deliberations were a good indication that the jury had found in my favor. But I was unsure until the court clerk read the jury's message:

"We, the jury, find in favor of the defendant, Jerry Thompson."

Then, and only then, did I breathe a sign of relief.

I was obviously elated with the jury's decision, but I was also angry that this gun-toting klansman had used "the system" to successfully circumvent the First Amendment and deprive me of my rights to freedom of speech and freedom of the press. His lawsuit had put a price on those freedoms, a price too high for Putnam to take a chance on paying. The result was that my freedom to speak out against the Klan and my freedom to publish what I had to say about the Klan was bottled up in a New Jersey book warehouse and stifled.

Those freedoms remained under lock and key until I was vindicated by the court. If I had not been successful, I don't suppose the books ever would have been released. However, when they finally were released, the initial interest in the book had waned, and Putnam apparently decided it would not be economically feasible to attempt to revive the promotional effort Torbert had so successfully squashed.

This book has been expensive in many ways. Not only did it cost me eighteen months of my life, it also has taken its toll on my family through the threats and harassment. I now realize that when I accepted the Klan assignment, I not only was making a commitment to do a story, but also was commiting my family to a change in lifestyle that we now expect to last for life.

Three years after the story broke, a fellow reporter from the *Chicago Tribune* came to Nashville to do a travel story. Linda and I accompanied him and his wife out for a night on the town. At a respectable night club I was confronted by a Klan member obviously proud of his affiliation. He termed me a "Judas to the white race" and said I was lucky he didn't have some of his buddies with him.

Just a year ago while taking two Cajun friends out for some

Middle Tennessee barbecue, we were confronted in my hometown by five Klan sympathizers. None of the five looked intelligent enough even to belong to the Klan, but they were smart enough to realize the foolishness of messing with two mad Cajuns.

Every time I mention the Klan story in one of my columns, it invariably results in threats. I don't suppose a fellow ever gets accustomed to having his life threatened; I'm certain it never becomes comfortable. However, it is a reality that I'm prepared to live with while I continue to ponder some of my past decisions.

I'm often asked if the story was worth it. My answer is always the same.

When I took the assignment, there were approximately 50,000 Ku Klux Klan members in active organizations in at least thirty-five states. Klan membership was doubling in less than every two years, and Klan-related violence was multiplying much faster than its membership. Seven Klan chapters were meeting regularly in Nashville and Davidson County.

Now Klan membership is down to what most experts estimate is less than 3,000 members nationwide, and it continues to decline. With the decline in membership, there also is a decline in Klan-related violence. Not a single Klan chapter meets regularly in Nashville or in Davidson County. So was it worth it? I think so.

The next most often asked question is whether I would do it again.

For every decision we make we have to weigh the cost against the potential gain. I know the price I have paid in doing the Klan story. When I weigh that cost against the gains made in helping thwart a rapidly growing menace of hatred and violence, I realize the answer to the second question is not yet clear.